PRAISE FOR *FRESH FRUIT, BROKEN BODIES*

"In *Fresh Fruit, Broken Bodies,* Seth Holmes offers up an important and captivating new ethnography, linking the structural violence inherent in the migrant labor system in the United States to the social processes by which it becomes normalized. Drawing on five years of fieldwork among the Triqui people from Oaxaca, Mexico, Holmes investigates local understandings of suffering and illness, casting into relief stereotypes and prejudices that he ties to the transnational labor that puts cheap food on American tables. Throughout this compelling volume, Holmes considers ways of engaging migrant farmworkers and allies who might help disrupt the exploitation that reaches across national boundaries and can too often be hidden away. This book is a gripping read not only for cultural and medical anthropologists, students in immigration and ethnic studies as well as labor and agriculture, and physicians and public health professionals, but also for anyone interested in the lives and well-being of the people who provide them cheap, fresh fruit."

Paul Farmer, Cofounder of Partners in Health and Chair of the Department of Global Health and Social Medicine, Harvard Medical School

"This book takes concepts from the world of scholarship to enrich the understanding of people's lives, while its vivid detail and empathetic portrait of the reality of people's lives enrich scholarship. Holmes leaves the reader in no doubt that economic arrangements, social hierarchies, discrimination, and poor living and working conditions have profound effects on the health of marginalized people, and he does so with the touch of a gifted writer. The reader lives the detail and is much moved."

Professor Sir Michael Marmot, Director, UCL Institute of Health Equity

"A tour de force ethnography. Holmes gives us the rare combination of medical, anthropological, and humanitarian gazes into the lives of Oaxacan migrant farmworkers in the United States. Their agricultural field work and his anthropological fieldwork intersect to produce a book full of insights into the pathos, inequalities, frustrations, and dreams punctuating the farmworkers' daily lives. Through Holmes's vivid prose, and the words of the workers themselves, we feel with the workers as they strain their bodies picking fruit and pruning vines; we sense their fear as they cross the U.S.-Mexico border; we understand their frustrations as they are chased and detained by immigration authorities; and we cheer at their perseverance when faced with bureaucrats and medical personnel who treat them as if they were to blame for their own impoverished condition. A must-read for anyone interested in the often invisible lives and suffering of those whose labor provides for our very sustenance."

Leo R. Chavez, Professor of Anthropology, University of California, Irvine

"In his first book, anthropologist and doctor Seth M. Holmes gives us an intimate look into the lives of migrant farmworkers. Through his exhaustive research, Holmes reveals the struggles of the millions who work in our fields, every year, to put food on our tables. In deliberations about immigration and farm policy, these are the stories that should be at the center. Holmes helps us put them there."

Anna Lappé, author *Diet for a Hot Planet* and founder of the Real Food Media Project

"In this book, Seth Holmes recounts the experience of Mexican workers who cross the border illegally at their own risk, hoping to be employed on the farms of the West Coast of the United States and, above all, to allow their children a better existence. His engaged anthropology provides a unique understanding of the political economy of migrant labor and of its human cost."

Didier Fassin, Professor of Social Science at the Institute for Advanced Study, Princeton, and author of *Humanitarian Reason*

"Like the reporting of Edward R. Murrow and the labors of Cesar Chavez, Seth Holmes's work on these modern-day migrants reminds us of the human beings who produce the greatest bounty of food the world has ever seen. They take jobs that other American workers won't take, for pay that other American workers won't accept and under conditions that other American workers won't tolerate. Yet except for the minority of farmworkers protected by United Farm Workers' contracts, these workers too often don't earn enough to adequately feed themselves. Seth Holmes's writing fuels the UFW's ongoing organizing among farmworkers and admonishes the American people that our work remains unfinished."

Arturo S. Rodriguez, President, United Farm Workers of America

Fresh Fruit, Broken Bodies

CALIFORNIA SERIES IN PUBLIC ANTHROPOLOGY

The California Series in Public Anthropology emphasizes the anthropologist's role as an engaged intellectual. It continues anthropology's commitment to being an ethnographic witness, to describing, in human terms, how life is lived beyond the borders of many readers' experiences. But it also adds a commitment, through ethnography, to reframing the terms of public debate—transforming received, accepted understandings of social issues with new insights, new framings.

Series Editor: Robert Borofsky (Hawaii Pacific University)

Contributing Editors: Philippe Bourgois (University of Pennsylvania), Paul Farmer (Partners in Health), Alex Hinton (Rutgers University), Carolyn Nordstrom (University of Notre Dame), and Nancy Scheper-Hughes (UC Berkeley)

University of California Press Editor: Naomi Schneider

Fresh Fruit, Broken Bodies

MIGRANT FARMWORKERS IN THE UNITED STATES

SETH M. HOLMES, PHD, MD

With a Foreword by Philippe Bourgois

UNIVERSITY OF CALIFORNIA PRESS
Berkeley Los Angeles London

University of California Press, one of the most distinguished university presses in the United States, enriches lives around the world by advancing scholarship in the humanities, social sciences, and natural sciences. Its activities are supported by the UC Press Foundation and by philanthropic contributions from individuals and institutions. For more information, visit www.ucpress.edu.

University of California Press
Berkeley and Los Angeles, California

University of California Press, Ltd.
London, England

Library of Congress Cataloging-in-Publication Data

Holmes, Seth M., 1975–
Fresh fruit, broken bodies : migrant farmworkers in the United States / Seth M. Holmes, PhD, MD ; with a foreword by Philippe Bourgois.
pages cm — (California series in public anthropology ; 27)
Includes bibliographical references and index.
ISBN 978-0-520-27513-3 (cloth : alk. paper) — ISBN 978-0-520-27514-0 (pbk. : alk. paper) — ISBN 978-0-520-95479-3 (ebook)
1. Migrant agricultural laborers—United States—Social conditions. I. Title.
HD1525.H685 2013
331.5′440973—dc23 2012045798

Manufactured in the United States of America

22 21 20 19 18 17 16 15 14 13
10 9 8 7 6 5 4 3

In keeping with a commitment to support environmentally responsible and sustainable printing practices, UC Press has printed this book on Rolland Enviro100, a 100% post-consumer fiber paper that is FSC certified, deinked, processed chlorine-free, and manufactured with renewable biogas energy. It is acid-free and EcoLogo certified.

To Ed and Carolyn Holmes, for introducing me to a life open to new questions

To the Triqui people in the United States and Mexico, for allowing me into your lives and guiding me toward new answers

. . . our work is not done.

Dolores Huerta

Contents

List of Illustrations ix

Foreword, by Philippe Bourgois xi

Acknowledgments xix

1. Introduction: "Worth Risking Your Life?" 1
2. "We Are Field Workers": Embodied Anthropology of Migration 30
3. Segregation on the Farm: Ethnic Hierarchies at Work 45
4. "How the Poor Suffer": Embodying the Violence Continuum 88
5. "Doctors Don't Know Anything": The Clinical Gaze in Migrant Health 111
6. "Because They're Lower to the Ground": Naturalizing Social Suffering 155
7. Conclusion: Change, Pragmatic Solidarity, and Beyond 182

Appendix: On Ethnographic Writing and Contextual Knowledge 199

Notes 203

References 213

Index 227

Illustrations

Map of migration fieldwork 4
The author, Macario, and their Triqui companions in the border desert 7
The author and Triqui men in the border desert 19
Triqui men sleeping under garbage bags in the border desert 20
Farm labor camp 48
Chart of labor hierarchy on the farm 51
A white teenage checker with Mexican pickers 70
Marcelina picking strawberries 74
Samuel pruning with children in California vineyard 82
Conceptual diagram of hierarchies on the farm 85
Abelino working in the field 91
Self-medication: cans behind a *cabina* 99

The village of San Miguel, Oaxaca 112

The center of San Miguel, where the Centro de Salud is located 145

Samuel's sister carrying firewood, returning to San Miguel with Samuel's father 149

Danger: pesticide storage area 173

A checker stands while pickers kneel in the strawberry field 175

Strawberry picker strike 178

Strawberry pickers on strike reading the list of grievances 179

FOREWORD The Symbolic Violence of Primitive Accumulation in the United States

PHILIPPE BOURGOIS

The good doctor tells us, "Eat fresh fruit—lots of it!" You, the reader—the tiny fraction of the world's population that has access to important critical and moving books, like this one by physician anthropologist Seth Holmes, are likely to take this healthy biopower dictate for granted. Most Americans who are not poor have learned to avoid the worst of the cheap, processed, and biologically engineered convenience foods saturated with sugar, salt, and fat (Moss 2013) that the global poor increasingly are condemned to eat because of transnational corporate domination of food markets. A few of the global privileged in the United States who remember reading Steinbeck's *Grapes of Wrath* and boycotting grapes in support of Cesar Chavez's United Farm Workers movement may be vaguely aware that the delicious, health-giving fruit they worthily devour is produced cheaply by literally breaking the backs, knees, hips, and other overstressed body parts of Latino farmworkers.

Holmes lets us know in no uncertain terms *why* we often fail to recognize the association between our "care of the self" and the suffering imposed on indigenous Mexican farmworkers that has been rendered invisible through the naturalization of racialized hierarchies. He shows us the urgency of recognizing that global assemblages are unequally structured and, although they impose themselves on all of us, they distribute embodied suffering differentially onto structurally vulnerable populations (Quesada, Hart, and Bourgois 2011). The stakes are high: these global inequities damage the body, and they are too often deadly. Holmes shows exactly who gets physically and emotionally hurt, and in what intimate ways, by the effects of racism, international trade policy, the everyday practices that normalize inequality, law enforcement, and disciplinary forms of knowledge. He explores the intellectual, political, practical, and ethical implications of the ideas of Marx, and especially of Bourdieu—not to mention the early Foucault—so that readers cannot continue to misrecognize the relationship between their biopower benefits and the damage inflicted on the bodies and lives of indigenous undocumented workers. In fact, as Holmes documents ethnographically, access to affordable fresh fruit in the United States, and in many of the wealthier parts of the world, is made possible by a symbolic violence that treats racism as a natural state of affairs. More concretely, he shows how this translates into abusive workplace hierarchies, residential segregation, and unhealthy living conditions.

The public secret of the politically imposed suffering of undocumented Latino farmworkers in the United States in the mid-2010s is unconscionably useful: It generates profits for transnational agribusiness and keeps U.S. citizens healthy. The suffering of the Triqui is arguably more useful, more noxious, and more invisible than was the human-engineered environmental disaster that expelled 2.5 million people from the Great Plains during the Great Depression of the 1930s and sent 200,000 "Okies" into migrant farm labor in California, contributing to the great boom in the multibillion dollar California agricultural industry. The Okies, too, were greeted with insults. Store entrances sported signs saying, "Okies and dogs not allowed inside." Holmes sought out a real live retired Okie, only to find that this elderly, upwardly mobile former migrant laborer spewed back the same venom that had been directed at him over half a century ago. He tried to convince Holmes that the latest wave of migrant farm laborers, the Triqui Amerindians, were culturally inferior and deserved their poverty. Their phenotype, body size, marriage customs, language, nationality, and even work discipline and exploitability become the pernicious symbolic markers of a racialized ethnicity that assigns them to a toxic occupational location in the global labor force.

The fresh fruit market niche that biopower, symbolic violence, old-fashioned racism, and xenophobic nationalism have rendered profitable and vibrant in the United States is actively enforced through the structural violence of U.S. immigration laws and the details of the Department of Homeland Security's border and workplace inspection enforcement policies. The political imposition of an "illegal" status on Mexican farmworkers in the United States was provocatively compared by Michael Burawoy in 1976 to the same mechanisms of unequally articulating modes of production (agricultural capitalism with subsistence agriculture) that enabled the mining industry of South Africa to thrive and to subsidize the living and working conditions of South African whites in the second half of the twentieth century through the political and legal enforcement of apartheid and the migrant homelands system. Almost forty years after Burawoy's critique, U.S. agriculture's relationship with indigenous rural communities of Mexico continues to institutionalize and, as Holmes demonstrates more subtly, to embody this dynamic. The costs of the reproduction of U.S. agriculture's labor force (the childhood nurturance and education of the laborers themselves) and their physical degradation (occupational injuries, pesticide poisonings, premature superannuation, and retirement) is displaced onto the home-sending communities. When farmworkers are rendered too sick, from physical exertion and exposure, to continue laboring, most "voluntarily" seek refuge in their rural communities throughout Latin America—but especially Mexico—and increasingly in its indigenous territories. The industry—even the well-intentioned mom-and-pop farm Holmes studied—exposes its workers to massive doses of sprayed carcinogens and imposes on them a choice between hunger and repetitive strain injuries that too often result in severe lifelong disabilities. When the desperation of the workers becomes excessively visible or costly, Homeland Security conveniently deports them, and they are blacklisted as criminals.

Those seasonal laborers who return home aching and exhausted to their formerly semi-autonomous subsistence farming communities find their remote villages and hamlets devastated by the North American Free Trade Agreement. Sooner rather than later, poverty forces most of them to drag themselves back across the militarized northern border for yet another harvest season of brutal labor. These indigenous communities used to supply local Mexican corn markets, but that valuable source of cash income and subsistence food supply has disappeared. Local markets have been flooded by corporate-grown U.S. corn imports and packaged convenience food that benefit from unequal access to tax subsidies and genetic technologies, because neoliberal practice is inconsistent with its own free-market ideology. This unhealthy, politically imposed structural violence can be thought of as a contemporary form of primitive accumulation akin to the enclosure movement of sixteenth-century England described by Marx as a prime example of the violent birth of "capital . . . dripping from head to foot, from every pore, with blood and dirt" (Marx 1972: 760). U.S. immigration and labor laws and, more distally, the unequal articulation of modes of production across international borders prevent agricultural laborers from organizing for their rights, or even from complaining about their superexploitation as seasonal laborers. This parasitical crossnational labor management strategy fosters a "conjugated oppression" that melds the experiences of racism and economic exploitation into an embodied symbolic violence.

As a physician anthropologist who has a commitment to being a public intellectual as well as a healer, Holmes has a privileged relationship to understanding and theorizing the embodied experience of conjugated oppression. He provocatively straddles two intellectual professional disciplines and epistemologies that see the world very differently: anthropology, with its productively schizophrenic foundation in the humanities and social sciences, and biomedicine, with its positivist commitment to pursuing statistically significant objective evidence. Holmes understands the body with the eye of a medical practitioner who knows technically how our organs, cells, and synapses operate. He has valuable practical skills for healing people, and he makes a U.S. doctor's high salary—even if significantly reduced by his being a university professor and primary care physician. Above all, Holmes is a border-crosser who is unambiguously on the side of the poor. He violates the apartheids of class, nationality, ethnicity, occupational status, space, and culture that organize most societies and are especially powerful and unequal in the hyperglobalized United States–Mexico nexus—along with gender, sexuality, normativity, age, and ability. He has the chutzpah to put the confrontational habitus of doctors (imposed on him by his rigorous training in medical school as well as his childhood socialization as the son of a doctor who specializes in radiology) to good use by betraying his guild of well-meaning physicians. He reveals from the inside the unintentionally depoliticizing logics of what is one of the most hermetically sealed and self-protected, privileged occupational niches in North America: that of practicing clinicians. In chapter 5, he accompanies his fellow farmworkers to an occupational health clinic to advocate for them, and through this practice-based ethical engagement he is able to open up analytically the operational mechanisms of the basic constitution of symbolic violence, so that naturalized, racist oppression can no longer reproduced itself as an unintended public secret among his colleagues in their clinical practice serving structurally vulnerable patients. At the same time, Holmes always maintains both an analytical and a personal hermeneutics of generosity that transcends Manichean political righteousness and avoids anthropology's cultural relativist and postmodernist pitfalls of failing to see the ugly contradictions and suffering imposed by political-economic, cultural, psychodynamic, and bodily forces. This political theoretical insight reveals why genuinely committed, caring, intelligent clinicians inadvertently blame patients for their own predicaments and remain largely clueless about social-structural inequality. In fact their misrecognition is largely a knowledge-power disciplinary product of all their years of miseducation in science and medical school. As a practicing physician who strives to work on behalf of the poor, Holmes knows what his colleagues contend with, because he too has to enter into unequal hand-to-hand combat with the byzantine insurance reimbursement illogics that are imposed on overpaid doctors in the United States by a medical system dominated by market forces that cut short patient-physician interactions, limit access to technologies and medication, and narrow the medical gaze. That same theoretically informed generosity allows him to show us how a genuinely nice and ethical family farm owner (whom he met in church) can enforce horrendous conditions on his most vulnerable workers. That farmer, too, is trapped in the same web of unequal global markets that harms the lives of his workers.

Finally, in addition to being an inveterate border-crosser in his intellectual, professional, and private lives, Holmes also proves himself in these pages to be a master artisan adept at the core methodology that makes cultural anthropology so exciting: the participant-observation version of ethnography. By living (and shivering at night) in decrepit farmworker shacks, picking berries for long hours (damaging his own sinews in the process and coughing from pesticide sprays); by accompanying his fellow farmworkers into clinics and advocating for them with physicians; by attending weddings and baptisms; by joining an extended family and migrating with them through California's Central Valley during the off-season in search of temporary, subsistence-level employment (in a journey reminiscent of the Okies'); by volunteering to drive one of the overcrowded cars that travel, in an awkward caravan, carefully below the speed limit to stay under the radar of hostile highway patrol officers; by bathing and camping out with these families in rest areas; by discreetly insisting on staking out a closet to sleep in at night, as a room of his own for the rest of the winter, when the family finally locates a slumlord willing to rent to them; and ultimately, by "going home" with his companions to their inaccessible rural hamlets in Mexico, Holmes conveys the stories of real people the way anthropology—for all its foibles and its more serious elitist sins—can do so well.

I envy those of you who have not yet read the opening chapter of this book. It is beyond gripping. Holmes throws you deep into the Arizona/Sonora desert with his Triqui companions, dodging rattlesnakes, helicopters, armed guards, and all-terrain vehicles. One could not invent a more brutally effective system for culling the best possible self-disciplined laborers if one tried. At the same time, however, Holmes rejects the traditional anthropological trope of macho heroism and omniscience. Despite his courage and ability to endure hardships, take the risks the poor routinely assume, and stand unashamedly for justice, Holmes is no Indiana Jones. He, like all of us, has his own personal vulnerabilities. He bursts into tears when scolded by authority, locked up in an Arizona detention cell. In revealing this detail of his own subjectivity he provides yet another example of how abusive power operates, gratuitously humiliating its detainees at the most intimate level of the body and the emotions.

Thank you, Seth, for being a public anthropologist and confronting an urgent high-stakes subject. The members of your generation of MD/PhDs have the potential to revolutionize medical anthropology and, more broadly, the social sciences and humanities through their hard work, intelligence, and embodied practical empathy as both critical intellectuals and hard-working healers.

Acknowledgments

I have received a humbling amount of support and encouragement during the processes of researching and writing this book. Most important, I want to thank the Triqui people who allowed me into their homes in Oaxaca, their shacks in the labor camps of Washington, their cars to sleep while homeless and in transit, their apartments in California, and their trust, especially in the border desert. Those who, over time, trusted me enough to enter into the events of their lives—from births to labor negotiations to border crossings—made my fieldwork possible. As I moved into my shack in the labor camp in Washington State, I expected to spend one or two years witnessing jarring realities, yet to my surprise I found myself also making friends. I have altered names and personal information to protect privacy, and I regret that I cannot thank everyone by name. More than anyone, I want to thank the person I call Samuel for trusting me and vouching for me with his family and friends. His family in Oaxaca was amazingly patient with and welcoming to this tall, white, bald visitor from the North, even when their neighbors treated me like the CIA agent or drug trafficker I was often believed to be. His family and friends (as well as some of his detractors) in the United States were instrumental in sharing their experiences with me and staying in touch after I traded the field for the computer keyboard. Specifically, Samuel, Joaquin, José, and Maribel have lent key insights and guidance for my thinking and writing. They have motivated me regularly with phone calls and visits, reminding me of the importance of letting broad publics know about their lives as indigenous migrants. In addition, I am grateful to their families, Marcelina, Crescencio, Abelino, Bernardo, Juana, those who befriended me in Oaxaca, those who trusted me to cross the border with them, and many others.

My research was made possible by many others in the field as well. The staff and friends of Tierra Nueva shared their insights and friendship with me during my first lonely months living in the Washington labor camp. The Tanaka farm gave me the go-ahead to live in its farm camps, observe and pick in the fields, and interview employees. Without this firsthand access to the farm, my research would have been watered down if not impossible altogether. I am grateful to all the employees on the Tanaka farm for allowing me into their worlds. Thank you, especially, to those whom I have called John, Rob, Mike, Sally, Jan, and Mateo. The neighbors of the farm and labor camps, residents of the Skagit Valley, shared with me important insights into agriculture in general and ethnic relations in rural America specifically. Thank you especially to my friends, the rabbit owners and runners, their bilingual friends down the street, my friends in the Skagit PFLAG, the caretakers of Cascade lookouts, and of course my long-bearded friend and his inspiring weekly courthouse vigils. I am grateful to the help from others in Oaxaca as well, especially Kris Olmsted, Alejandro de Avila, and Fray Eugenio, for moral support and intellectual community. I enthusiastically thank all the staff of the migrant clinics in Washington State and California who welcomed me to learn about the medical problems and health care of this population. I hope to work together with all of them toward positive social and health change in the future.

I want to thank the institutions that generously provided financial support for my work during this project: the Martin Sisters Endowed Chair at the University of California, Berkeley (UCB), School of Public Health; the UCB Department of Anthropology; the University of California, San Francisco (UCSF), Department of Anthropology, History and Social Medicine; the Medical Scientist Training Program at UCSF; the University of California Institute for Mexico and the United States; the Mustard Seed Foundation; the UCSF Graduate Division Dean's Fellowship; the UCSF Center for Reproductive Health Research and Policy; the UCSF School of Medicine Rainer Fund; the University of Pennsylvania Physician Scientist Program; and the Robert Wood Johnson Foundation Health & Society Scholars Program at Columbia University. I want to thank the following organizations for other forms of support: Tierra Nueva and Jesse Costello-Good for quiet space to think and write; the individuals involved in the Society for Humanities, Social Sciences and Medicine (including Vinh-Kim Nguyen, Jeremy Green, Walt Schalick, David Meltzer, Helena Hansen, Jennifer Karlin, Adam Baim, Ippolytos Kalofonos, and Scott Stonington) and in the Harvard Department of Global Health and Social Medicine (especially Allan Brandt, Paul Farmer, and Arthur Kleinman) for believing in my multidisciplinary career path; and the University of Rochester Division of Medical Humanities (especially Stephanie Brown Clark, Jane Greenlaw, and Ted Brown) and Department of Anthropology (especially Robert Foster) as well as the CRUX NYC climbing community for quiet space during my writing in upstate New York.

I must thank my family for introducing me from an early age to realities outside of our comfortable semiurban family life. I doubt my parents knew how these experiences of transnational inequality would start a process of questioning my received understandings of society and the world, eventually leading me back to challenge many of my parents' own paradigms. My family has taken an active role during my training, reading and commenting on papers, as well as simply visiting and corresponding during some of my lonelier months. My brother, Wynn, has been an especially valuable co-thinker and co-theorizer. Thank you for your ongoing invaluable support, Mom, Dad, Wynn, Deb, Na, Laura, Aidan, Kellan, and grandparents. My grandmother's last question to me before she passed away this spring was, "Have you finished your book?" Thank you also to my friends who visited me in cards or in person during my fieldwork: Corey and Bethanie, Adam, Kai, Jack, Ippy, Kelly, Rachel, Tim, Cale, Mark and Gwen. Thank you to Cale and to Lane for supporting me during the sometimes angst-filled months of writing, revising and grappling with writer's block.

Thank you to Vincanne Adams, Philippe Bourgois, Nancy Scheper-Hughes, Lawrence Cohen, and others in the UCSF/Berkeley Joint Program in Medical Anthropology; Tris Parslow, Jana Toutolmin, Kevin Shannon, Catherine Norton, and others in the UCSF Medical Scientist Training Program; Helen Loeser, Maureen Mitchell, and others in the UCSF School of Medicine for believing in the possibility of joint training in medicine and the social sciences; Lisa Bellini, Gary Koretsky, Richard Shannon, Ilene Rosen, Robby Aronowitz, David Asch, Skip Brass, and others at the University of Pennsylvania for finding creative ways to give me writing time and support during an incredibly intense internship and residency; and Bruce Link, Peter Bearman, Lisa Bates, Gina Lovasi, Julien Tietler, Beth Povinelli, Lesley Sharp, Kim Hopper, Zoe Donaldson, Kristen Springer, Kristin Harper, Jason Fletcher, Mark Hatzenbuehler, Kerry Keyes, Jennifer Hirsch, Helena Hansen, Cate Taylor, and others at Columbia University for interdisciplinary intellectual discussions, helping me clarify my language and writing. Without the joint support of these individuals and institutions, this project would not have been completed. I am grateful for being able to train in universities open to unconventional career paths and interdisciplinary perspectives.

I am grateful to many official and unofficial colleagues and advisers: Chris Kiefer for being amazingly accessible and responsive to my writing; Lawrence Cohen and Vincanne Adams for supporting my explorations into new ideas; Gay Becker for close and constructive readings of my work; Donald Moore for one of my favorite social theory seminars during graduate school; Judith Justice and Jeanne Simonelli for modeling an anthropological engagement in the world of global health; Paul Farmer and Adrienne Pine for modeling different forms of passionate and strategic solidarity; Catherine Maternowska, Steffanie Strathdee, Wayne Cornelius, Lois Lorentzen, Jennifer Burrell, and the manuscript workshop at SUNY Albany for myriad insights into research on migration; Jim Quesada, Rosemarie Chierichi, Xochitl Castañeda, Heide Castañeda, Sarah Willen, Liz

Cartwright, and Kurt Organista for engaging discussions on migration as well as for moral support; Donna Goldstein and Laurie Hart for long-distance encouragement on writing and career path; the UC Berkeley Center for Latin American Studies for creating spaces for scholars engaged in contemporary issues in Latin America; the UC San Diego Center for Comparative Immigration Studies for providing a spatially extended community of immigration scholar mentors and colleagues; Tom Boyce, Nancy Adler, Paula Braveman, Ray Catalano, Len Syme, Denise Herd, Merry Minkler, Rachel Morello-Frosh, and Mahasin Mujahid for supporting my research and questions even though I used methods largely different from their own; Jeff Gaines, John Fife, and BorderLinks for believing my writing was important in seeking social justice; No More Deaths, Jennifer Hill, and Daniel Ramirez for giving me a place to recover from my time in the Arizona desert and the Border Patrol jail; Joe Figini and Heather Williams for legal advice before and after my encounter with the Border Patrol; John Hughes, Walt Odets, Chris Bartlett, Jeff Darcy, and Susan Phillips for keeping me sane in the midst of this wonderful and tiring work; and Steve McPhee for modeling deep compassion for those who are suffering.

Above all, I am grateful for the invaluable advice, comments, and moral support of Philippe Bourgois. Thank you for the multiple meetings and long-distance conversations over the past several years, complete with academic advice, theoretical ideas, and a listening ear for an anthropologist sometimes depressed by the realities he was experiencing. Thank you for making critical theories of social inequality and struggle come to life. Thank you to my formal mentors: Nancy Scheper-Hughes for modeling passionate and engaged writing as well as an impressively eclectic combination of theoretical perspectives, Loïc Wacquant for precise explanations of critical social theory as applied to contemporary social situations, Stanley Brandes for supportive writing advice and facilitation of a wonderful writing group, and Tom Denberg for challenging insights into the integration of anthropological research and academic medicine. Thank you to my colleagues in anthropology, especially Maya Ponte, Ippolytos Kalofonos, Meg Stalcup, Thurka Sangaramoorthy, Ben Hickler, Scott Stonington, Angela Jenks, Adrienne Pine, Katya Wesolowski, Jelani Mahiri, Johanna Crane, and the Violence in the Americas Writing Group of the UCB Center for Latin American Studies, who read early drafts of this project. Thank you to Daniel Mason for joining this group and sharing your insights as a writer. Finally, I am grateful to the University of California Press, including the two anonymous reviewers and the faculty editorial board reviewer for critical theoretical feedback as well as Naomi Schneider for invaluable editorial suggestions to improve narrative flow.

On many levels, I am indebted to the Triqui people of San Miguel. Despite my errors and imperfect rendering, I hope their stories and experiences are communicated in these pages, dismantling stereotypes that normalize unequal social structures and naturalize social suffering.

Seth M. Holmes
Berkeley, CA
Summer 2012

ONE Introduction

"WORTH RISKING YOUR LIFE?"

THE ROAD FROM SAN MIGUEL[1]

It is early April and our group is leaving the Triqui village of San Miguel in the mountains of Oaxaca, Mexico,[2] each of us wearing dark-colored, long-sleeved clothes and carrying a small, dark-colored backpack with one change of clothes, a plastic bag with coyote fur and pine sap made by a Triqui healer for protection and called a suerte *[luck], along with many* totopos *[smoked, handmade tortillas] and dried beans to eat. I was instructed by Macario to bring these things. Each of us carries between $1,000 and $2,000 to pay for the bus ride to the border, for food at the border, for rides on either side of the border, and some for the* coyote *[border-crossing guide].*

Our journey begins with a two-hour trip in a Volkswagen van from San Miguel to the nearby mestizo[3] town of Tlaxiaco. After buying our bus tickets, we walk around the town's market, buying food to share with each other on the bus. Joaquin chooses mangoes, Macario oranges and peanuts, and I miniature sweet bananas. Macario buys a slingshot to use against rattlesnakes in the desert and asks if I want to carry one, but I don't have much experience with slingshots. When we return to the bus, the two nuns from San Miguel are waiting to wish us well as we board. The younger nun explains to me that they go there every weekend to pray for the border crossers.

The bus ride in itself is exhausting. The bus is packed with people, mostly men, all headed to the border except a half dozen who plan to go to Baja California to harvest tomatoes. We ride from 3:00 P.M. *on Saturday until our arrival in Altar at 4:00* P.M. *on Monday, a total of forty-nine hours. We pass through five army checkpoints between the state of Oaxaca and the border. The checkpoints all have signs that say in Spanish, "Permanent Campaign Against Narcotraffic." Before each checkpoint, the bus driver or his assistant announces loudly that all the bus riders should say that they are going to Baja California to work so that the stop would not take too much time with questions about crossing the border into the United States. Each time, the driver tells me to say that I was just hitchhiking to the next tourist town—Mazatlán, Hermosillo, Guadalajara, depending on where we are at the time. Before each checkpoint, the bus becomes quiet, and people seem nervous about the possibility of being interrogated or sent back south. Two or three soldiers board the bus each time in green army fatigues and ask a few seemingly random people for identification and search a few bags while other soldiers look through the windows with rifles over their shoulders.*

Interestingly, there are three army soldiers riding the bus with us, going to their base in northern Mexico. They, as well as everyone else, play along with the story. The oldest of the soldiers, seated next to me, is convinced I am the coyote leading my friends to a job in the United States. He explains to me that these military checkpoints are paid for by the U.S. Drug Enforcement Agency in order to stop drug smuggling across the border and to stop undocumented immigration to the United States. He tells me to take the driver's assistant to "El Norte" for free since he is so nice to everyone on the bus. The driver's assistant—who collects fares from the passengers, enforces the schedule at the food stops, and makes sure everyone makes it back on board after meals—simply smiles in response. I reply that I am not a coyote. The soldier laughs and asks in Spanish, "Then why are you taking all these guys?"

FIELDWORK ON THE MOVE

For one and a half years full-time, followed by shorter field visits, I used the classic anthropological research method of participant observation in order to understand the complicated issues of immigration, social hierarchy, and health. This method involves long-term immersion in the everyday lives and practices of people while often including more specific tape-recorded conversations and interviews. Due to my interests in interactions and perceptions among different groups of people, I also collected media accounts of migration and reviewed clinical charts of migrant patients. This book corresponds to the "follow the people" multisited fieldwork outlined by George Marcus as one way to do ethnography that takes seriously the interconnections inherent in the contemporary world.[4]

For the first several years after 2000, I actively searched for an interesting and important ethnographic project to undertake. Given the critical social, political, and health issues related to U.S.-Mexico migration, I chose to work in this context. James, director of a nonprofit organization working with migrant laborers in the Skagit Valley of Washington State and an acquaintance through mountaineering networks, encouraged me to work with the Triqui people from San Miguel, Oaxaca. He explained that this group of people was especially interesting and important because they had only recently begun migrating to the United States, had a reputation for being violent, and lived and worked in unhealthy environments in Washington State and California.

In spring 2003, I decided to visit San Miguel, the rural hometown in the state of Oaxaca of many Triqui migrants in Washington and California. San Miguel is located at an elevation of almost nine thousand feet and has approximately three thousand inhabitants. During most of the year, however, almost half of them are in the United States, working. Upon arriving in Tlaxiaco, the nearest primarily mestizo city, I was told by several residents not to go to San Miguel. By long-term Protestant missionaries, waiters, and drivers of *suburbans* (eight-passenger vans providing rides between towns), I was told explicit and detailed stories of people being kicked out of San Miguel, being shot, or having their cars

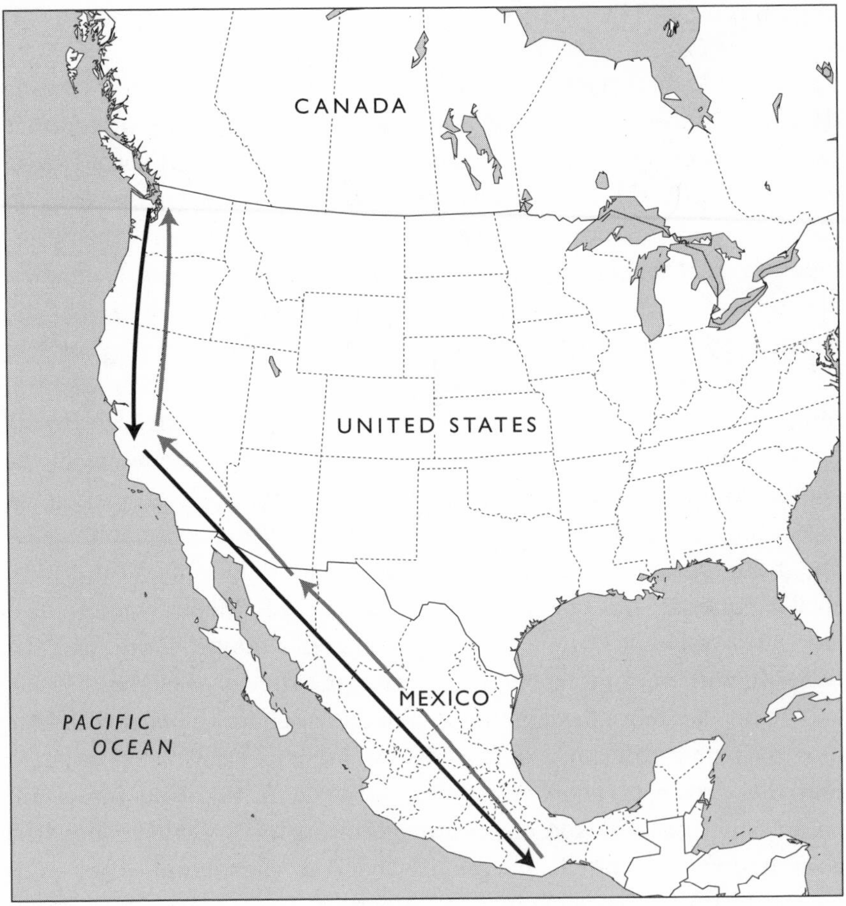

Migration fieldwork beginning in 2003 in northwestern Washington State through central California to rural Oaxaca State in Mexico and back again in 2004.

stolen. After getting off the suburban and walking up the several-mile dirt road to San Miguel, I approached *la presidencia* (the town hall). I told the four men there that I was a friend of James, the social worker and chaplain in Washington State. I was greeted with cold silence, followed by the authorities speaking quickly in Triqui that I was not able to follow, and then one of them asked, "¿Cuál Jaime?" (Which James?). When they seemed convinced we knew the same James, the man with the white plastic sombrero invited me to his house to eat. We walked up the dusty hill in silence, as I wondered what I had gotten myself into. I tried various questions like, "For how long have people from San Miguel been going to the U.S.?" "Have you heard of a social movement called the MULT here?"[5] "When was the first time you went to the U.S.?" I was greeted with dusty wind and silence. The whole meal proceeded the same way, in silence. Afterward, I thanked the man and his wife for the food and returned to the main road, where I would catch the next passing suburban.

After returning to the United States and processing this experience, I remembered Eric Wolf's article describing "closed corporate communities" in Mesoamerica.[6] According to Wolf, due to pressures from Spanish conquerors, indigenous groups separated themselves from each other in language, dress, and trust. Latin American indigenous communities became suspicious of all outsiders. I decided it would not be easy, perhaps impossible and even dangerous—as several people had suggested—to begin my fieldwork in San Miguel.

With the help of James and one of my childhood neighbors who now lived in the Skagit Valley, I began my fieldwork in northwestern Washington State. My childhood neighbor had become the pastor of the church attended by the president of one of the larger farms in the region. She helped me get permission from the farm's president to live and work on the berry farm. James and his coworkers introduced me to several families of Triqui, Mixtec, and mestizo Mexican migrants in the area. With this tenuous entrée, I moved into my one-room shack in the farm's largest migrant labor camp in early summer 2003. I lived there the rest of the summer and fall, surviving the labor camp conditions described by one close friend as "one inch above squalor," squatting down all day picking berries with the rest of the people from the camp, slowly getting to know migrant workers and other farm employees, and observing and interviewing migrant clinic workers and other area residents.

In November I accompanied an extended family of twenty-three Triqui people as they drove from Washington to the Central Valley of California. We drove below the speed limit in a caravan all night, eating homemade tacos and napping at rest stops along the way. We spent a week homeless in Madera, California, sleeping in our cars and washing ourselves in city parks. Each day we drove the town's street grid looking for housing until we found a three-bedroom, one-bathroom slum apartment. That winter, nineteen of us shared this apartment, looked for work, visited the local migrant clinic and Department of Social and Health Services, and occasionally found work pruning grapevines.

I spent spring 2004 living in San Miguel, Mexico. I lived in a partially constructed house with the extended family of Samuel: his father, who did not know his exact age but considered himself old *(viejo);* his twenty-eight-year-old sister; and his nieces and nephews, who were considered too young to cross the border with their parents. The house was made of plain concrete slabs built piecemeal with money sent by Samuel, who remained working in California. Along with Samuel's family, I used the snake-inhabited latrine, visited the government health center when sick, carried water from the well, harvested and planted corn and beans, and took the bulls and sheep to pasture. During this time, I experienced more intimately the "closed corporate community" aspect of this town. This rural Triqui town proved to be very suspicious of and unfriendly to me early on. I was repeatedly warned about violence by townspeople themselves as well as accused of being a spy for the U.S. police. A handful of times, I was threatened with being kidnapped and put in jail explicitly because "*gabachos* [white Americans] should not be here."

In April 2004, I accompanied a group of nine young Triqui men from San Miguel as they prepared to cross the border *(la línea),* trekked across the desert into Arizona, and were apprehended by the Border Patrol and put in Border Patrol jail. They were deported back to Mexico, and I was eventually released with a civil offense and a fine. I spent the rest of the month conducting interviews with border activists, Border Patrol agents, border residents, and vigilante members. In May I met up with my Triqui companions in Madera, California, after all but one of them had successfully recrossed the border. I spent the rest of May living in Central California in another slum apartment with Samuel and his extended family, and then we all migrated back to Washington State. I spent that

The author, Macario, and their Triqui companions in the border desert. Photo courtesy of Seth M. Holmes.

summer living in the same shack in the same labor camp as the year before. As I continued in my medical training and worked on this book over the next several years, I returned to visit my Triqui companions in Washington, California, and Oaxaca on numerous short trips and kept in touch over the phone.

TRAVELING TO THE BORDER

Three times a day, the bus stops. Two stops a day for food, each time for thirty minutes at a roadside restaurant I would never choose to visit. The restaurants are dirty, with flies all over and a few workers trying frantically to get food for all of us. I begin feeling sick before I even eat the food because of the smells and unsanitary sights. There are two or three choices of food that all entail meat, rice, and soda. Each time, I eat with four of my Triqui companions from San Miguel, including Macario and Joaquin. We take turns buying meals for each other and then eat all together, usually standing up since there isn't enough room to sit. The driver and his assistant are given free meals in exchange for bringing all of us to these restaurants. The conversation during these meals most often revolves around past experiences of violence and suffering on the border. Everyone appears to be on edge, nervous about what might lie ahead. People talk about whether or not we will be caught by the Border Patrol and whether or not we will die trying to cross.

Once a day, we stop to fill the bus with gas as we all attempt to use the restroom as fast as possible. These restrooms most often have two stalls for a bus full of over thirty men. As I sit on the toilet, people often say to me, recognizing my shoes under the stall door, "Hurry up, gabacho!" or "Finish, already!" They say the same things to anyone else they recognize by their shoes. Some of the stalls have no doors such that the line of waiting people directly faces the person on the toilet. The bus drives throughout the night, and we all try to sleep as much as we can since we know we will need all the energy possible for the upcoming desert trek. The bus is reminiscent of one that may have been owned by Greyhound decades earlier, the seats reclining only two or three inches. It is cramped, full of people and small backpacks, as well as fear and anxiety.

SUFFERING THE BORDER

During the first year of my fieldwork, over five hundred people died in the Tucson sector of the border alone. Most died of heat stroke and dehydration, some from direct violence. Migrants face many mortal dangers in the borderlands. There are Mexican and American assailants and kidnappers after their money; heat, sun, snakes, and cacti after their bodies; armed American vigilantes after their freedom; and Border Patrol agents after their records.

My Triqui companions often explain their everyday lives in terms of *sufrimiento* (suffering). But one of the sites of sufrimiento most frequently described by Triqui migrants is crossing the border from Mexico into the United States.[7] Many times throughout my fieldwork, my migrant companions told me stories of their harrowing experiences.

One of my friends was kidnapped for ransom with her four-year-old boy. They escaped with one other hostage through a window from the house where they were held captive for several days in Phoenix, Arizona. They found a pay phone and called their relatives in California, who immediately drove to pick them up. One young man I know described burns on his skin and in his lungs after being pushed by his coyote into a chemical tank on a train. Another man explained that he was raped by a Border Patrol agent in exchange for his freedom. All my migrant companions have multiple stories of suffering, fear, danger, and violence at the border.

Early in my fieldwork, I realized that an ethnography of suffering and migration would be incomplete without witnessing firsthand such an important site of suffering for Latin American migrants. I had read several powerful accounts of border crossings.[8] However, there have been very few firsthand accounts since the significantly increased militarization of the border after 9/11, and most of these are rather limited. For example, the Pulitzer Prize–winning "Enrique's Journey" published in the *Los Angeles Times* in 2002 (September 29) involved powerful photographs and stories from a train ride through Mexico to the border, but the photographer and his team did not actually cross the border with the Mexican and Central American migrants.

I began asking Triqui friends what they thought of the possibility of my crossing the border. They warned me of robbers, armed vigilantes, rattlesnakes, and heat. At the same time, they reminded me that the border crossing is a principal experience of sufrimiento that I should understand and began introducing me to people who might let me cross with them. In addition, I communicated with lawyers in the United States about this idea. They warned me about death by dehydration and sunstroke, death by kidnapping and robbery, and death by rattlesnake bite, as well as the possibility of being mistaken for a coyote and charged with a felony. One of the lawyers from Arizona, who specializes in immigration and the border, told me sternly not to cross but gave me her cell phone number in case I decided to try. Finally, I spoke with my family and friends. My mother shared my desire to understand inequalities and to work toward their amelioration.

At the same time, she became quite scared for me. She made me promise to call her immediately after crossing so she would know I was still alive and safe. After considering the dangers and risks, I began looking for a group of Triqui people whom I could accompany across the border.

SPRING IN SAN MIGUEL

In March 2004 I was invited to cross the border into the United States with a group of Triqui men. We planned to start together in the village of San Miguel, take a bus north through Mexico, and then trek through the border desert into Arizona. The group included nine young men from San Miguel and one from a neighboring Triqui village. Two of the men were in their late teens, hoping to enter the United States for the first time. One of these young men was the nephew of the coyote we planned to meet at the border for the final leg of the journey. The remainder of the men were in their mid- to late twenties and were returning to California. These men left their families in different agricultural areas of Central California to return home to San Miguel, share money with their relatives, help with the corn harvest, and attend the village's patron saint festival in November.

One of these men, Macario, was my neighbor in the labor camp shacks in Washington the previous summer. He was a twenty-nine-year-old father of three, with a reputation for being one of the fastest strawberry pickers. I remember being invited, during the first few months of my time in the labor camp, to his baby daughter's baptism party outside his shack. Macario's two youngest children, born in the United States, were in Madera, California, with his wife. His two older children lived in San Miguel with his parents to attend elementary school there until they were old enough to cross the border themselves. Over the few weeks prior to our departure, Macario introduced me to several of the others in the group. Joaquin was Macario's good friend and planned to return to his wife and baby boy in a berry-growing region along the coast of Central California, close to Watsonville.

I had already tried unsuccessfully to join other groups from San Miguel crossing the desert into the United States. One coyote told me a time to meet him to go with his group on a weekend morning, but when I arrived at his house it was locked and empty. I heard from my Triqui friends later that this man had wondered if I might be a spy for the U.S. Border Patrol and decided to leave without me.

Every Saturday in March and April, a full bus of border-crossing hopefuls leaves the small town of Tlaxiaco. Each of these buses includes one or two groups of five to ten people from San Miguel planning to cross. As I left San Miguel to start the journey north, almost all the Triqui people I knew from Washington and California had already returned to the States. Most people—including all the women and children—attempt to cross before the desert gets too hot in late April and May. Our trip was saturated with anxiety and fear, and it was under rather ideal circumstances: trekking with all healthy, young, fast hikers. Many groups with older or younger migrants from San Miguel hike three to five days through the desert. In addition, my Triqui friends are fortunate to cross with coyotes from their hometowns, people they know, sometimes extended family members. In general, this brings more trust and safety. Those who arrive at the border—for example, from South or Central America—and search for a guide in one of the border towns cannot know if they will find a coyote or a con man.

THE MEXICAN SIDE OF THE BORDER

Altar, the desert town where we stop in northern Mexico, is small, with several hundred residents and probably two thousand others preparing to cross the border. As the bus approaches Altar, the bus driver tells everyone to get their backpacks and get ready to disembark. Outside of town, at an abandoned gas station, he makes all of us quickly jump off and walk into town because "Altar está caliente" [Altar is hot]. Macario says to no one in particular, "De por si, Altar es caliente" [That's how it is, Altar is hot]. This brings nervous chuckles from those within earshot. "Caliente" in this context means both "hot" and "dangerous."

Laughing quietly, perhaps to cover up our anxiety, we enter the scorching sun, curse the bus driver for dropping us off so far away, and follow one of the young men in our group, who is the nephew of the coyote we plan to meet in town. My skin is already peeling from the dry, hot wind in the bus and the sun that came in through the window. Now, I begin sweating profusely.

This town scares me. It's impossible to know which person dressed in dark clothing is an assailant wanting money from easy targets and which is a person hoping to cross the border. Macario tells me to guard my money well. He remarks, "People know how to take your money without you even noticing." I push an empty soda bottle in my pocket above my money, and I feel a bit safer. There are people, mostly men, from all over Mexico and Latin America; some appear to be chilangos *[people from Mexico City] but most look like campesinos from rural Mexico. The only shops in town are small moneychangers, a Western Union, a few restaurants, grocery stores with aisles full of water bottles and Gatorade, and open-air markets full of dark-colored clothing and small backpacks. I try to figure out when to mail the three anthropology textbooks I carry in my backpack to my address in the United States so I won't have to carry them on the trek.*

The Catholic church at the center of town has hand-drawn posters along the inside walls facing the pews describing the many dangers in crossing the border: rattlesnakes, scorpions, desert insects, several species of cacti, dehydration, heat, and assailants. Each poster asks in bold, red letters in Spanish, "Is it worth risking your life?" The church has a small side room where people light candles and pray for safe passage. Macario and I plan to do this but run out of time.

Everything is so clearly and obviously set up for border crossers in this town. I wonder to myself why the whole operation hasn't been shut down by the U.S. Border Patrol if their primary goal is really to stop undocumented entry.

EXTERNALIZATION AND EXTRACTION

As described by the sociologist Michael Burawoy,[9] systems of migrant labor are characterized by a physical and temporal separation of the processes of reproduction of the labor force and the production from that labor force. The migrant laborer can survive on low wages while contributing to economic production in one context because the family, community, and state in the other context provide education, health care, and other services necessary for reproduction. In this way, the host state externalizes the costs of labor force renewal and benefits even further from the phenomenon of labor migration. In the case of my Triqui companions, this analysis holds well, as primarily healthy young men and women come to the United States to work after being raised and educated in Oaxaca. Beyond Burawoy's analysis, my Triqui companions often return to their hometown when they are unable to work due to old age, sickness, or injury. Thus that which is necessary for both reproduction and convalescence is provided in Mexico, and the United States provides only what is necessary while the migrants are working.

The separation of these processes is not a natural or a voluntarily chosen phenomenon but must be enforced through the meeting of contradictory political and economic forces. Systems of labor migration involve economic forces inviting and even requiring the cheap labor of migrants at the same time that political forces ban migrants from entering the country. Such systems must include a set of political and legal mechanisms that presuppose that the migrant is without citizenship rights and has only limited power in the state of employment. The reproduction of a system of migrant labor hinges on the inability of the migrants, as individuals or as a group, to influence the institutions that subordinate them to the other fractions of the labor force and to the employer. Ever renewed and updated legal, political, and symbolic separations produce the maximal extraction of labor as well as the inherent suffering and danger linking one side of the border to the other. Such separations include Proposition 187 in California and similar initiatives in Arizona and Colorado that make it legal for U.S. companies to pay workers only enough for daily survival and illegal for government money to go toward their health care, education, or other social services.

FROM BORDER TOWN TO BORDER

The man leading our group takes us down a residential street several blocks and then into a doorway. It opens into a one-room apartment with no furniture. This is where we will stay until our coyote arrives. The damp concrete floor is covered in several places by swaths of old, grimy carpet, presumably for sleeping. The bathroom has no water service and reeks of old garbage and urine. The shower behind the apartment is made of a hose connected to an iron rod with wet sheets for minimal privacy and a mud floor. The shower is shared by several apartments with back doors to the same yard. We eat our food in the backyard on the cement that has stains and pieces of rotten food. A skinny yellow cat meows at us, hoping for handouts.

As we sit in the hot, smelly apartment, every hour or two someone walks in unannounced. First, our coyote, who had been working in the United States, arrives and greets everyone in a mixture of Triqui and Spanish. He explains that we will leave the next evening, and then he goes out to get us all food. Macario goes with him to explain who I am and why I am there. I am nervous, wondering if this might be the end of my journey with the group. Macario returns later and tells me that he explained that I am a student who wants to experience for himself how the poor suffer. The coyote agrees to let me come along and says he will not charge me since I am trying to do this to cooperar *[lit., "cooperate," though with more of a tangible, material meaning, like doing one's part or paying one's share for a group expense] with those who suffer.*

Later comes a middle-aged Mexican man who tells us that he owns the place, asks which coyote we are with, and tells us we have to pay him to stay there. One man pays him; the rest of us keep our money hidden and tell him our coyote will pay him. As he walks out, he asks if we are hot, and a few reply in the affirmative. He turns on the hollowed-out air conditioner which is now just a see-through fan with no protection from the spinning blades. Another man walks in a couple times and asks where our coyote is by name. One of us asks who he is, and he replies, "Your raitero *[driver] for tomorrow." He asks me who I am several times and seems nervous about my being there. He tells my friends that they cannot be sure that I am not a spy for the* migra *[Border Patrol] or the police.*

I silently ponder words. Raitero, *the word used to denote our van driver, sounds unnervingly like* ratero, *which means "assailant" or "robber." The semantic confusion comingles in my mind with my tangible uncertainty about the identities and intentions of everyone we meet.*

Several hours after we go to sleep—in the wee hours of the morning—three young men walk in, turn on the bare lightbulb hanging from the ceiling, and talk loudly to each other for what feels like hours. I hide under my blanket to avoid drawing attention to my white self. In the morning, one of them announces that they are from Michoacán, that they tried to cross the day before and were deported. One slept on the seat from a van in the middle of the floor. They are much louder than any of my Triqui friends, who watch them in silence. The men from Michoacán change the TV channel from the one we had been watching, and I speak up; their disrespect of my companions pisses me off. Later, Macario tells me they are rateros and that is why they act so rude. We did not rest well. After our forty-nine-hour bus ride and this night of intrusions, I am fatigued and wonder if this desert trek is doomed before we even begin walking.

The next day, we walk through town, some in our group call their relatives asking them to wire money because they do not have enough, and we all buy gallons of water and Gatorade. Our coyote directs us to buy mayonnaise to put our money in so that it is hidden if we are attacked by rateros along the way. Apparently, we are not the only group doing this since the grocery store has aisles and aisles of each of five sizes of small mayonnaise jars. Every time we run into other people from our bus from Tlaxiaco, they wave or greet me. They all seem to think I am a coyote, and several ask me when I will take people north. Macario and his friends tell me to joke around with the others and offer to drive them to Arizona for two thousand dollars. I am too focused and nervous for this kind of game. After the preparations, we wait—trying to play cards—for our ride.

In the afternoon, a man I don't know comes in suddenly and tells us to run out the back of the apartment for our ride. The man who said I might be a spy earlier looks at the driver of the tan van behind the apartment and says in Spanish, pointing at me, "See what I mean?" The driver is a tall, light-skinned Mexican man wearing a cowboy hat, clean jeans, and a button-down shirt. The ten of us pile into the farthest back seat of a twelve-passenger van already holding thirteen people, for a total of twenty-three adult passengers. Joaquin finds an old teen tabloid magazine behind the seat, reads it out loud, and laughs. That lightens the mood some.

We drive very fast, without air conditioning or vents, for approximately three hours along dirt roads through the desert sun. Dust from the desert road filters in through the top of the closed windows and lands on our sweaty skin and clothes, turning us slowly more beige from head to toe. During this time, we pass at least two buses, ten other vans, and a handful of cars and pickups headed back toward town. The driver tells us it is caliente today and that he is nervous about getting caught.

Suddenly, after three hours on the road, the driver swerves off the road into the cacti and drives even more quickly through soft sand. He stops at a small outpost of a few houses made of bricks, cardboard, and tin piled together without mortar. Outside, there are several light-skinned mestizo men with cowboy hats and large pistols talking in the sun, squatting on concrete blocks and overturned buckets. I feel like I am entering the Mad Max movie with Tina Turner and crazy motorcycle cage fighting: an outpost of lawless rebel gangs with large guns and makeshift shelter. Some of the men turn and watch me as I get out of the van. I clearly stand out. I move into the shade, hoping to hide from the sun and their watching eyes.

Our coyote leaves with the driver for about a half hour without explaining to us what is happening. We stand together silently, waiting, thinking. Again, I worry about the identity and intentions of everyone we meet. Which of the men outside is trustworthy? Which is an armed ratero ready to steal our money, knowing that we each carry a large sum of cash? Could this whole situation be a setup?

Without explanation, our coyote motions for us to pile into the back of an old pickup truck with two other men. The floor has several cracks and holes large enough for us to see through clearly to the desert below. We ride standing up, looking alternately ahead and through the floor below for over an hour. Every once in a while we seem to be followed by another car. The pickup seems to take several unnecessary detours only to return to the main road once again. At this point, there is no option but to go forward.

A few minutes after we drop off the two other men at a smaller outpost, a camo-colored Humvee of the Mexican Grupo Beta (the Mexican Army organization whose mission it is to stop border violence against migrants) stops and asks us—especially me—questions. Luckily for me, one of the Grupo Beta soldiers is from Oaxaca and knows that I answer all the geographic questions about where I was in Oaxaca correctly. My friends from San Miguel support my story as well. The soldier looks at my passport and seems satisfied: "To my countrymen, good luck; to my friend from our sister country, God bless."

INDIVIDUALISM IN MIGRATION STUDIES

Traditional studies of migration focus on the motivations for an individual to choose to migrate. These motivations are often categorized as "push" and "pull" factors. "Push" factors are understood to be located in the "sending community" and include such things as poverty or racism in the hometown of the migrant. Conversely, "pull" factors are located in the "receiving community" and include such aspects as social networks and economic opportunities. Many experts who study what are called "risk behaviors" in the field of public health might say that these push and pull factors are weighed in the individual's "decisional balance" when this person chooses whether or not to engage in a risky behavior.[10] Such a view assumes a rationally acting individual, maximizing her self-interest and having control over her destiny through choice. Minimized in these analyses is a focus on the central importance of structural context and the ways in which structural forces constrain and inflect individual choice and direct the options available to people.

As discussed further in the concluding chapter, much of traditional migration studies assumes a dichotomy between voluntary, economic, and migrant on the one hand and forced, political, and refugee on the other. The logic behind this dichotomy states that refugees are afforded political and social rights in the host country because they were forced to migrate for political reasons. Conversely, migrants are not allowed these rights because they are understood to voluntarily choose to migrate for economic reasons. The "push" and "pull" factor school of migration studies tends to assume that labor migration is entirely chosen, voluntary, and economic.

However, my Triqui companions experience their labor migration as anything but voluntary. Rather, they have told me repeatedly that they are forced to migrate in order for themselves and their families to survive. At one point during our trek across the border desert, Macario told me, "There is no other option left for us."

CROSSING

The pickup drops us off in the middle of the desert. We thank the driver and walk over to the tall cacti to hide in their partial shade. Our coyote sneaks ahead for several minutes, then comes back and tells us there is a lot of Border Patrol activity and we need to wait here. We sit in a circle, a few people pull out their food, and we all share their totopos and dried beans. It feels good to share food with each other. It feels like family, solidarity, almost like a communion ritual before a dangerous trial of biblical proportions. Two people in our group have diarrhea and ask me for antidiarrheal pills I have in my bag. One sprained his ankle the week before on a hill by his house and asks for ibuprofen. Each time we hear the sound of an automobile, we know it could be assailants or other migrants planning to cross. We sit silently on edge. Macario pulls garlic cloves out of his bag and rubs one on his boots. He instructs me to do the same to keep away the rattlesnakes. After an hour of nerve-wracking waiting, we put on our backpacks and follow the coyote in a single-file line farther into the desert, toward the north. I can see another single-file line of border-crossing hopefuls walking in the distance as the sun begins to set. Deep in my pocket, I hold my suerte tight.

The coyote tells us to duck down and wait. He walks ahead, then motions down low with one arm, and we all run as fast as we can to and through—mostly under—a seven-foot barbed-wire fence. We run across a sand road and through another barbed-wire fence and keep running until we cannot breathe anymore. Now we walk quickly. It is around 6:30 P.M., and the sun just finished setting. We do this at least ten more times—through, under, and over tall wood and barbed-wire fences. Though I am a runner and backpacking guide in the summers, we move faster than I have ever moved without taking breaks. My mouth gets dry quickly as I hike, and I drink through a gallon of water every few hours. I carry five gallons of water and several bottles of Gatorade and Pedialyte.

We continue walking and running, occasionally ducking under or climbing over fences. We pull cactus spines out of our shins from cacti we did not see in the dark night. We walk without talking, just breathing loudly and thinking. I

The author and Triqui men in the border desert. Photo courtesy of Seth M. Holmes.

think of the mountains to our right and how the desert might be beautiful under different circumstances. I hear a dog bark and think of the towns to our left and how the people living there are likely asleep and comfortable. Macario tells me we are in Arizona now. I see no difference.

After hiking several more hours, we stop in a dried-up creek bed. I am thankful that there are no hidden cactus spines when I sit down. Again, we sit in a circle, three people pull out food, and we all share. We rub garlic on our shoes again and a few of us ready slingshots in our hands. The moon is almost full, and the desert is eerily quiet.

After hiking and running another hour, we hear a helicopter. I try to hide under tall cacti. Joaquin tells me not to look at the chopper because it can see my eyes. I remember that Triqui hunters in the mountains of Oaxaca use flashlights at dusk to find the eyes of rabbits in order to shoot them. I feel like a rabbit, vulnerable and hunted. Macario hides under a cactus that has a rattlesnake rattling at him, but he does not move for fear of being seen. The helicopter flies off into the distance until we barely hear it.

Triqui men sleeping under garbage bags in a dry creek bed in the border desert. Photo by Seth M. Holmes.

After two more hours of hiking, we stop again in a dry creek. One of the younger men enlists help pulling large cactus spines from one of his legs. We sit in a circle sharing food. Two people share cooked grasshoppers from the open-air market in Tlaxiaco. The tastes link us to loved ones and Oaxaca.

After we have hiked through blisters for many miles and I have shared all my ibuprofen with the others, we stop to rest in a large, dry creek bed under the cover of several trees. We fall asleep, using torn-open plastic trash bags as blankets. Our coyote leaves to talk with his contact on a nearby Native American reservation about giving us a ride past the second border checkpoint to Phoenix. He returns, anxious, telling us his contact no longer gives rides because of the increased Border Patrol activity. We discuss pooling our money and buying a car to drive ourselves or looking for someone else to drive us. Two of the men try to convince me to drive them into Phoenix, past the internal Border Patrol checkpoints. I tell them that would be a felony and would mean I would go to prison and lose the ability to work. They seemed satisfied by my response, respecting the need to be able to work. After we decide to look for another ride, our coyote sneaks off to look for a different driver. We wait for a few hours. We rest quietly, drink Gatorade, and brush our teeth in the creek bed.

Suddenly, our coyote runs back speaking quickly in Triqui. Two Border Patrol agents—one black and one white—appear running through the trees, jump down into our creek bed, and point guns at us.

FRAMING RISK ON THE BORDER

As I rested in the creek bed, I remember being haunted by the church's posters. "Is it worth risking your life?" At first blush, it seems clear that for the thousands who cross the border to work in the United States, the answer is a resounding "Yes." However, taking this question at face value misses an important opportunity to question its framing. As Judith Butler points out,[11] frames shape our perceptions of an entity. Frames allow an entity to break from its original context in order to be meaningful in other times and spaces.

Like much of the media discourse about migrant deaths in the borderlands, the question "Is it worth risking your life?" frames the crossing of the border as an individual choice, a choice to take on mortal risk. In the United States, this framing is used regularly to justify a lack of grief for those who die and a lack of action to achieve meaningful equality and change.

However, the reality of survival for my Triqui companions shows that it would be riskier to stay in San Miguel without work, money, food, or education. In this original context, crossing the border is not a choice to engage in a risk behavior but rather a process necessary to survive, to make life *less* risky.

APPREHENDED

The agents tell us in Spanish to put our hands up and not to move. They instruct us to take out any pens, knives, and toothbrushes from our bags and leave them on the ground and then raise our hands in the air. The agents separate me from my friends and lead us all toward the road, leaving scattered pens, nail clippers, toothbrushes, and other items littering the desert.

We wait on the curb outside a church to be taken to Border Patrol jail. The white Border Patrol agent says to me in English, "This doesn't look good for you, with a bunch of illegals." He asks who I am, and I explain I am a medical and anthropology student working on my thesis and show him the letters I brought from school and my passport.

The agents call their supervisor to let him know that they caught a "U-S-C" [U.S. citizen] with a "group of illegals." The supervisor arrives thirty minutes later and interrogates me. He stands above me and raises his eyebrows, reminding me of an angry, patronizing schoolteacher. He puts me in the back of one Border Patrol truck and my friends in another. My truck stops once to pick up two Guatemalan men who were just apprehended, once to let us urinate on the side of the road at my request, and once to take one of the two agents to the nearby Indian Health Service hospital to be treated for a rattlesnake bite he sustained as he chased us. The air-conditioning unit is not working in the back cell of our truck, and it feels like we are baking inside. While we wait in the back of the truck at the Indian Health Services hospital, I bang on the windows and ask the agent who is walking by to do something about the rising heat. He cracks open the back door and secures it with handcuffs.

As we are led into the jail, Border Patrol agents shake their heads at me and ignore my companions walking by. An older man, who appears to be in charge, stares me in the eyes and asks, "Do you really think your thesis is worth breaking federal law?" Part of me wants to say that it is not just for a thesis, but to understand our globalizing world and help work for positive social change. Part of me wants to explain that I consulted with immigration lawyers and knew all the legal ramifications of my actions and decided ahead of time it was worth it. I lower my gaze and say sheepishly, "I guess not." I don't want to make him angrier than he already seems to be since he is in control now. He tells me they are booking me for "alien smuggling," and if that does not hold they will get me for a $5,000 fine for "Entry Without Inspection."

I know the charge of alien smuggling is unlikely to stick, but it freaks me out. I know Entry Without Inspection is a civil offense and am not too worried about that on my record. As though reading my thoughts, the agent tells me that Entry Without Inspection is what drug smugglers are charged with and that will make it difficult for me to travel ever again. I wonder to myself why the agents seem so focused on and angry at me when there seem to be much more clearly dangerous criminals in the borderlands on whom they could focus their time and energy. I wonder why they are charging me with alien smuggling if they all seem to admit they knew I was doing this "for my thesis." After all, I think to myself, what crazy smuggler would carry heavy anthropology textbooks as well as letters from university officials explaining his plans?

Once in jail, my Triqui friends are put in one cell and I alone in another. After being held in my cell for a few hours and quietly singing childhood Sunday School songs to try to distract myself, I notice that my Triqui companions are being led single-file past the front desk, being fingerprinted, and having their photos taken. I wonder what this will do to their possibilities of applying for green cards in the future.

I remember reading in the pamphlet given to us by Grupo Beta that I have the right to one phone call as well as food and drink every six hours. I decide I want to call one of the immigration lawyers with whom I had already spoken. I look at a female red-headed agent through the window and motion like I am talking on the phone. The agent simply forms her mouth in the shape of "no" and looks away. I make the same motion to a young male agent, and he quickly shakes his head and furrows his brow. Three different times, agents walk up to my cell and shake their heads at me exaggeratedly and walk away. One tells me not to look at the cell where my friends are sitting. Apparently, he is afraid of what we might communicate with our faces. At one point, I count fourteen agents looking on as one of them rummages through my backpack, examining my camera, tape recorder, anthropology books, passport, and letters from people in San Miguel to loved ones in the United States.

I read the scratches on the door in my cell. Many are from women to their loved ones. Many of the messages are addressed to specific people: sisters, friends, husbands, children. I wish I had a pen and paper to write them all down. Instead, I read them over and over, trying to memorize them. I see many versions of the same Spanish phrases "100% Mexican" or "proud to be Mexican," along with statements like "don't lose hope," "God will care for you," "don't let them get you down." There are also many messages of return such as "I'll be back as soon as they drop me off" or "see you in Chicago." Unexpectedly, these messages comfort me.

When a young Latino agent comes to my cell to ask permission to look at the pictures in my digital camera, I tell him I should be allowed to talk with my lawyer. He takes me to the front desk and fingerprints me in front of the other cells of apprehended migrants. Several agents look on idly as I call the Arizona lawyer with whom I consulted earlier. She lets me know she will come in the next day to meet with me. She says the Arizona courts are overloaded, and it may be a month before I have a hearing and am allowed another phone call. She offers to call my friends and family. I start giving her phone numbers for mother and father, brother, another lawyer, and a few of my closest friends. I begin to cry, exhausted, imagining life in prison as I wait for the legal system to process my case. That is the last moment my friends from San Miguel see me. As I cry on the phone, they are taken away, put on a bus, and deported back to Mexico.

After my phone call, I am taken back to my cell. I wonder how my Triqui friends are being treated. I am forced to look at the wall on the other side of my cell and not allowed to look out my cell's window, even after my Triqui companions are gone. I want to use the toilet but avoid it since the toilet is in the open for everyone to see at the end of my cell. Besides, there is no toilet paper in the cell. In addition, I am starting to feel hungry and thirsty. Again, I remember reading that Border Patrol detainees have the right to food and drink every six hours during detention. I look at the clock on the wall. It has been over eight hours. I remember the cold responses I received asking for my phone call through the window and decide not to try.

I am deeply relieved when an agent comes to my cell and lets me know they decided not to prosecute me with smuggling and would be giving me simply the $5,000 fine for Entry Without Inspection. I wonder to myself who made this decision and want to thank them for being reasonable, saving their own time and mine. I ask for something to drink and eat and some toilet paper. He comes back with six crackers and a tiny bottle of an orange-colored drink (with 0% juice, according to the label), no toilet paper.

On my way out, I file a formal complaint against the two officers who did not let me call my lawyer. The manager taking my complaint asks me three times, "You do understand the nature of your crime, right?" It seems that she feels the need to remind me that I am the one in the wrong, not the Border Patrol agents. I wonder why law enforcement officers seem often to lack respect for the other human with whom they are interacting. I wonder how I will pay the fine. I wonder how my Triqui friends are doing and how it would feel to know you had to attempt the long trek again.

"IS IT WORTH RISKING YOUR LIFE?"

In much public health and global health discourse, as in the case of border death, the focus remains on individual risk behaviors. In much of the mainstream media, migrant workers are seen as deserving their fates, even untimely deaths, because they are understood to have chosen voluntarily to cross the border for their own economic gain. However, as pointed out above, my Triqui companions explain that they are forced to cross the border. In addition, the distinction between economic and political migration is often blurry in the context of international policies enforcing neoliberal free markets as well as active military repression of indigenous people who seek collective socioeconomic improvement in southern Mexico.

Especially important is the U.S.-initiated North American Free Trade Agreement (NAFTA) banning economic barriers, including tariffs, between signatory countries. Thus, the Mexican government was forced to erase tariffs, including that on corn, the primary crop produced by indigenous families in southern Mexico. However, NAFTA and other free trade policies do not ban government subsidies. Thus the U.S. government was allowed to increase corn subsidies year after year, effectively enacting an inverse tariff against Mexican corn. In addition, such subsidies are only possible for relatively wealthy countries and could not be enacted by the relatively poor Mexican government. During my fieldwork in San Miguel, I watched genetically engineered, corporately grown corn from the U.S. Midwest underselling local, family-grown corn in the same village.[12]

How can the immense dangers on the border be worth the risk? On the other side of the equation are heartless global politics and economic markets. At this point, staying in San Miguel means not having enough money for food and not being able to buy the school uniforms required to allow your children to attend public schools. The calculus involves slow but certain death on one side of the equation and immense risks on the other. Staying in San Miguel without sending a family member north involves a slow, communal death by the unequal, "free" market. Staying in San Miguel today means putting your life at risk, slowly and surely.

It is critically important for anthropologists as well as global and public health professionals to reframe suffering, death, and risk to incorporate analyses of social, political, and economic structures. In order to ameliorate suffering and death in the borderlands, we must focus together on the legal and political apparatuses that produce labor migration in the first place. Policies that shore up inequalities, like NAFTA and the Central American Free Trade Agreement (CAFTA), must be renegotiated and health reform legislation must be broadened to include structurally vulnerable populations, such as migrants. Without this reframing, we will continue to see not only an externalization of the costs of reproduction but also an individualization of risk and responsibility. When risk and blame are individualized, the solutions imagined and interventions planned focus on changing the behavior of the individual. However, attempting to intervene on individual behavior in such contexts draws attention away from the structural forces producing mortal danger and death in the first place. Without reorienting our understanding of risk and our subsequent interventions, we will continue to witness hundreds of human beings dying each year in the borderlands and suffering throughout the rest of their migration circuits.

AFTER BEING RELEASED

After calling an acquaintance in Phoenix, I walk through the deserted town in the dark to a Greyhound bus station and catch a Phoenix-bound bus. I rest three days in the house of this acquaintance—who, ironically, studies and writes about border death—recovering from the trip physically and emotionally. There is an intense thunderstorm with downpours of rain and flooding, and I worry for the safety and health of my friends if they are again in the desert. Not knowing what else to do, I fly back to California a few days later.

I wait in California, calling Macario's cell phone every few days to see if I can reach him. One of my anthropology classmates offers to throw a fund-raising party for me to help me pay off my fine. The party never happens, but the offer feels supportive. After a week, my Triqui companions arrive in Madera, California. One of the younger men doesn't make it back during my fieldwork because he did not have money to pay the coyote and drivers a second time. Instead, he returned to his family in Oaxaca.

When Macario and I meet again in Madera the next week, he tells me that he suffered a lot crossing the second time. He briefly speaks of blisters and more rattlesnakes, but he does not want to talk much about it because he is afraid others would make fun of him for not being tougher. He shows me the large, popped blisters on his feet and the holes in his socks. He tells me that a couple of the guys in the group blamed me for bringing bad luck. He also says that just as they were being deported, arriving at the border in Nogales, Arizona, the driver of the Border Patrol bus turned around. He took them back to the station and had them sign a statement in English that they could not read. They were told it said that I was their friend, had lived in their hometown, and was not a coyote. They finally arrived in Mexico well after dark.

BOOK ORGANIZATION

Although I have written this book with the primary format of substantial chapters, I attempt to present the unfolding narrative nature of the experience of migration. This strategy demonstrates the everyday joys and suffering involved in migration as well as the bodily experiences of multisited fieldwork in transit. Conversations, interviews, and quotes are based on either tape recordings or my own handwritten and typed notes. Translations are my own unless otherwise noted. While I have changed the names of the people and some places described in this book to protect the identities of those who entrusted me with entrée into their lives, I maintain to the best of my ability the details and richness of real experiences and observations throughout.

In Chapter 2, I explore the critical significance of understanding U.S.-Mexico migration as well as the importance of an ethnography that focuses not only on the bodies of the people under study but also the body of the anthropologist. In Chapter 3, I describe firsthand the labor segregation in American agriculture that leads to highly structured hierarchies of ethnicity, citizenship, and suffering. Here I use ethnicity not as a genetic or biological given but as a somatic and social category. As described by Mary Weismantel and others,[13] the social and economic histories of people not only reshape their bodies over time but also shape the perceptions of those bodies in such a way as to establish their ethnicity. In addition, ethnicity can be understood to be something akin to Althusser's concept of interpellation,[14] in which a human subject is positioned by social and economic structures in a specific category within power hierarchies and simultaneously recognizes oneself and others to be members of these specific categories. Sickness as the embodiment of violence is the focus of the fourth chapter, drawing on the experiences of three Triqui migrant laborers to show that illness is often the manifestation of structural, symbolic, and political violence, as well as, at times, resistance and rebellion. Chapter 5 endeavors to make sense of the acontextual lenses through which physicians and nurses see the plights of their migrant patients and, thereby, inadvertently add insult to injury by blaming the victims of structural inequalities.

Chapter 6 considers the crucial issue of how such hierarchies become taken for granted by analyzing the normalization of social and health inequalities as an example of symbolic violence.[15] For those at each rung of the social ladder, perceptions and assumptions naturalize the position of those above, of those below, and—perhaps more disturbingly—of one's own group and oneself. This chapter prompts worries about representations of marginalized people, keeping in mind the important critiques of the "culture of poverty." However, along with Philippe Bourgois,[16] I believe it is important to portray marginalized people as full human beings, showing the odds and prejudices they are up against. In line with Laura Nader's call to "study up"—to analyze the powerful and not just the marginalized—this book takes a "vertical slice," exploring every level of the social hierarchies related to the farm.[17] The conclusion of this book deals with the future for Triqui migrants, the possibility of hope, and the difficulty of resistance and change. It issues a call to listen to migrant laborers, enact solidarity with their social movements, and work toward equality at multiple levels from micro farm practices to macro global issues.

I attempt to portray and analyze the lives and experiences of Macario and my other Triqui companions in order to understand better the social and symbolic context of suffering among migrant laborers. I hope that understanding the mechanisms by which certain classes of people become written off and social inequalities become taken for granted will play a part in undoing these very mechanisms and the structures of which they are part. It is my hope that those who read these pages will be moved in mutual humanity,[18] such that representations of and policies toward migrant laborers become more humane, just, and responsive to migrant laborers as people themselves. The American public could begin to see Mexican migrant workers as fellow humans, skilled and hard workers, people treated unfairly with the odds against them. I hope these recognitions will change public opinion and employer and clinical practices, as well as policies related to economics, immigration, and labor. In addition, I hope this book will help anthropologists and other social scientists understand the ways in which perception, social hierarchy, and naturalization work more broadly. With these hopes in mind, I invite you, the reader, into the journey of migration along with me, Macario, and the other indigenous Mexican farmworkers in these pages.

TWO "We Are Field Workers"

EMBODIED ANTHROPOLOGY OF MIGRATION

> We dedicate everything to the fields, we are field workers. We are workers; ever since we're born we're planting. . . . Poor people from Oaxaca come here; we come here to give away our strength and everything and they don't do anything for us. . . . Because of our will this government survives.
>
> *Samuel, 31-year-old Triqui Mexican father, speaking with his family and me over tamales in his labor camp shack, rural Washington State, summer 2004*

The Triqui migrants and I are field workers. They harvest strawberries and blueberries in the fields of Washington State and grapes and asparagus in the fields of California year after year. My Triqui companions live far from their extended families and their native lands in the mountains of Oaxaca, Mexico. They "dedicate everything to the fields" in the United States, their labor and skills, their energy and time, and their identities and reputations, as well as their minds and bodies. The time they might have spent learning in school is spent instead working in the fields to earn money to survive. Their bodies that might have labored calmly with their family members in their own multicolored cornfields in Oaxaca or, alternatively, sat quietly working behind a desk are offered the sole prospect by the transnational market of picking fruit bent over all day, every day, moving quickly, exposed to pesticides and the weather. As a result of their dedication to the U.S. agricultural fields, their bodies ache, decay, and are injured.

My field, though spatially overlapping theirs for some time, involves a different kind of labor. I seek to understand the political and economic, cultural and social components of migrant labor and migrant health by spending time in what anthropologists call "the field." I am grateful that I have been allowed entrée into the lives of the Triqui migrant laborers described in this book through their migration in Washington, Oregon, California, Oaxaca, and the borderlands of Sonora and Arizona. During this time, I have dedicated my mind, my body, and my social experiences to the production of field notes. Ultimately, I hope that my field research and writing will work toward ameliorating the social suffering inherent to migrant labor in North America.

Broadly, this book explores ethnographically the interrelated hierarchies of ethnicity, labor, and suffering in U.S. agriculture as well as the processes by which these become normalized and invisible. The exploration begins by uncovering the structure of farm labor, describing how agricultural work in the United States is segregated according to an ethnicity-citizenship hierarchy. The book then shows ethnographically that this pecking order produces correlated suffering and illness, particularly among undocumented, indigenous Mexican pickers. Yet it becomes clear that this injurious hierarchy is neither willed nor planned by the farm executives and managers; rather, it is produced by larger social structures. Of note, these structures of inequality are very rarely problematized by any group of people on the farm, even the most exploited. In the ethnographic data, we find that this structure becomes invisible via perceived bodily differences, including ethnic conceptions of pride. Utilizing Bourdieu's theory of symbolic violence, I argue that the taken-for-granted nature of these social and health asymmetries contributes to their justification and reproduction. The book concludes with possibilities for pragmatic solidarity and beyond for positive change.[1]

EXPLAINING AND BEING EXPLAINED

Like most researchers, I have struggled with explaining my research project to different audiences. With other cultural anthropologists and sociologists, I have become accustomed to using social theory terms like "Bourdieuian" and "Foucauldian," "governmentality" and "biopower," receiving knowing looks in response, some sympathetic and others critical. However, anthropology at times seems especially difficult to explain to those outside the discipline. We do not use methods most commonly pictured with the term "research," like pipetting into test tubes or amplifying genetic markers, handing out surveys or leading structured interviews in an enclosed room. Instead, we perform participant observation over the *longue durée,* gaining field data from observations of and embodied participation in the conversations and activities of everyday life. In 1922 Bronislaw Malinowski laid out his conception of participant observation as a scientific enterprise, explaining that "there is a series of phenomena of great importance which cannot possibly be recorded by questioning or computing documents, but have to be observed in their full actuality." However, for much of the world, this appears to be primarily hanging out, asking naive questions and using a tape recorder or writing in a notebook. In fact, Clifford Geertz and James Clifford recently went so far as to use the phrase "deep hanging out" to debate the immersion fieldwork central to anthropology.[2]

As an anthropologist and a physician, my positionality has been somewhat complicated. As I began my fieldwork, I found that most people did not know the word *anthropologist,* or assumed it meant someone who studies bones and ruins somewhere like Egypt. When I moved into a berry farm's labor camp in Washington State, I tried explaining that I was a medical *and* anthropology student wanting to learn about health, labor, and ethnic relations throughout a cycle of migration. This seemed to make some sense to people and slowed down the barrage of questions as to why I, a *gabacho,*[3] was living in a labor camp. However, it also led a few pickers to come to my shack to ask for medicines for backaches and toothaches and led the labor camp foreman to introduce me as "Doctor Seth." After explaining to several people that I had no medicines and was in the camp primarily to learn, I began to assume that the other pickers put up with me in the camp as an incompetent, useless, yet interested doctor.

I was out of place in the farm hierarchy in many ways—social class, ethnicity, citizenship—and this evoked variously respect, laughter, and suspicion from people in different social locations on the farm. Of course, the confusion existed outside the farm as well. While spending the winter in California, my fellow picker, Samuel, and I drove to a laundromat to wash his family's and my clothes. At that time, Samuel was thirty-one, the father of one young boy. He grew up in the village of San Miguel in the mountains of Oaxaca and had been sending money for the past few years from the United States to his sister, nieces, and father, who remained at home. He drove an Aerostar minivan, listened to Mexican rock music, had light brown skin, wore his hair long in something of an extended mullet, and was nicknamed "Goat-head" in Triqui because of his goatee. While we were unloading our dirty clothes, another Mexican migrant in the laundromat asked Samuel in Spanish why he was doing laundry with his *jefe,* his boss. Samuel answered that I was not his boss but rather a friend. The other man was not easily convinced. "No really, why are you here with your boss?" he said in Spanish. Samuel explained that I lived in the labor camp, picked strawberries on a farm with them, and was learning their indigenous language. Samuel then summarized, "He wants to experience for himself how the poor suffer." Although I had never spoken of my work in this way, this phrase became my Triqui companions' explanation of why I was with them and what I was doing.

In many ways, this was a clear, brief description of the embodied anthropology of migrant labor I have attempted to perform for this book. This explanation also succeeded in satisfying the curiosity and suspicion of the Triqui, Mixtec, and mestizo Mexican listeners to whom it was directed.[4] My confusing presence in the lives of Triqui migrant laborers was considered legitimate, even sensible, once its goal was understood to be "experiencing how the poor suffer."[5] Poverty, violence, and embodied suffering are central experiences of their lives and are some of the primary topics of this book.

EMBODIED ANTHROPOLOGY

Anthropologists historically have imagined themselves plainly documenting facts from the outside world. As Nancy Scheper-Hughes states,

"They pretended that there was no ethnographer in the field." She argues that they treated "the self as if 'it' were an invisible and permeable screen through which pure data, 'facts,' could be objectively filtered and recorded."[6] Our selves, our bodies, have been taken for granted and assumed to be simply a tool utilized for observation (if thought of at all). By and large, we have failed to consider our bodies in the experiences of fieldwork. While the documentation of "facts" is important and may be a matter of life or death, it is also essential for anthropologists to reflect on their own embodied experiences of fieldwork. Paul Stoller calls for "sensuous scholarship," which would "incorporate into ethnographic works the sensuous body—its smells, tastes, textures, and sensations."[7] Though Stoller focuses more on the bodies of his Songhay informants than on his own embodied experiences, a focus on the ethnographer's body could be considered an intimate form of sensuous scholarship or embodied anthropology. Loïc Wacquant, the ethnographic sociologist, uses the word *carnal* to indicate field research that reflects upon the body of the ethnographer.[8]

I use the word *body* not as a reiteration of Western assumptions of a mind-body dichotomy but rather something akin to Margaret Lock and Nancy Scheper-Hughes's concept of a "mindful body."[9] In this phrase, the authors attempt to undo the disconnection between mind and body common in Western societies by arguing that the body itself feels and thinks, is "mindful." In a similar fashion, Maurice Merleau-Ponty offers a phenomenological philosophy in which the body is a subject-object interacting actively with the world, all parts of which are also subject-objects.[10] Thus the body is not something that "I have" or that "I use" to find data; rather, "I am" my body, and my body "itself/myself" produces field data.

In my own fieldwork, my bodily experiences lent valuable insights into social suffering, power hierarchies, and the implications of field work relationships. It was not only my eyes and ears that collected valuable field observations but also the back of my neck as cold rain seeped down the inside of my farm-issued rain gear; my sore knees, hips, and lower back from bending over all day in strawberry fields; my acidic stomach showing signs of stress before a day of racing against the clock to keep my picking job; my foggy and tired mind from night after night of sleep interrupted by rain leaking on my face as well as freezing wind and noises surging through the permeable walls in the migrant camp; my sore legs and hungover mind after a night of dancing, drinking, and celebrating a Triqui child's baptism; my stiff neck from living homeless out of a car while migrating from Washington to California and looking for a slum apartment; my dry throat, tired legs, and overactive imagination in the midst of running through the deadly Arizona desert after days of struggle to reach the border. These were several ways in which my body offered important field notes on social suffering. Without paying attention to my bodily experiences, I would have missed out on much of the valuable data about the everyday lives of migrant laborers.

Of course, though our living and working conditions were shared, our experiences were not always the same. After living homeless out of cars for a week in Central California, my Triqui companions and I found a slum apartment available to rent to migrant workers without credit histories. Nineteen of us (including four children under five years old) moved into this three-bedroom apartment with thin walls and hollow doors. I asked for permission to sleep in the hall closet of the apartment for privacy instead of in the doorless living room with two adults and an adolescent girl. The closet was just large enough for me to lie down if I did not use a mattress but rather positioned my body diagonally with my feet and my head in opposite corners. For me, this privacy felt absolutely necessary in order to decompress and remain sane at the end of each full day. I could not imagine sleeping in the living room to be woken up whenever one of the young children cried on the way to the bathroom or kitchen. However, my Triqui companions were visibly embarrassed and amused by my choice to be so uncomfortable instead of sleeping on a mattress in the living room with the other housemates. They repeatedly joked with other Triqui friends about the *gabacho chakuh'*[11] who chose to sleep in their hall closet when there was a perfectly roomy living room available.

This difference is clarified in Bourdieu's concept of *habitus*.[12] Bourdieu explains habitus as the mixture of bodily comportments, dispositions, tastes, and desires accreted (sequentially layered) over a lifetime of experiences. My lifetime bodily experiences (for example, living in my own bedroom in a semiurban home as a child) had accreted into a habitus needing privacy in order to relax. On the other hand, the habitus of my Triqui companions (who grew up in dirt floor huts with several people sharing one room and watching globalized television and movies depicting the physical comforts of wealthy lifestyles) could be understood to prioritize the physical comforts of space and a mattress.

My body offered insights not only via experiences of the living and working conditions of migrant laborers but also as I generated particular responses from those around me. In many circumstances, my light-skinned, tall, student-dressed, English-speaking body was treated very differently from the bodies of my Triqui companions. The supervisors on the farms never called me deprecatory names like they did the Oaxacan workers. Instead, they often stopped to talk and joke with me, all the while picking berries and putting them into my bucket to help me make the minimum required weight. The social categories inscribed on bodies led to my being treated as an equal, a friend, even a superior, while the Oaxacans were treated most often as inferiors, sometimes as animals, or machines.

Usually on payday, one or more of the Triqui families I knew went to Burger King for dinner. By the end of my fieldwork, I had become an invited guest. On one such day, I went with Samuel and his family of five in their minivan to the local Burger King. We ordered the usual: four Whoppers, four large fries, and two kid's meals. This time, however, the four Whoppers and two kid's meals came with three medium fries. Without thinking about social status, I suggested one of us go and ask for the right fries. Samuel and his wife, Leticia, looked at each other with furrowed brows. They explained to me that they could never do such a thing because they would not be given different fries and would likely get in trouble for asking. Samuel told me to go up to see what they would do to a gabacho. As I expected, they gave us four large fries and apologized kindly-resentfully. Samuel was amazed. My body was treated as though it had and deserved power, whereas theirs have been treated repeatedly as underlings, undeserving of respect.

All too often similar inequalities of treatment played out in other contexts. Multiple times in the clinics of Washington, California, and Oaxaca, Triqui companions of mine were charged incorrectly, given the inappropriate medicines, or treated generally as inferiors who should obey unquestioningly. After observing or hearing about these events, if I approached a clinic staff member for help, I was greeted with a kind (if sometimes insincere) apology and a quick rectification of the situation. When my Triqui friends asked for help, they were often brushed off or told there was nothing that could be done, "period."

My Triqui companions regularly slunk down fearfully as they asked me if a car or truck with a sign on the side was the border patrol or the police. I hardly ever noticed these cars before they were pointed out to me. My Triqui friends kept their own cars in perfect shape, every windshield crack filled, every light bulb functioning well, every sticker in its assigned place, and of course the speed always under the limit in order that the police would not pull them over. I, on the other hand, hardly ever thought of these details. Some of the migrants spoke of "Driving While Brown," indicating the effect of racial-citizenship profiling. Any minuscule problem with their cars or their driving could become an excuse for pulling them over, which, in turn, could lead to their deportation. Though the law in Washington State did not allow local police to perform racial profiling, police officers sometimes contacted Border Patrol officers for translation. Once present, the Border Patrol agent could check for documentation and would often deport those without it, breeding distrust of law enforcement officers in general. I knew that I would likely never be pulled over for a small crack in my windshield or a brake light out, and if I were I would likely get a simple if authoritarian verbal warning. After many months of living, eating, seeking medical treatment, and driving with migrant workers in the United States, it became clear that everyone around us recognized my body as belonging in a significantly different place in our society's power structure than did the bodies of my Triqui friends.

In addition to the comprehension of social suffering and strong social hierarchies, my embodied experiences led me to recognize the impossibility of separating research from human relationships. Despite my training in social theory and reading of many ethnographies, I subconsciously assumed I simply would spend a year migrating with Triqui people in order to understand and write about an important and possibly difficult reality. Given that most ethnographies give the impression of an unchanged and often uninvolved anthropologist, I did not consider seriously how I myself might be changed. Unlike the portrayal of the unchanged anthropologist using his body objectively to observe facts, my experience of anthropological fieldwork required many levels of personal involvement and changed me in unexpected ways.

First, I have become more involved in the social requirements of friendship than I had imagined beforehand. As people slowly allowed me into their lives, homes, and confidences, I became more an odd friend than simply a researcher. After living together in the same labor camps, picking berries together, going to the same clinics, and sleeping in the back of the same cars, my Triqui companions began to trust me. When I first moved into the labor camp in Washington State, rumors spread around the camp that I might be a CIA agent or a drug smuggler looking for a good cover. After I lived there for several months, Samuel and the other pickers I had come to know countered these rumors, using what had become the most common explanation of me as the *gabacho chakuh'* who wanted to experience how the poor suffer. This increasing trust led me to be invited to meals, births, baptisms, healings, and even a strike. It also led me to be an unwitting part and recipient of alliances, family feuds, hatred, rumors, and possibly sorcery. The unexpected reality of these relationships has led to regular calls from across the country asking for help dealing with a clinic, the people who stole my friend's car, or the police. It brings expectations of cross-country flights for visits and of regular communication.

Friendship, of course, has meant that I participate in a version of the gift exchange practices of my companions from the Triqui Zone of Oaxaca. In exchange for trusting me with their everyday lives, I spent money, time, and anxiety bringing more than my airplane- and bus-share of bags full of Triqui food, bright pink hairpins, birth certificates, photographs, cactus needles for sewing, hundred dollar bills, broken cameras, and new stereos to and from Oaxaca, California, and Washington on behalf of family members who could not travel as freely across borders as I. I also gently and nervously turned down many requests to take cars, vans, and U.S.-citizen children of undocumented parents across the border.

These relationships brought not only the foreseeable requirements and benefits mentioned above but also expectations of solidarity, advocacy, and activism. A body cannot live the reality of another category of people without being changed in some sense. In my case, I see this in my altered experience of the fruit I eat and the rural vistas I encounter, in my remembering the often hidden complexities of the social structures in which I and my living conditions are embedded, as well as in my lingering back and knee pains. In addition, I have had a growing desire to be involved in actions for local and larger-scale structural change. Every week of my fieldwork, I was approached by at least one Triqui companion for assistance in interactions with stores, clinics, traffic police, or state health care programs for U.S.-citizen children. Without these invitations to extremely micro, local forms of advocacy, I would not have understood the inordinate amount of time and energy spent by my companions negotiating interactions with U.S. society. I would not have understood how poorly migrant workers are treated or how much this treatment might change in the presence of an educated white American.

These regular experiences of prejudice and hierarchy fed my desire to work for larger social change. Although most of my Triqui friends took for granted their position in the world the majority of the time, sometimes they questioned the organization of this society and of the world. In these moments, I was asked to stay involved in their lives, to keep talking and writing about their lives, and to join them working for a better future. I have been asked to invite them to speak to other gabachos—and have been shocked how often conferences on migration include no migrants, even though they are presumably experts on the topic. In the conclusion of this book, I attempt to flesh out some suggestions for positive change, from my Triqui companions and from my own analysis.

From experiences of the living and working conditions of migrant laborers to the intricacies of becoming involved in a web of relationships to the corollary expectations and desires for active solidarity, my embodied experiences enriched my fieldwork in unexpected ways. Alongside the imperative role of record keeper is the critical anthropologist's responsibility to acknowledge the field notes offered by the body.[13] This embodied experience offers thickness and vividness to the ethnographic description of everyday life, including such critical realities as social suffering, inequality and hierarchy, and local and global solidarity. In this book, I attempt a critical *and* reflexively embodied anthropology of the context and everyday lives of indigenous Mexican migrant laborers.

THE IMPORTANCE OF MIGRANT FARMWORKERS

The phenomenon of migration is especially important to understand in the contemporary world given the growing number of migrants and the negative ways they are perceived and treated. The United Nations Population Division estimates conservatively that there are 175 million migrants in the world, nearly 50 percent more than a decade earlier.[14] In the United States, researchers estimate that there are over 290 million residents, including 36 million immigrants,[15] approximately 5 million to 10 million of whom are unauthorized.[16] In addition, it is estimated that approximately 95 percent of agricultural workers in the United States were born in Mexico, 52 percent of them unauthorized.[17]

However, it is not only the sheer number of migrants but also the ways they are perceived and treated that make this topic important. Of note, the United States deports approximately 4,000 people a week, mostly to Mexico, and the Board of Immigration Appeals has a backlog of 56,000 cases.[18] Approximately 5,000 immigrants under eighteen years of age are apprehended and detained each year, most along the border with Mexico.[19] Regardless of the financial status of these child-detainees, the U.S. government does not provide defense attorneys. In addition, the U.S.-Mexico Border Counties Coalition has claimed that seventy-seven hospitals along the border are in a state of financial emergency and lobbied for reimbursement for the costs of emergency treatment of migrants along the border.[20]

Beyond these policy issues related to the border, several anti-immigrant policies have been enacted in the United States. In 1994 the voters in California passed the "Save Our State" initiative, Proposition 187, denying public services (including health care and education) to anyone "reasonably suspect[ed]" to be undocumented. In 2004 Arizona voters passed the Arizona Taxpayer and Citizen Protection Act, requiring proof of citizenship in order to vote, proof of immigration status in order to receive all public benefits, and criminal charges against public employees who do not report people suspected of being undocumented. Similar policies have been passed in other states far from the border, such as Colorado.

Despite the importance of these anti-immigrant policies, it is more precisely international economic policies that form the root of contemporary global labor migration. As mentioned in the introduction, on January 1, 2003, the North American Free Trade Agreement (NAFTA) began deregulation of all agricultural trade.[21] The Mexican government has pointed out that since NAFTA's initial implementation in 1994 the United States has raised farm subsidies 300 percent.[22] Throughout the past two decades, a cash-strapped Mexican government, on the other hand, has reduced financial supports for corn producers, most of them indigenous campesinos from southern Mexico,[23] leading more and more to migrate in order to survive.[24] Mexican activists are pressing the Mexican government to renegotiate NAFTA so that more farm owners and workers will not be forced by poverty to emigrate for wage labor.[25]

In various areas of rural Mexico, rebel groups have risen up, some armed and some not, to demand a change to the structural violence of these neoliberal international policies justified by "development" and "free trade." They demand "work, land, housing, food, health, education, independence, freedom, democracy, justice, and peace."[26] Several communiqués from such groups point out migration or displacement as a specific motivation for their uprising.[27] In response, military and paramilitary groups have enacted massacres and disappearances of anyone suspected of being related to these rebel movements.[28]

Clearly, migration is a significant and often violent and painful reality in the contemporary world. It is intimately related to other modern problems—neoliberal market policies, increasing global inequalities, representations of "development," decentralized warfare, and more. What is often called "the migrant problem" is particularly compelling in the United States as it relates to diasporic Mexican farmworkers.[29] These laborers are threatened by various brutalities in Mexico and the United States and are the focus of ongoing debates on immigration law and policy in both countries. Yet we know relatively little about the everyday lives of this largely hidden population. In order to confront these distressing realities, it is vital that we begin to understand more fully what causes people to migrate, the suffering effected by the living and working conditions of Mexican migrants in the United States, and the responses of migrant health clinicians and policy makers, as well as the perceptions and stereotypes that might normalize these problems.

According to my farmworker companions, migration is a recent phenomenon for the Triqui people. In the late 1980s and early 1990s, Triqui migrant workers began coming to Washington State for the berry picking season in the summer and fall and returning to San Miguel in the winter to attend the town's patron saint festival and to help their families with the corn harvest. Since 9/11 and the increasing militarization of the border with Operation Gatekeeper and other programs whose explicit goal it is to "close the border," most Triqui migrants have taken to staying in the United States several years at a time before returning. Ironically, the forceful efforts to keep immigrants out has caused many of them to stay longer. Most have a specific financial goal such as saving enough to build a house or to pay a bride-price in order to get married. It is simply too dangerous and financially costly to cross the border each year. Everyone in San Miguel knows someone who has died in the deserts of Arizona and someone who was kidnapped or robbed along the way. While most Triqui migrants make between $3,000 and $5,000 a year, each crossing now costs between $1,500 and $2,500 for rides, food, and a coyote. Some of the migrants in their late teens and early twenties still attempt to return home each year for the patron saint festival in early November and stay through Christmas. Because of this, the population of San Miguel is largest in November and December and then shrinks slowly as winter turns to spring and people take buses north to the border to risk another crossing.

At this point researchers estimate that there are one million indigenous Mexicans, mostly Mixtec and Triqui from the state of Oaxaca, in the United States.[30] Triqui people come from several villages in the mountains of the region known as La Mixteca. They now make up the majority of farm labor in northwestern Washington and are increasing in number in other parts of the United States, including a few towns in Oregon, a few farms in California, and the rural area near Albany, New York. Their history is defined by domination from many sides—Spanish conquerors, American Protestant and Mexican Catholic missionaries, and Mexican politicians, as well as neighboring mestizo and indigenous groups. Their present is permeated by a well-known reputation for violence both from outside and from within. Each of these experiences of domination and violence has led to displacement for the Triqui people, who now have to respond to structural violence and inequality with another form of displacement, migration. Triqui migrants are especially important to understand, due to their relatively recent move into migrant labor, their growing number in various migration circuits, and their position at the bottom of many social hierarchies.

In addition, as Daniel Rothenberg demonstrates, there are intimate connections between migrant farmworkers and the rest of the American public.[31] It is likely that the last hands to hold the blueberries, strawberries, peaches, asparagus, or lettuce before you pick them up in your local grocery store belong to Latin American migrant laborers. How might we respect this intimate passing of food between hands?

THE VIOLENCE OF MIGRANT FARMWORK

This ethnography endeavors to uncover the linkages among suffering, social inequalities related to structural violence, and the normalizing symbolic violence of stereotypes and prejudices. It attempts to do this while telling the stories of indigenous Mexican migrant laborers who are largely hidden from public view. By structural violence, I mean the violence committed by configurations of social inequalities that, in the end, has injurious effects on bodies similar to the violence of a stabbing or shooting. This is what the English working men described by Friedrich Engels called "social murder."[32] Much of the structural violence in the United States today is organized along the fault lines of class, race, citizenship, gender, and sexuality.[33]

Symbolic violence is a concept from the French sociologist Pierre Bourdieu, indicating the interrelations of social structures of inequalities and perceptions.[34] For Bourdieu, the lenses through which we perceive the social world are issued forth from that very world. Because of this, our lenses of perception match the social world from which they are produced. Thus, we come to (mis)recognize the social structures and inequalities inherent to the world as natural. Symbolic violence works through the perceptions of the "dominating" and the "dominated" (in Bourdieu's words), while it tends to benefit those with more power.[35] Each group understands not only itself but also the other to belong naturally in their positions in the social hierarchy. For example, the powerful tend to believe they deserve the successes they have had and that the powerless have brought their problems on themselves.

Structural violence—with its pernicious effects on health—and symbolic violence—with its subtle naturalization of inequalities on the farm, in the clinic, and in the media—form the nexus of violence and suffering through which the phenomenon of migrant labor in North America is produced. This book attempts to make sense of the lives, labor, and suffering of Triqui migrant laborers in Mexico and the United States through these concepts. More broadly, it engages a critically embodied anthropology to confront the ways in which certain classes of people become written off or deemed less human.

THREE Segregation on the Farm

ETHNIC HIERARCHIES AT WORK

THE SKAGIT VALLEY

In fall 2002 I visited northwestern Washington State to explore the possibility of field research with migrant farmworkers in the area. Driving north from Seattle into the Skagit Valley, I was struck by the natural beauty of the landscape. The large Skagit River flows west from the snow-covered peaks of North Cascades National Park to the Pacific Ocean's Puget Sound, pouring through some of the most scenic vistas in North America. The river is located roughly halfway between Seattle, Washington, and Vancouver, British Columbia, about an hour and a half drive from each. The valley is made up of berry fields, apple orchards, and the dark green evergreen tree stands common in the rainy Pacific Northwest, with the occasional brightly colored tulip field or brown dirt field lying fallow. Skagit County uneasily links upriver logging towns in the mountains such as Concrete, railroad towns at the base of the mountains like Burlington, floodplain farming towns including Bow in the flats, coastal upscale villages like La Conner at the mouth of the river, and Native American reservations such as Lumi Island. The area is most famous for its tulip festival every spring, though it also receives many visitors who patronize the Skagit Valley Casino run by the Upper Skagit Indian Tribe as well as take advantage of the area's many hiking trails. When I was a child in eastern Washington, the northwestern part of the state figured in my imagination as a place of idyllic farmland with views of mountain peaks and Puget Sound islands.

As I came to discover during my first visit to Skagit County, most of the agriculture is found in the low, flat floodplain of the Skagit River. This land is protected from the tides of the Puget Sound by a grassy dirt dike some five feet high that gently curves along the meeting of the valley and the bay. The wide dirt path atop the dike has some of the most stunning three-hundred-sixty-degree views I have ever seen. To the west, the sun sets amid the San Juan Islands. The coastal mountains of Washington and British Columbia lie nearby to the north. To the east rises the glacier-covered volcano, Mount Baker, surrounded by several other snowcapped mountains. Large, dilapidated wooden barns peep out from patchwork tulip and berry fields to the south. One might notice as well the exhaust hovering over the ocean near a paper mill in the distance.

The valley is made up of several towns lining Interstate 5, with charming turn-of-the-century brick and wood town centers surrounded by ever-expanding strip malls, apartment buildings, and housing developments. The homes of the local elite boast magnificent views from the wooded hilltops and the coastline at the edges of the valley. Most of the land covered by the uninspiring strip malls was a flower or berry field in the late 1990s or early 2000s. In the valley, one commonly hears heartrending stories of the difficult state of family farming in the United States—stories of neighbor Benson's dairy farm closing after five generations because he could not compete with corporate agribusiness in the Midwest after recent federal policy changes, farmer Johnson's berry fields being shut down after nearly a century due to increasing competition from China and Chile, and orchardist Christensen's shame at selling his land to the developers of a new Wal-Mart after his family had been growing apples since arriving from Scandinavia. A common bumper sticker in the valley rails against this phenomenon: "Save Skagit Farmland, Pavement Is Forever." The remaining agricultural land is still cultivated by several family farms, relatively small in comparison with much of U.S. agribusiness.

MIGRANT FARMWORKERS IN THE SKAGIT VALLEY

As I came to discover over the course of my fieldwork, the Skagit Valley is an important site in multiple transnational circuits of Mexican farm laborers,[1] including indigenous Triqui and Mixtec people from the southern Mexican state of Oaxaca. A few thousand migrate here for the tulip-cutting and apple- and berry-picking seasons in the spring and live several months in squatter shacks made of cardboard, plastic sheets, and broken-down cars or in company-owned labor camps, often in close proximity to the multilevel houses of the local upper class that have picturesque views of the valley. The migrant camps look like rusted tin-roofed tool sheds lined up within a few feet of each other or small chicken coops in long rows.[2] In the labor camp where I came to live, the plywood walls are semicovered by peeling and chipping brown-pink paint. There is no insulation, and the wind blows easily through holes and cracks, especially at night. Each unit is elevated a foot off the ground and has two small windows on one side, some of which are broken and most of which are covered by pieces of old cardboard boxes. The ground around the camps is often deep mud or a dust storm waiting to be triggered by a passing car. During summer days, the rusty tin roofs of the units conduct the sun's heat like an oven, regularly bringing the inside to over 100 degrees Fahrenheit. At night, the air is damp and cold, reaching below 32 degrees Fahrenheit during the blueberry season in the fall.

During the first and last phases of my fieldwork, I lived in a 10-by-12-foot unit that the farm calls a *cabina* (cabin) in the middle of the largest labor camp on the farm. It might be more appropriately called a "shack." Normally, a minimum of one family would share a shack of this size. Mine had one old, damp mattress with rust stains from the springs on

Farm labor camp. Photo by Seth M. Holmes.

which it rested, a tiny sink with orange-colored water from separate hot and cold hoses, an old and smelly refrigerator, and a camping-style dual-burner gas stove. The bathrooms and showers were shared in separate, large, plywood buildings with concrete floors. Shacks like these, where thousands of workers and their families live in the county, are most often hidden away from public view, in compounds behind the farm company's tree stands or behind other farm buildings.

THE TANAKA BROTHERS FARM

The Tanaka Brothers Farm is the largest farm in the Skagit Valley, employing some five hundred people in the peak of the picking season, late May through early November. During the winter, employment dwindles to some fifty or so workers. This family farm is owned and run by third-generation Japanese Americans whose parents' generation lost half their land during the internment of the 1940s. The part of the family with hundreds of acres on Bainbridge Island near Seattle was interned suddenly, and all their land was seized by the government. The part of the family in the Skagit Valley had time to entrust their farm to an Anglo-American family with whom they were friends and thus avoided the same fate. Today the farm is famous for strawberries, many from the "Northwest variety" cultivated by the father of those currently running the farm. The business is vertically integrated, incorporating everything from a plant and seed nursery to fruit and berry production and even a processing plant. However, most of the fruit and berries produced on the farm are sold under the label of larger businesses, from berry companies like Driscoll to dairy companies like Häagen-Dazs. The farm consists of several thousand acres, much of the land visible to the west as one drives Interstate 5 through the valley. The majority of the land is planted with expansive rows of strawberry plants, although significant numbers of fields are dedicated to raspberries and apples, as well as organic and so-called traditional blueberries.

At the base of a forested hill, abutting one of the blueberry fields on rural Christensen Road, lies the largest migrant labor camp on the farm, housing some 250 male and female workers and their families every summer. This camp is made up of plywood shacks with no insulation, no heat, and no wood layer under the tin roof. Immediately above this camp, on Christensen Heights Road, stands a group of five beautiful, relatively large houses partially hidden by trees with floor-to-ceiling windows that capture the panorama of the picturesque valley. The other two labor camps are relatively hidden behind the large, warehouse-sized concrete processing plant and the farm headquarters. The camp closest to the road houses about fifty year-round employees, is insulated and heated, and has a layer of wood under the tin roofs. The other camp, located a few hundred yards from the road, holds almost one hundred workers and their families in the summer. The shacks in this camp have a wood layer under the tin roof and insulation but no heating. Diagonally across from two of the labor camps and the concrete processing plant are the houses of some members of the Tanaka family. The one most visible from the main road is a one-story brick house behind a large white, wooden fence, reminiscent of a small Jeffersonian plantation house. A public elementary school sits directly across from the main entrance to the smaller two labor camps.

The Tanaka farm advertises itself as "a family business spanning four generations with over 85 years experience in the small fruit industry." The farm's stated business goal is to produce high-quality fruit and sell it for profit. This farm specializes in berries with high taste content sold for use in dairy products (ice creams, yogurts, etc.) that use few or no preservatives, artificial flavors, or colors. Their Northwest variety strawberry is red throughout, with an incredible amount of tasty juice and a shelf life of minutes, distinct from the fresh-market "California variety" strawberries sold in grocery stores that are white in the middle with less flavorful juice and a much longer shelf life. Several of the Tanaka farm's fields produce organic blueberries and are comanaged with and sold under the label of a large organic food producer. On a practical level, employees on the farm plant, grow, harvest, process, package, and sell berries, supporting the explicit goals of the company.

On a subtler level, the structure of farmwork inheres an intimate and complex segregation, a "conjugated oppression."[3] Philippe Bourgois coins this term in his analysis of a Central American banana plantation to show that ethnicity and class work together to produce an oppression experientially and materially different from that produced by either alone. After my first few weeks living in a migrant camp and picking berries, I began to notice the intricate structuring of labor on the farm into a complicated hierarchy. In the case of contemporary U.S. agriculture, the primary fault lines of power tend to fall along categories of race, class, and citizenship. The structure of labor on the Tanaka farm is both determined by the asymmetries in society at large—specifically around race, class, and citizenship—and reinforces those larger inequalities. The complex of farm labor involves several hundred workers occupying many distinct positions, from owner to receptionist, field manager to tractor driver, berry checker to berry picker. People on the farm often described the hierarchy in vertical metaphors, speaking of those "above" or "below" them, of "overseeing" or of being "at the bottom." Responsibilities, anxieties, privileges, and experiences of time differ from the top to the bottom of this labor organization. The symbolic vertical

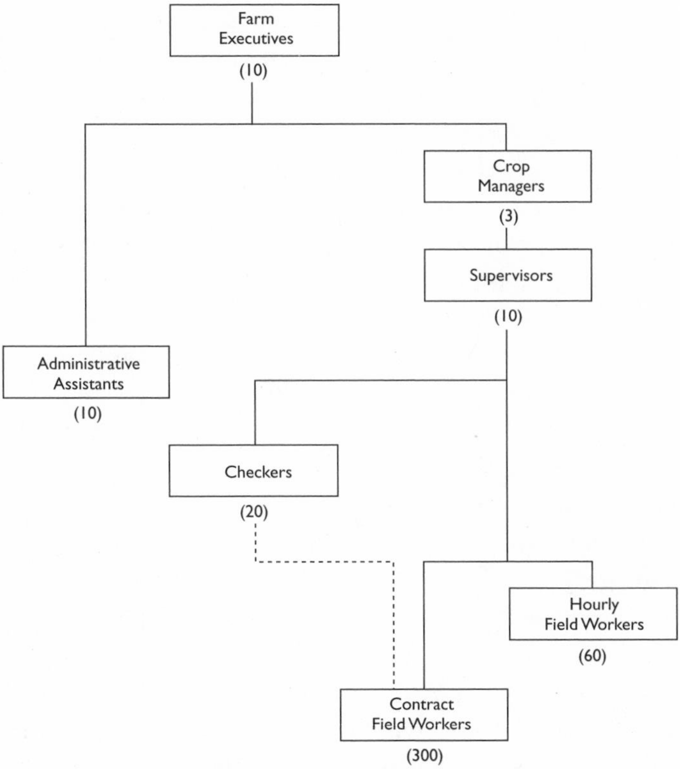

Labor hierarchy on the farm. Solid lines denote direct oversight; dotted lines, less formal oversight.

metaphor also corresponds to hiddenness and visibility, with those at the top most visible from outside the farm and those at the bottom most hidden. In congruence with the vertical metaphors used by those on the farm, the remainder of this chapter uncovers the social stratification of farm labor, moving from "the top" to "the bottom."

FARM EXECUTIVES

Today the third generation of Tanaka brothers makes up the majority of the farm's executives; the rest are Anglo-American professionals brought in from other agricultural businesses. They worry primarily about farm survival in a bleak landscape of competition in the midst of increasing corporate agribusiness, expanding urban boundaries, and unequal economic globalization.

Over the course of my fieldwork, many of my friends and family who visited me in the labor camp quickly blamed the farm management for the poor living and working conditions of berry pickers. They automatically assumed that the growers could easily rectify the situation. This supposition is supported by other writings on farmworkers, many of which describe the details of pickers' lives but leave out the experiences of the growers.[4] The fact that the perspectives of farm management are generally overlooked inadvertently encourages the assumption that growers may be wealthy, selfish, or unconcerned.

The stark reality and precarious future of the farm serve as reminders that the situation is more complex. The corporatization of U.S. agriculture and the growth of international free markets squeeze growers such that they cannot easily imagine increasing the pay of the pickers or improving the labor camps without bankrupting the farm. In other words, many of the most powerful inputs into the suffering of farmworkers are structural, not willed by individual agents. In this case, structural violence is enacted by market rule and later channeled by international and domestic racism, classism, sexism, and anti-immigrant prejudice.[5] However, structural violence is not just a simple, unidirectional phenomenon; rather, macro social and economic structures produce vulnerability[6] at every level of the farm hierarchy.

The structural nature of the labor hierarchy comes into further relief when the hopes and values of the growers are considered. The Tanaka farm executives are ethical, good people who want the best for themselves, their workers, and their local community. They want to live comfortably, treat their workers well, and leave a legacy for their children and grandchildren. They have a vision of a good society that includes family farming as well as opportunities for social advancement for all people. Several of them are involved in local nonprofits working toward such hopes for society. At different points during my fieldwork, several of them wanted my opinions on how the labor camps could be improved for the workers. After the picker strike described in chapter 6 in which explicit racist treatment of the pickers in the fields was brought to light, the growers were visibly surprised and upset. They promptly instructed the crop managers to pass along the message that all workers are to be treated with respect. Of course, the executives share some complicity with the unfair system, and some are more actively racist and xenophobic than others. Overall, however, perhaps instead of blaming the growers, it is more appropriate to understand them as human beings doing the best they can in the midst of an unequal and harsh system.

The current farm president, John Tanaka, now in his fifties, is the second oldest of the brothers. He grew up on the farm and upon graduating from college joined the military. After serving as an army officer for twenty-six years, John returned to the farm and became its president. He has the quick speech patterns and erect posture one might expect of a military officer, as well as the ability to maneuver conversations through controversial issues one might expect of a political leader. As president, one of his roles is to help promote a positive view of the farm in the local community. Toward this goal, he heads a nonprofit organization to protect farmland, meets regularly with several community groups, and recently ran for the County Council. His primary role, however, is to oversee all the operations of the farm in such a way as to ensure profitability.

I met John Tanaka on my first trip to the Skagit Valley, as I was looking into the possibility of doing full-time field research with Triqui migrant workers in the area. After flying to Seattle, I drove north on Interstate 5 and arrived in the beautiful agricultural valley at the current home of my childhood neighbor. This woman, now in her early thirties, grew up next door to me in eastern Washington and attended the same junior high, high school, and church. Her first job after graduating from college and seminary was as pastor of a small Methodist church in Skagit County. During the week I stayed with her and her husband, she told me that the main farm with Triqui migrant laborers was the Tanaka Brothers Farm. On Sunday I attended her church service, during which she introduced me to John Tanaka and his wife and let John know that I was interested in doing anthropological fieldwork in the area related to migrant laborers, ethnic relations, and health. He and his wife were friendly, and he seemed intrigued by the idea. The next day, I met him at 5:30 in the morning in his office at the farm to discuss the possibility of my living in the farm labor camp where most of the Triqui families lived and picking berries over the course of the summer. John indicated that he would be interested to learn more about the indigenous Oaxacan migrant workers, as he had only relatively recently been made aware of the distinction between "regular" Mexicans (as most people in the area referred to mestizo Mexicans) and indigenous Mexicans. We kept in touch over the remainder of the spring, and I moved into the labor camp in early June.

John's work schedule is influenced by weather, the growth rate of plants, the meetings of community groups, the hours of berry markets, and the current state of the farm's workforce. He begins his workdays usually before 6:00 A.M., takes a break in the middle of the day to work out at a nearby gym or eat lunch with his wife, and comes back to work until the late afternoon. He works seven days a week on the farm, except during the winter, when he works at the affiliated plant nursery in California. He explained to me that in California farms are required to pay overtime if anyone works more than six days a week. In Washington there is no such regulation. Most of John's time is spent indoors behind his desk, though he also visits the fields from time to time to see how things are going and to make his presence known. He explained to me that the farmworkers liked seeing him when he visited the fields. His daily worries orbit around such things as profitability, with its many inputs related to weather, bird activity, market price, and labor crew retention. Over several conversations, John told me about the difficulties of attempting to manage all the variables playing into the business side of the farm. Sitting behind his desk in his private office in the trailer that functions as the headquarters of the farm, John elaborated on some of the difficulties of running a family farm: "It's different than other businesses, where you grow a business and then sell out or reach a certain profit level that you're comfortable with. In our business, we grow it for the next generation. Which means that when I retire, you know, I can't pull dollars out of the company, because it would leave the next generation with a big gap. We know that, and that's what we focus on."

During my second summer in the Skagit Valley, John agreed to a conversation with several interested area residents organized by a local nonprofit working with migrant laborers. The conversation took place in a conference room on the second floor of the farm's processing plant that had a large window overlooking the assembly-line workers in yellow rubber aprons and hairnet caps. John took questions from the primarily white audience of twenty-some people, and the answers were translated into Spanish for the two Spanish-speaking area residents who attended. Here, he responded to questions about the main issues faced by the farm.

John: The challenge for us at a management level is to maintain our fair share of the market. . . . The difference is that in South Carolina, they have federal minimum wages, $5.75 an hour. In Washington, I'm paying a picker $7.16, the state minimum wage, competing in the same market. That's a huge difference, huge difference.

I would say the largest challenge . . . is probably offshore competition. For example, China: they could take a strawberry and bring it to San Francisco and deliver it to a restaurant cheaper than we can. And a lot cheaper to Japan. We pay $7.16 an hour. In most countries that we're talking about here, China or Chile or wherever, they don't pay that a day!

Now, the other side . . . is a labor issue. That's the next—probably the largest issue that faces agriculture today. Right now, we feel comfortable—today—with the labor forces that we have and that we believe are available to us. But, as we look into the future, I think that's going to be a problem. What we're looking at is either we have to find a way to do what we do today with machines. Or we've got to find the right kind of labor market that will keep providing us that labor force that we're going to need to harvest our crops.

It's a multidimensional issue. What happens is that the first generation comes over and they're willing to work in the fields. But the next generation, they're schooled here, and they don't quite see the same passion for the fields.

Female area resident: Fourteen dollars an hour putting up drywall starts to look good *[laughs].*

John: Given education and other opportunities, they do other things, which is fine. I don't have any problem—I mean, our family did the same thing. I go back into the forties and we've seen Canadian Indians;

> we've seen the Hispanics, not out of Mexico, but inside of eastern Washington and Oregon, California, Texas. That was the first part. And then we saw the Cambodians, the Vietnamese. Then we started to see the migration of the Hispanics out of Mexico. And then they went further. They went out of the state of Oaxaca, where a lot of them come from today. What you see is that same generational trend: the first generation works in the fields, a lot of them stay with you; the next generation, fewer of them stay with you, and more of them are educated and do other things. It's my belief that once any particular group of people go through a three-generation move, they'll no longer be in agriculture. Unless they own the farm and are running it themselves.

John recognizes that the living and working conditions of pickers are so undesirable that each group will move out of this position as quickly as possible. The pickers come from the most vulnerable populations at any given time. As each group advances socially and economically, a more exploited and oppressed group takes its place. Over the course of my fieldwork, the children of Triqui migrants have been learning English in school and hoping to find other kinds of work, though there have been very few options available to them thus far, due largely to the prejudice and ethnic hierarchies that exist in the United States. In one sense, this narrative of ethnic succession functions to justify the plight of the group currently at the bottom of the hierarchy. That is, it appears to foster the sense that it is all right that certain categories of people are suffering under poor living and working conditions at present because other groups have had to endure these conditions in the past. Some people begin to perceive this as a natural, evolutionary story.

John's younger brother, Rob Tanaka, is responsible for the direct agricultural production of the farm. Rob is a tall, bearded man with a kind, gentle personality. He plans everything from planting to harvest and oversees those in charge of each crop. His office is located in a small house in the middle of the berry fields, several miles from the main offices. He spends most of his time in this office, although he works also via laptop in the small lounge of the main office building and visits the fields often. Over several conversations in the small lounge in the main office building, Rob described to me his anxieties related to his work. His primary concerns related directly to farming—weather, insects and birds, soil quality, labor—though he was concerned also with competition and the survival of the farm.

Seth: What things could cause the most problems?

Rob: For us, it's labor. We can grow the best crop there is, but if we don't have the people to harvest, we're pretty well sunk. Also weather. There's flooding, freezing. A frost kills the growing buds, so you can lose anywhere from 5 to 40 percent of your crop. And regulations somewhat. Regulatory issues which change your practice usually pick the edge off, and it goes to someone else.

It's also urban growth. There will be battles for preserving farming if that's what one wants. If we plan on trying to farm and hand it down, and all of a sudden here's all these buildings being built, we'd go, "Oh, wait a minute, I thought we were going to continue farming for another hundred years in the valley." Wherever the border of growth is, the guy on the other side of the fence is just waiting to sell because it's all economics. I understand that. Would you rather have two hundred bucks or two hundred thousand? How can farming compete with that? Especially now, as the processors move out and production is going offshore where it's cheaper.

Costs are up on everything, pricing's pretty much stayed the same. In the old days, those were all separate companies: the plant nursery, the farmer, the processor, the broker. Now, we're making it all in-house, and we hope this'll help us survive.

There are a lot of worries I have about expanding. Any time we decide to do something bigger, it's like, "Wow, you want to take this headache and make it bigger? Are you sure?" *[Chuckles]* And we're trying to look to the future for our kids and the next generation and the future of the community. . . .

Right now, the growing crop is blueberries, which gained popularity through a pretty good marketing campaign. Health benefits of blueberries have really taken off in the last ten years. If it wasn't for that, I think we'd be hurting.

Seth: Some of your blueberries are organic, right? The ones by labor camp 2?

Rob: Yeah. That's just to spread the risks out. We lowered our risk for debt, but then the return isn't as great either. Hopefully, it would be stable instead of doing this *[moves his hands up and down]*. And if we dump everything else, it would provide steady income, just like buying a pretty conservative mutual fund versus speculating on a tech stock. Look at it like we're creating a portfolio of crops. Some have more risk than others; it's the same thing. For example, apples—we were planning on taking 20 acres out this year, but it looks like we're going to make some money on it, so . . .

Seth: Probably not *[chuckles].*

Rob: Yeah.

In another conversation, Rob told me about a recent meeting of the farm executives regarding becoming a "great company" or a "level five company." He explained that every time he heard the word *great* all he could see in the discussion was profitability to shareholders. He recounted getting angry and saying, "We already are a great company, and if this is what being a great company means, then I want to be a good company." He described his frustration with the farm becoming more corporate and more bureaucratic. He liked it more when it was a small, family business, and he "didn't have to go through all these hoops to write a check." Later, he explained his goals with relation to the pickers: "Fair and consistent is what we're going for. Without one of those, you don't have a leg to stand on. I hope we keep in touch with our community, both migrant and stationary. I hope they view me as a fair person." Rob Tanaka is in a double bind, needing to expand operations to compete on the market while attempting to "keep in touch" with the pickers and resist the farm becoming another impersonal corporate agribusiness.

Tom, another of the executives, a lean white man in his late forties, was brought in by the Tanaka family to help the farm compete on the international small fruit market. He has an office in the trailer with the other executive offices, although he has taken more care to decorate it than the others, proudly displaying a colorful painting of Chinese workers picking strawberries in China—one of the very places against which he is competing. Previously, Tom was in charge of processing and marketing for a large Mexican strawberry producer. At the Tanaka farm, his job starts before sunrise, when he calls his competitors and potential buyers in Poland, China, and Chile. Later in the day, he can take breaks to meet friends or eat out. He attempts daily to find a competitive advantage by buying fruit from other farms to process and then sell. Over the course of several months, Tom described to me the stark competitive disadvantages of the farm in domestic and global terms.

Tom: In Oregon, Washington, you have Totem [variety of strawberry]. Let's call it the Northwest variety. In California, the big one right now is Camarosa. California is for the preserve and fresh market. That's where they make the big bucks. Preserves, fillings, juice concentrates, like Pop-Tarts, jellies, anytime you get strawberry as a sweetener, food science–related stuff. This is my enemy, food science. They're taking a not very flavorful strawberry—you've tasted the Camarosa. It's not very flavorful. It's white in the center. It dissolves pretty easily if you cook it down. What they do is add sugar, sweeteners, and coloring agents to stretch that strawberry out. So you're taking a very cheap strawberry, adding things to it, and stretching it out. So when you taste a Pop-Tart, you're tasting something sweet that might be reminiscent of a strawberry. Northwest variety is for dairy. The market I go after is yogurt and ice cream because the strawberry itself in its natural form has to carry the product. Northwest is red throughout. So, Häagen-Dazs, for example, if you look at the ice cream, you're going to see vanilla, cream, sugar, strawberry. If you buy one from California, you're going to find emulsifiers; there could be twenty of them.

Seth: Why isn't Northwest more fresh market?

Tom: Because you can't ship them across the street; you can hardly get them to Seattle. You see how they arrive at our own plant, juice dripping off. California, I ship them from Oxnard forty hours, and they arrive in better condition than when we see our own fruit in the plant here. Camarosa is a dream to run; they're like potatoes; they're rock hard. I compete primarily with Poland because their variety is closest to what we're doing up here. If Poland has a short crop, I've moved products to France for Häagen-Dazs Europe. Chile and China have more a California type. Last year, they introduced Totem into China, so that's our next major threat.

I think the competitive disadvantages we have aren't just Northwest versus California. I think the U.S. strawberry industry as a whole has problems. We're forced to do total traceability back to the farm to make sure we're not overspraying. Whereas in China, they don't do that.

I'm not an optimist on the future of the Northwest strawberry. It's expensive. For example, if you talk to a grower here, they'll tell you they

> want fifty cents a pound in the field. I can buy finished product landed here from China, grade A frozen Camarosa, for probably forty cents a pound. That's why they're paying R&D [research and development] people eighty thousand bucks a year to make it stretch. It comes down to economics. So, I'm just hanging on to a totally shrinking customer base. A half-million-pound buyer walked away earlier this year. They went to Chile. I can't blame them; it's just the way it is. I just hope Häagen-Dazs keeps buying.

The farm executives profiled above are anxious to ensure the survival of the farm for future generations despite the bleak agricultural and economic trends. They work long days, worrying about many variables only partially within their control and attempting to run an ethical business that treats its workers well. They have some degree of control over their schedules. They take breaks when they choose to eat or work out, talk on the phone, or meet with a friend. They have relative financial security and comfortable, quiet houses with private indoor bathrooms and kitchens, insulation, and heating. In addition, they have private indoor offices with phones and computers as well as employees working "under them" (as they put it).

ADMINISTRATIVE ASSISTANTS

Most of the administrative assistants are white, along with a few Latina U.S. citizens. All are female. They work seated at desks in open spaces without privacy. They are in charge of reception, interacting with both local white residents and businesspeople as well as with Mexican farmworkers.

Sally is the year-round front desk receptionist. She is a lean white woman, approximately forty years old, often with a smile on her face. She grew up in the same town in which the farm is located and lives with her husband and children in a relatively small house. The reception desk used to face away from the front counter such that anyone entering approached the receptionist's back. Sally tries to treat the workers well, and turning the desk around when she first arrived was one step in this direction. She helped arrange loans for the Mexican farmworkers one year when the picking date was moved back and the workers were living out of their cars, waiting without money or food. Crew bosses and farm executives occasionally reprimand her for being too nice to the workers. She has been told to be "more curt" and "quick," "less friendly." At times, she feels disrespected by the people "above her" (as she states), treated like a "peon." She complained to me that they often give her advice on her work and give her jobs to do without the common courtesies of "please" or "thank you."

Samantha is a white bilingual administrative assistant in her mid-fifties who was hired two summers before to help work with Spanish-speaking employees. Before working here, she was a travel agent specializing in Spain and Latin America. She lives alone on a small plot of land several miles from the farm with a few of her own farm animals. Her desk is located in the hallway between the main entrance and the private offices of the executives. She first became aware of the difference between "regular Mexicans" (as she stated) and indigenous Mexicans during her first year on the Tanaka farm. Over the course of our interactions, she described indigenous Mexicans from Oaxaca as "dirty" and "simple" and told me such things as "they don't know how to use bank accounts."

Maria is thirty years old, a bilingual Latina from Texas. Her great-grandparents moved to the United States from Mexico. She lives in the year-round labor camp with heating and insulation that is located closest to the farm headquarters. She works several positions from May through November, sometimes at the front desk with Sally, sometimes in the portable unit where pickers can ask questions and pick up mail in the afternoon. On Fridays, she works in the wooden shed where paychecks are passed out to workers as they wait in a long line. Her first summers on the farm, including the summer she was pregnant, she picked berries and worked with a hoe. After four years of working with the hoe, she was moved up to desk work due largely to her ability to speak English fluently. Like Samantha, she first met indigenous Mexican people while working on the farm. She explained her work to me while we sat in the portable unit, occasionally interrupted by a picker seeking his or her mail.

> I'm pretty easy to get along with. I guess that's why I've been in the office for five years. I try to help these people—like a guy just came about his tickets [papers marking how much he picked]. I can get in trouble if I do anything with those tickets, because it's not my job. But I tend to do it because I understand them. I started out like they did; I started out at the bottom.
>
> This season was wild and busy. Last week I worked 108 hours. Then trying to get answers to [the pickers]; sometimes you try asking for answers and you get all this runaround. One of the Tanakas is really helpful. If I have a problem, I go to him right away. He tends to listen, and he's pretty understanding.

The administrative assistants are responsible for completing tasks for the farm executives, providing a cheerful face to those outside the farm, and managing sternly those within. They work six or seven days a week indoors at desks without privacy and frequently answer phone calls that distract them from their other tasks. They worry about the moods and opinions of their bosses. They are paid minimum wage without overtime, since agriculture falls outside U.S. overtime labor laws.[7] They have lunch breaks and can take breaks to use the bathroom as long as there is not someone needing direct help at that moment.

CROP MANAGERS

The crop managers are in charge of all the details involved in the efficient production of a specific crop, from plowing to planting, pruning to spraying, picking to delivery to the processing plant. They have private offices in the field house amid the blueberry and strawberry fields close to the largest labor camp on rural Christensen Road, although they spend a fair amount of time walking through the fields overseeing. During harvest, they begin by 5:00 A.M. seven days a week and finish in the early evening. They can take a break when they choose, to eat, run errands, or go home. The crop managers worry about the availability of machinery, the effects of weather on the crops, and the docility of their labor force. They have some control over how much the pickers are paid, and they have several field bosses below them enforcing their directions.

Jeff is a thirty-year-old white man who recently finished a degree in agricultural marketing at a university in California. He manages blueberries and raspberries. Jeff told me about his job as we rode together in his extended white pickup, two large dogs in the back. We drove to an agriculture store and bought large concrete drains for the blueberry fields and to Costco to buy tri-tip steaks for him to take to a potluck at his church. He explained several simultaneous tasks in the raspberry fields to help me understand the many things a crop manager has to oversee at once. The thing that causes him the most anxiety is having numerous bosses on a family farm without a strict chain of command. He also worries about weather and harvest crews. "It is what it is," he told me. "Sometimes people walk out, and sometimes people pick. It's kind of like the weather; you can't really predict it and you don't really have control over it, but usually it ends up working out all right." He went on, "We make the prices fair, so if the crew walks out [on strike], we just say, 'Hey, we'll be here tomorrow,' and that's the way it is. They can come back if they want." He told me that all the people who work on the raspberry machines are Latinos from Texas, whereas those picking blueberries are "O-hacan" (Oaxacan), although he also told me that he cannot really tell the difference. That week, Jeff was in the midst of budgeting for the following year, trying to predict the crop yield. Each year he predicts based on bud count: for each fruit bud in the fall, he expects seven berries the following summer, although a freeze could make the fruit smaller or kill the buds altogether.

Scott is a tall, thin, middle-aged white man who came to the Tanaka farm from a larger apple orchard in eastern Washington. He manages the strawberry and apple crops. He spoke with me in his private office in the field house as well as in the fields as I picked strawberries and he walked around talking with people and occasionally eating berries. He explained to me the number of workers on the farm—approximately five hundred in summer and fifty in winter—and what is done in the different seasons. His primary worries relate to managing the labor force, "which is sometimes pretty overwhelming." The following interview took place after a brief strawberry picker strike late in the summer.

Seth: What things worry you as crop manager?

Scott: Numerous *[laughing]*. Damn near changes daily. Once we get closer to strawberry harvest, the big push is to see the camps start to fill up, "Am I going to get enough pickers?" The concern's not really that I have too many, it's always, will I get enough? Once I see that we have 300 guys living in the camps, then that starts to ease down a little bit. I can pick strawberries with 300 guys, but 350's a lot nicer. You get up to 400, then you're concerned about getting too many guys. Now, they're only getting to come out and work four hours a day. You get 400 guys, and you go through the field pretty quick. So we try to keep it between 350 and 400, which gives everybody a good day's work. They can go out and make decent enough money and feel they got a good day's work. They've made their wages and get plenty of rest for the next day. If strawberries goes well, the other crops just kind of fall into place.

But, we couldn't do it without the people that come and do it for us. The [strike] we had this year was a big deal. It was a worry. Since I've worked here, I've gotten to know some of the Tanakas. They want to treat everybody right. That's a big push for them. So when that kind of thing happens, they've really stepped back to take a look at exactly what's going on. You'll almost always find a Tanaka out in the field. They're still real hands-on.

Seth: That's different from other farms you've seen?

Scott: Oh yeah. The farm I ran in eastern Washington had 150 acres. I'd only see the guy who owned it twice a year. It was a big change to come over here and the guy that owns the farm is out there working on the site. I think it's good for morale all the way around. That's just Tanakas' work ethic. They're—they're real hands-on people. If you're out there working 14 hours, 7 days a week, so are they, and usually they're working more than anybody else. You'll see John coming in at 3:00 in the morning, and he might be there until 7:00, 8:00, 9:00 at night. Daylight to dark, it's just the nature of farming.

There's a lot of talk today about immigration and the border and stuff like that. They end up spending a whole lot of money to get up here to work. I think we should tell the politicians, even if it's not popular or whatever, there's a lot of need that they have to work here. That's a given.

After I turned off my tape recorder, Scott asked about my interest in crossing the border with some of the Triqui workers. First he told me I should get permission from the federal government. Later he changed his mind and said that the problem with that would be that they would ask for all my information about where I crossed. He was afraid the government would then shut down that route, "and we wouldn't have any workers anymore." He explained that 90 percent of the pickers were probably undocumented.

The profiles of the crop managers bring into focus the practical attempts by the management to run a good, ethical farm in the midst of difficult conditions. In addition, Scott is clearly concerned about the direct effects of immigration and border policies on his labor force. Like many farmers I interviewed, he knows that the current structure of U.S. farming would be impossible without undocumented Latin American migrant workers.

SUPERVISORS

Several supervisors, often called crew bosses, work under each crop manager. They are each in charge of a crew of approximately ten to twenty pickers. They walk through the rows, inspecting and telling workers to pick faster without leaving too many berries behind, allowing too many leaves into their berry buckets, or picking too many pounds of berries per bucket. The crew bosses are constantly under the supervision of the crop managers, although they can take short bathroom breaks, and they often carry on lighthearted conversations with coworkers. Most of the crew bosses are U.S. Latinos, with a few white U.S. citizens, a few mestizo Mexicans, and one indigenous Mixtec Oaxacan. Most crew bosses live in the insulated, year-round labor camp. The crew bosses of the "Mexican crews" (as they are called) work outside all day, walking and supervising, giving directions and reprimands. The one field boss of the local white crew has her own private office in the main building of the farm, though she spends time regularly in the fields supervising. Some of the crew bosses treat the indigenous pickers with respect; others call them explicitly derogatory and racist names. The crew boss most often accused by pickers of such racist treatment has a daughter, Barbara, who also works as a crew boss.

Barbara is a bilingual Latina from Texas in her early twenties who has worked the harvest at the farm for eleven years. She attends community college in Texas every spring and hopes to become a history teacher. She gets upset that other crew bosses call Oaxacan people "pinche Oaxaco" (damn Oaxacan) or "indio estúpido" (stupid Indian). During one conversation, she explained to me that the Oaxacans are afraid to complain or demand better working conditions because they do not want to lose their jobs. She described a farm policy stating that if one crew boss fires a picker, they can never be hired by anyone else on the farm. She told me, "It's unfair. I think there should be checks and balances. This isn't a dictatorship." Her family learned English in Texas as well as in the farm-sponsored English classes each night after work. The farm executives intend for these classes to be open to anyone on the farm. Others on the farm believe that the courses are open to all workers except pickers. This unofficial, yet effective exclusion of pickers from the English classes inadvertently shores up segregation on the farm.

Mateo is a twenty-nine-year-old Mixtec father of two young children. He has worked on the Tanaka farm for twelve years and has taken the farm's English classes for five years. His family had enough money to allow him to finish high school in Oaxaca before emigrating. He is fluent in his native language, Mixteco Alto, and Spanish and is the only Oaxacan person on the farm who speaks English. He is also the only Oaxacan with a job other than picker. He oversees pickers in the strawberry and blueberry harvests. He hopes to continue studying English and to be promoted on the farm until he can "work with the mind instead of the body *[trabajar con la mente en vez del cuerpo]*." Mateo worries about the pregnant women in his crew picking long, hard days in close contact with pesticide-covered plants. During one interview, he explained that many give birth prematurely due to the difficulty of their work. He also worries about the low pay of the pickers. The pay for strawberries has gone up only a few cents per pound in the past decade, and the pay for blueberries has gone down in the past several years.

Barbara and Mateo expressed their desire to treat workers well, even though the structures within which they work are, as they say, "unfair."

Some of the crew bosses who were rumored to be more blatantly racist were not interested in being interviewed by me. Mateo's position as the only Oaxacan crew boss indicates the importance of having the resources to be able to study Spanish and English in order to have social and occupational mobility.

Shelly is a relatively short white woman in her early forties. She started working on the local picking crew when she was seven years old. After college, she came back to work on the farm as an administrative assistant, then married Rob Tanaka, and now is the supervisor for the local white teenage crews and checkers. She sees the local crew as serving the purposes of inculcating the value of agriculture in local families and teaching white teenagers to respect diversity. Of course, the perceptions and outlooks of the white pickers and checkers are more complicated, as discussed below. In her office, Shelly told me that she missed the days when mestizo Mexicans, whom she called "traditional Mexicans," made up the majority of pickers on the farm. On another occasion, she told me she was "fed up" with the Oaxacan pickers and described them as "more dirty," "less respectful," less work-, family-, and community-oriented.

As I came to learn over the course of my fieldwork, I could not take interethnic perceptions and descriptions at face value. Of course, in a literal sense, the indigenous Mexicans were dirtier than their mestizo counterparts, simply because they worked picking strawberries bent over in the dirt, as opposed to the mestizos, who worked seated on raspberry machines or walking through the fields as crew bosses.[8] I never saw or heard of any disrespectful actions on the part of indigenous workers. However, the language barrier made this difficult to know. Shelly did not speak any Triqui or Mixteco and spoke poor Spanish, while the Oaxacan pickers did not speak English and many of them did not speak fluent Spanish. The idea that the Oaxacans were less work-oriented was directly contradicted by some of the crew bosses of Triqui pickers, who explained that the latter were displacing mestizo and Mixtec pickers on the farm because they worked so hard and fast. Given the fact that the Triqui pickers usually migrated as entire families and I attended numerous Triqui family baptism and birthday parties in the camps, while mestizos tended to migrate solo, leaving their families in Mexico, Shelly's understanding of Oaxacans as less family- and community-oriented appeared to me a misperception. Instead, it appears that the physical dirt from the labor of the indigenous pickers had become symbolically linked with their character,[9] and at the same time the limited possibility of relationships between Shelly and the indigenous workers because of the language barriers had become symbolically projected as assumed character flaws onto the indigenous pickers themselves.[10] In addition to bringing into relief the "de facto apartheid" on the farm,[11] the profiles of the supervisors exemplify the range of responses to ethnic and class difference within an exploitative system.

CHECKERS

Local white teenagers punch the beginning and ending times as well as the weights of each bucket of berries brought in on each picker's daily work tickets. The first day I picked berries, I arrived at 5:10 A.M., but the checker marked me as arriving at 5:30. Each day I picked, I was marked as arriving at or after—never before—the time I started picking. Later that summer, one of the supervisors explained to me that each morning the supervisors tell the checkers one specific time to mark on all the cards. He considered this standardization simply a measure to make the process easier for the supervisors and checkers. However, as a picker, I experienced this standardization as unfair. Also, at the end of the day the checkers were told a certain time to mark on the cards, often before most of the pickers finished working. During the day, the checkers try to make sure the berries brought in are ripe without being rotten or having leaves attached. They sit or stand in the shade of overhead umbrellas or in the sunshine as they talk and laugh with each other. They speak English with an occasional Spanish word to the pickers. Some occasionally hurl English expletives—and perhaps even a berry—at the pickers, who are often old enough to be their parents. Some speak of the Mexican pickers as "grease heads" and joke about them driving low-riders, although I never saw a single low-rider in any of the labor camp or berry field parking lots. The following tape-recorded field note excerpt describes the checking stations during one of my first days picking.

> There were different stations where you could have your berries weighed. The first station I went to had three checkers, and they were slow. They weren't mean and they weren't really nice, just kind of slow and disorganized, which was frustrating, because they were taking away my time to get pounds [of berries]. And I might not get the minimum weight for the day because they were slow. On top of that, even though my berries weighed 28 pounds, I was marked for 26. The next place I went to weigh my berries, there was somebody teaching someone else how to do it: "If you see more than ten green stems when you look at the berries, take them out. Throw out the bad berries. You've got to look through the berries that are underneath, too, because sometimes they try to hide the bad berries." I was thinking to myself, "You don't have time to try to hide anything. You just go; you do it as fast as you can!" The next place I went, there was a girl and the one Chicano guy. The Chicano guy didn't talk. He just moved berries back and forth, and the girl was weighing really fast; I liked how fast they were. The next place I went, they seemed kind of rude to people—throwing berries out in a disrespectful way. They were throwing berries out, looking at people and telling them "No!" without speaking Spanish enough to explain what they meant by "No," and just refusing to weigh the bucket of berries.

During my second summer on the farm, a white female college student came up to me and said, "So, I hear you're writing a book." Laura grew up in the area and worked assigning pickers to rows and checking ID badges. She was studying Spanish in college in Seattle and enjoyed talking with and learning about the pickers. She was frustrated with the way her supervisor, Shelly, dealt with the pickers. Laura explained, "One day we were walking back to the cars, one girl was talking to one of the pickers, practicing her Spanish. I don't know if they were even talking to each other, but Shelly said something to her like she didn't want her to talk to pickers. It's like she doesn't trust them. She gets frazzled a lot. I was surprised, like, 'Why didn't she want you to talk to them?'"

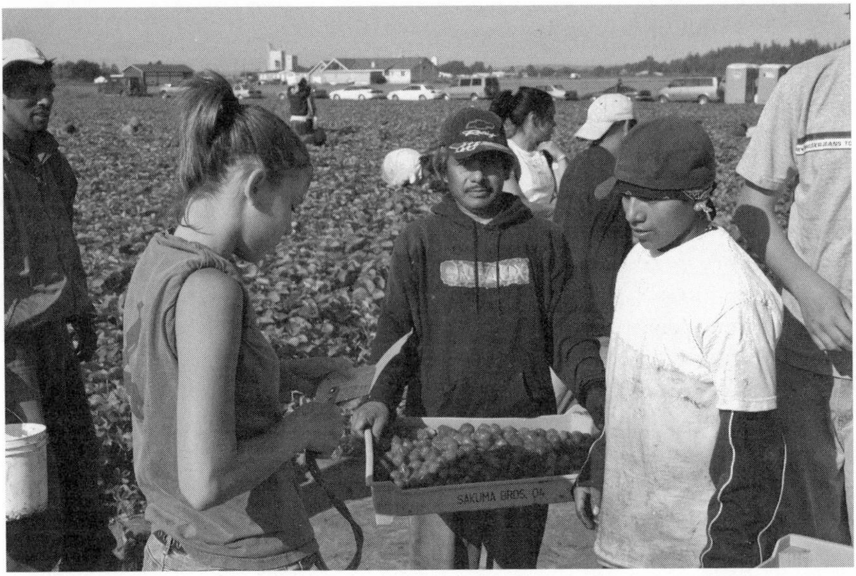

A white teenage checker with Mexican pickers. Photo by Seth M. Holmes.

Although the farm management—including Shelly, who supervises the white picking and checking crews—sees the employment of white teenage checkers as developing positive values toward agriculture and diversity in the valley, checkers learn also that they deserve to have power over Mexicans, even those old enough to be their parents or grandparents. The teenagers are paid minimum wage while being allowed to talk and sit most of the time; the pickers have to kneel constantly and work as fast as possible in order to keep their jobs. The white checkers are given power over how many pounds are marked for the pickers, and I observed more often than not that checkers marked less weight on the cards than the scale displayed. Numerous times over the course of my fieldwork, I observed supervisors telling checkers that the laborers should not pick more than thirty pounds of berries per bucket. Supervisors indicated that more weight would damage the berries. In addition, they indicated that the pickers would try to "get away with" putting more berries per bucket because they were "lazy." Of course, there was no way for me to estimate precisely how much the berries in my bucket would weigh. And I experienced picking strawberries as anything but lazy. The checkers are also allowed to treat the pickers as people who do not deserve equal respect. This serves to further develop the lenses through which symbolic violence, the naturalization of inequality, is effected.[12] In addition, Laura pointed out that the farm's management sometimes works directly to keep labor positions and ethnicities segregated.

FIELD WORKERS PAID PER HOUR

Several small groups of field workers are paid minimum hourly wage. All live in the labor camps with wood under the tin roofs but no heat or insulation. They work seven days a week from approximately 5:00 in the morning until the early evening. Approximately one dozen men, mostly mestizo Mexicans along with a few Mixtec Oaxacans, drive tractors back and forth between the fields and the processing plant. The tractors carry stacks of berry containers several feet high, and the drivers are exposed to direct sun or rain all day. In addition, small groups of mostly mestizo Mexican men and women, and a handful of Mixtecs, work in other capacities, from tying off the new raspberry growth to covering blueberry bushes with plastic, from spraying chemical or concentrated vinegar (for organic fields) pesticides to using hoes between rows of plants.

Thirty-some raspberry pickers work twelve to eighteen hours a day, seven days a week, for approximately one month. Two or three people work on each raspberry harvester, which is approximately one story high, bright yellow, and shaped like an upside-down "U" tall enough for the row of raspberry bushes to pass beneath its middle. The machine shakes the bushes such that the ripe berries fall onto a conveyor belt and then onto a crate. One worker drives the machine; the others move the full berry crates and remove bad berries and leaves. They are all seated and have minimal shade from umbrellas attached to the machine. All the raspberry pickers are Latinos from Texas; most are relatives of the raspberry crew boss.

FIELD WORKERS PAID BY WEIGHT

"The White Crew"

Pickers are the only group not paid by the hour. Instead, they are paid a certain amount per pound of fruit harvested. The white teenage pickers are paid fourteen cents per pound of berries, but because they are under sixteen years old they have no minimum wage and therefore no minimum weight to meet each day. They live in the relatively comfortable houses of their parents. They work bent over six days a week, though they have no time pressure and take frequent breaks. Often I observed their parents helping pick into their buckets for part of the day. They are treated well and cheerfully by their supervisor, Shelly. Some of them hope to be promoted to the level of checker; others decide not to do manual labor and stop working at the farm at the end of the season. They complain of knee and hip pain, as well as not getting to spend time playing with their friends. The knee and hip pain is temporary because these workers not only take breaks from bending but also pick only a few summers at most.

There were fundamental differences between the work of the teenage white pickers and that of the Mexican pickers, including, importantly, the fact that white pickers do not have a minimum weight to pick each day in order to keep their job, are allowed to work at their own pace and take breaks, and work a few summers at most. Despite these crucial differences, several white area residents and friends of mine responded to my description of my research with migrant berry pickers by saying that they "know what it's like" because they picked on a white teen crew when they were growing up. Several of them even went on to conclude, "It's not that bad, really."

"The Mexican Crew"

Like the white teenage crew, the Mexican pickers are not paid by the hour. Instead they are called "contract workers" and are paid a certain amount per unit of fruit harvested. Most live in the camp farthest from farm headquarters, which has no heat or insulation and no wood under the tin roof. Each day, they are told a minimum amount of fruit they must pick. The crop manager calculates the minimum to make sure that each picker brings in more than enough to be worth paying them at least the legal state minimum wage. If they pick less on two occasions, they are fired and kicked out of the camp. The first contract picker I met, a Triqui man named Abelino, explained, "The hourly jobs, the salaried jobs are better because you can count on how much you will make. But they don't give those jobs to us."

Approximately twenty-five people, mostly mestizos with a few Mixtec and Triqui men, pick apples. The field boss, Abby, explained to me that picking apples is the hardest job on the farm. Apple pickers work five to ten hours a day, seven days a week, carrying a heavy bag of apples over their shoulders. They repeatedly climb up and down ladders to reach the apples. This job is sought after because it is known to be the highest-paid picking position.

However, the majority of pickers—350 to 400—work in the strawberry fields for one month, followed by three months in the blueberry fields. Other than a few Mixtecs, they are almost all Triqui men, women, and teenagers (agricultural workers can legally be fourteen or older). Most Triqui pickers come with other family members, and most hail from the same village, San Miguel, in the mountains of Oaxaca. The official contract pay for strawberry pickers is 14 cents per pound of strawberries. This means that pickers must bring in fifty-one pounds of deleafed strawberries every hour because the farm is required to pay Washington State minimum wage—$7.16 at the time. In order to meet this minimum, pickers take few or no breaks from 5:00 A.M. until the afternoon when that field is completed. Nonetheless, they are reprimanded by some crew bosses and called *perros* (dogs), *burros*, *Oaxacos* (a derogatory mispronunciation of "Oaxacans"). Many do not eat or drink anything before work so they do not have to take time to use the bathroom. They work as hard and fast as they can, arms flying in the air as they kneel in the dirt, picking and running with their buckets of berries to the checkers. Although they are referred to as contract workers, this is misleading. On a few instances, the pay per unit was changed by the crop managers without warning or opportunity for negotiation.

Strawberry pickers work simultaneously with both hands in order to make the minimum. They pop the green stem and leaves off of each

Marcelina picking strawberries, wearing bandanas to protect herself from the sun. Photo by Seth M. Holmes.

strawberry and do their best to avoid the green and the rotten berries. During my fieldwork, I picked once or twice a week and experienced gastritis, headaches, and knee, back, and hip pain for days afterward. I wrote in a field note after picking, "It honestly felt like pure torture." Triqui pickers work seven days a week, rain or shine, without a day off until the last strawberry is processed. Occupying the bottom of the ethnic-labor hierarchy, Triqui pickers bear an unequal share of health problems, from idiopathic back and knee pains to slipped vertebral disks, from type 2 diabetes to premature births and developmental malformations.[13] The brief profiles below highlight the economic and physical hardships of the pickers on the farm and on the U.S.-Mexico border, touching on the importance of language, ethnicity, and education in the organization of the farm labor hierarchy.

Marcelina is a twenty-eight-year-old Triqui mother of two. She is a cousin of Samuel (introduced in chapter 1), grew up in San Miguel, and is one of the other people with whom I would share a slum apartment in

Central California in the winter. Every summer, a local Skagit Valley non-profit organizes a seminar on migrant farm labor. The seminar involves a visit to a farm and labor camp as well as several brief presentations and live interviews with people from all aspects of migrant labor, from pickers to growers, Border Patrol agents to social workers. Most of the attendees are white, middle-class adults who live in the area, along with a handful of mestizo and indigenous Mexican farmworkers. Late in my first summer of fieldwork, Marcelina was invited to speak at the seminar about her experiences migrating and picking. Shyly, she approached the translator, holding her one-year-old daughter, and spoke in Spanish, her second language.

> Good afternoon. I am Marcelina. I come here to the United States to work. A man left me with two children. I wanted to come here to make money, but no. I don't even make enough to send to Oaxaca to my mom who is taking care of my son. Sometimes the strawberry goes poorly, your back hurts, and you don't make anything.
>
> I am sorry; I don't speak Spanish well. Pure Triqui. *[Chuckles]* Pure Triqui.
>
> It's very difficult here. The farm camp manager doesn't want to give a room to a single woman. So I am living with this family over here *[pointing to a Triqui family of five in the audience]*. One gains nothing here, nothing to survive. Besides that, I have a daughter here with me, and I don't make anything to give her. Working and working. Nothing. I've been here four years and nothing.
>
> It's very difficult for a person here. I came to make money, like I thought, "Here on the other side [of the border] there is money and good money," but no. We're not able to make enough to survive.
>
> And then sometimes [the checkers] steal pounds. Sometimes rotten berries make it into the bucket—"Eat that one!" they say, throwing it into your face. They don't work well. And there are hardly any good berries this time of year, pure rotten ones.
>
> This is not good. You don't make enough even to eat. I have two children, and it is very ugly here, very ugly to work in the field. That's how it is. Sometimes you want to speak up, but no. You can't speak to them.

After speaking about the difficulties of farmwork in Washington State, Marcelina was asked to talk about the migration process in general. She continued:

> There in Oaxaca, we don't have work. There are no jobs there. Only the men work sometimes, but since there are many children in my family, the men didn't make money for me and my son. That's why I wanted to come here, to make money, but no—no—no. You don't make anything here; you don't have anything to survive. I wanted to work, to move ahead *[salir adelante]* with my children, to take them ahead *[salir adelante].*
>
> I have been here four years without seeing my son.
>
> In California, there is no work, just pruning, and you don't make any money because of the same thing, we don't know Spanish, and that is because we don't have enough money to study. Parents have to suffer in order to send their children to school, buy food and school uniforms. I have lots of sisters back there, studying, but I couldn't study. There are many children who don't go to school because they lack money. I had to leave Oaxaca so I wouldn't suffer from hunger. I hoped I would make enough to send back to support my sisters in school. I had to give up school myself.

One of the Triqui families who welcomed me most into their lives was that of Samuel, his wife, Leticia, and their four-year-old son. As described earlier, after moving from the farm in Washington to Madera, California, I shared a three-bedroom, one-bath slum apartment with Samuel, Leticia, and their son; Marcelina and her daughter; Samuel's sister and her son; Samuel's brother, his wife, and his daughter; and two other families of four. One night in the farm labor camp, while we watched a Jet Li action movie with the sound turned down and drank blue Kool Aid, Samuel described in Spanish their lives as migrant farmworkers.

> *Samuel:* Here with Tanaka, we don't have to pay rent, but they don't pay us much. They pay 14 cents a pound. And they take out taxes, federal taxes, social security. They pay $20 a day.
>
> . . . They don't pay fairly. If a person has 34 pounds of strawberries, 4 pounds are stolen because the checker marks only 30. It is not just. That is what bothers people most. People work a lot. They suffer. Humans suffer.
>
> It is easy for them, but for us it is not.
>
> In the blueberries, they steal an ounce from the little boxes and that is why the people can't move ahead *[salir adelante].* We pick a lot of fruit, and we don't make money.

The people don't say anything. They are afraid of speaking, because the farm will fire them. We want to say things to them, but we can't because we don't have papers. Sometimes the bosses are really mean, and they'll deport you. Sometimes, when one of us says something, they point to the police, and the police can do something to us. That's why people are silent.

Seth: How much do you make each year?

Samuel: One person makes $3,000 to $5,000 a year. We are not asking to be rich. We don't come here to be rich. Yes, it's very little. They say the boss doesn't want us to earn money, and I ask myself, "Why?"

Some supervisors explain how we are going to pick or what we're supposed to do, but other supervisors are bad people or have bad tempers and don't explain well what we do or what we pick. They even scream at us, using words you should not say. If you treat people badly, they're not going to work calmly or happily. And if we tell the boss, he might not believe us. They scream at us and call us "dumb donkeys" or "dogs." It's very ugly how they treat us.

One of Marcelina and Samuel's cousins, Joaquin, nicknamed "Gordo" or "Lobo," also lived in the slum apartment in Central California. Late in the first summer of my fieldwork, Joaquin's 1990 Aerostar minivan broke down. Most of my Triqui companions had bought old American minivans because they often cost less than $500 and could carry several people to and from the fields, the grocery store, and the local church, which gave away free food on Tuesday evenings. I stood with several of Joaquin's Triqui friends as we took turns watching and helping work on his car. At one point, the conversation turned to work, and Joaquin elaborated on the stresses and contradictions of picking.

The supervisors say they'll take away our IDs and fire us if we don't pick the minimum. They tell us we're dropping too many berries, we have to go slow so we don't drop so much. When we go slowly, we don't reach [the minimum] and "Go faster!" They tell us, "You don't know how to work," "Indian, you don't know!" We already know how to work and why the berries drop. If we go slowly, we can't make any money and we get in trouble. If we hurry up, we drop berries and they come and castigate us. "Dumb donkey!" "Dog!" We are afraid.

The first day I picked, the only people who were as slow as I was were two Latinas from Southern California and one Latino who commuted from a suburb of Seattle. After the first week, the two Latinas began picking into the same bucket in order make the minimum and keep one paycheck. The second week, I no longer saw the man from Seattle. I asked a supervisor where he had gone, assuming he had decided the work was too difficult and given up. She told me that the farm made a deal with him that if he could make it through a week picking, they would give him a job paid hourly in the processing plant. He has been "one of the hardest workers" in the plant since then. I then inquired about why the indigenous Mexicans could not get processing plant jobs. The supervisor replied, "People who live in the migrant camps cannot have those jobs; they can only pick." She considered it a farm policy without any need for explanation.

Thus marginalization begets marginalization. The indigenous Mexicans live in the migrant camps because they do not have the resources to rent apartments in town. Because they live in the camps, they are given only the worst jobs on the farm. Unofficial farm policies and practices subtly reinforce labor and ethnic hierarchies. The position of the Triqui workers, at the bottom of the hierarchy, is multiply determined by poverty, education level, language, citizenship status, and ethnicity. In addition, these factors produce each other. For example, a family's poverty cuts short an individual's education, which limits one's ability to learn Spanish (much less English), which limits one's ability to leave the bottom rung of labor and housing. Poverty, at the same time, is determined in part by the institutional racism at work against Triqui people in the first place. Segregation on the farm is the result of a complex system of feedback and feed-forward loops organized around these multiple nodes of inequality.

OUT OF PLACE

In many ways—ethnicity, education, citizenship, social class—I did not take the appropriate position in the labor hierarchy. For the purposes of my research, I picked berries regularly alongside the Triqui people and lived in the labor camp that housed the majority of Triqui families. Our labor camp was the farthest from the farm headquarters on rural Christensen Road, and each shack was made of plywood walls and a tin roof. When I first met one of the white families who lived directly above the labor camp on Christensen Heights Road, they explained to me that the Mexican migrants partied so hard and drank so much that they could hear horns honking each morning around 4:00. However, like my Triqui neighbors in the camp, I was awakened each morning by the honking of the vans arriving before dawn to pick up the children enrolled in a local daycare before both parents left to pick. During blueberry harvest in the fall, when the vans arrived after sunrise, we were awakened instead by cold rain inside our shacks as the tin roofs, on which our breath had condensed and frozen overnight, were thawed by the morning sun. In fact, I observed relatively little drinking in the camp. When a Triqui family threw a baptism or birthday party, tacos, soda, and beer would be served, Mexican *norteño* and *chilena* music would be played, and a few people would dance. On these occasions, one or two people, always men, would become intoxicated. Most people drank no or very little alcohol.

Although I worked and lived in the same conditions as the Triqui migrants, the farm executives treated me as someone out of place, giving me special permission to keep my job and my shack even though I was never able to pick the minimum. At times they even treated me as a superior due to my social and cultural capital, asking me for advice related to the future of labor relations and housing on the farm. Crop managers, field bosses, and checkers treated me as a sort of jester, respected entertainment. They often joked with me, laughing and using rhetorical questions like, "Are you still glad you chose to pick?" As they walked through the fields, they regularly stopped where I was and talked with me, picking into my buckets to help me keep up, something they did not do regularly for other pickers.

On the other hand, the other pickers interacted with me with a mixture of respect and suspicion. For example, there were the rumors that I was a spy for the police or a drug smuggler looking for cover. When I first moved into the camp, many Triqui people wondered why a gabacho would live there and pick berries. Some people complained that I "pick[ed] really slowly"; "He always comes behind," they would say. In a conversation late in my first summer on the farm, Samuel complained about the problems in his hometown due to lack of resources. He said they need a strong mayor. I asked him if he would be mayor someday, and he replied, "No. You need to have some education and some money and some ideas. You will be president of San Miguel, Set', and you can do a lot of good! We need a water pump and paved roads. You could set up a pharmacy and build a house and marry a Triqui woman *[laughing]*."

During my first few months living and working among the Triqui people, I noticed that even the children in the camp seemed to recognize the farm segregation. Given that the adults in the camps were suspicious of me, I spent a fair amount of time in the beginning of my fieldwork playing with the children. After asking many sets of children where they were from and which languages they spoke, I found that all the children who came to visit me were Triqui. None of the Mixtec or mestizo children ever came to my shack. Apparently, the children recognized (or were explicitly instructed by their parents)[14] that I was positioned in a Triqui location in the farm hierarchy and responded to me accordingly.

Near the end of my research, Samuel told me, "Right now we and you are the same; we are poor. But later you will be rich and live in a luxury house *[casa de lujo]*." I explained that I did not want a luxury house but rather a simple little house. Samuel replied, looking me in the eyes, "But you will have a bathroom on the inside, right?"

CALIFORNIA

At the end of the berry season in the Skagit Valley, after living on the Tanaka farm for almost five months, I was invited to drive south to California with Samuel and his extended family. His youngest cousin, Juan, did not yet have a driver's license, was not accustomed to driving on freeways, and needed someone to drive his recently purchased used Ford Taurus. Juan was sixteen years old and single. He had come to the United States from San Miguel for the first time at the beginning of the berry season several months earlier. After our last day picking, Juan and I loaded up his car, and I drove the Ford Taurus in a caravan along with six Aerostar minivans. We drove directly, below the speed limit and through the night, from northwestern Washington to Central California, stopping for short bathroom and meal breaks at rest stops along the way. We ate homemade tacos and cilantro salads we had brought with us. At the rest stops, we napped, joked around with the children, who were energetic from being cooped up in the cars, and reminisced about moments when different people were scared we might be pulled over by a police car.

Once we arrived in Madera, California, it took a week to find a landlord with an open apartment who would rent to Mexican migrants with no credit history. During this week, we washed in the bathrooms of city parks before they were locked at dusk, and we tried to find safe places to sleep in our cars. One night, we parked and slept in our cars near a Triqui friend's rental house so that the children could use the bathroom in the middle of the night if needed. However, we were woken up by a white neighbor woman yelling in the middle of the night, forcing us to drive away because she did not want us sleeping in front of her house. Each day, we drove up and down the streets looking for housing. Several times in the first few days, we found relatively comfortable, large apartments for rent but were turned down because of my companions' lack of credit history. As time wore on, we learned to look for apartments that were poorly advertised, with handwritten "For Rent" signs in the windows. These were more likely to be dirty, smelly apartments in bad repair, but they were also more likely to take us seriously as renters. After eight days, we found the three-bedroom, one-bathroom slum apartment that nineteen of us—most of Samuel and Juan's extended family, including four young children—shared for the winter. Each week, we went to the Mexican flea market in town where we saw other Triqui friends from San Miguel who had been on the Tanaka farm. We regularly looked for work, occasionally doing short stints pruning grapevines.

The general features of the ethnic-labor hierarchy in California agriculture was the same as that in Washington, although the specifics differed. White people still had the best jobs, followed by U.S. Latinos, then mestizo Mexicans, and finally indigenous Mexicans and a few Central Americans. Most California farms worked through contractors,

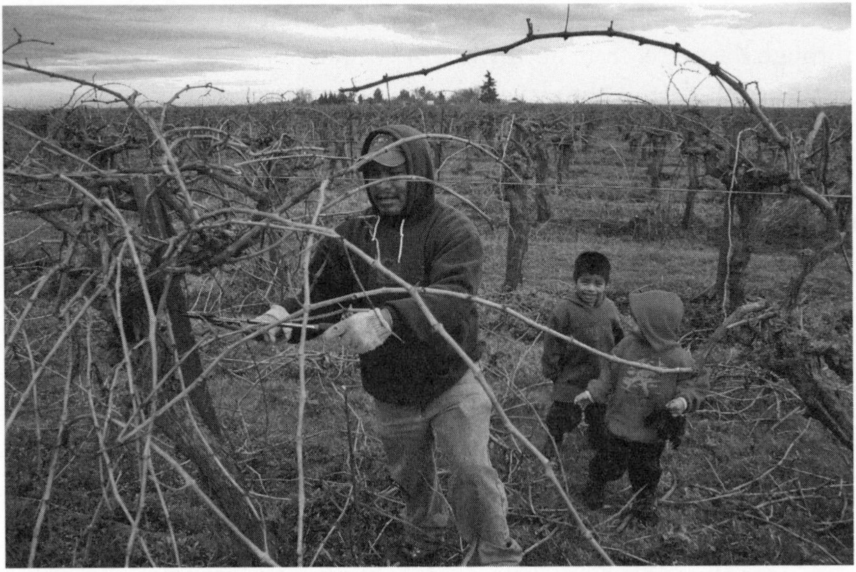

Samuel pruning with children in a California vineyard. Photo by Seth M. Holmes.

without making each individual picker an employee of the farm or having any record of their employment. These farms paid their contractor a lump sum for getting a particular field pruned or picked. The contractor, then, paid each worker a certain amount per vine pruned. During the five months I lived and worked in the Central Valley of California, my companions and I were consistently paid less than minimum wage. On top of that, most contractors prohibited driving oneself or walking to the field. We had to get a ride from the "ride-giver" (*raitero*), almost always a relative of the contractor, for $5 to $7 a day. In the end, we were paid close to $10 for a five-hour workday and a commute of up to two hours each way. In addition, most farms in California did not provide housing, so that some of our salaries went to pay the rent for our slum apartment. And the state of California did not provide childcare for farmworkers like Washington did. Thus one parent gave up his or her paycheck to stay home with the children, or the parents paid $10 to an unofficial childcare program in a nearby slum apartment, or the parents took the children to the vineyard with them while they pruned.

The Triqui pickers also reported more explicit racism in California, specifically from Latinos who were U.S. citizens. Though the general shape of the social hierarchy remained the same, the specifics of the everyday lives of the Triqui people in California were worse in several respects. Despite my numerous attempts, most contractors in California would not consider letting me work. I attribute this partly to their recognition that I did not fit in that position in the hierarchy and partly to their fear that the poor and unfair working conditions might be exposed.

HIERARCHIES AT WORK

Responsibilities, stressors, and privileges differ from the top to the bottom of the labor hierarchy described ethnographically above. The workers at every level of the ladder worry about factors over which they have little control. Everyone on the Tanaka farm is structurally vulnerable,[15] although the characteristics and depth of vulnerability change depending on one's position within the labor structure. For example, opportunities decrease and anxieties accumulate as one moves down the pecking order. Those at the top worry about market competition and the weather. The middle managers worry about these factors and about how they are treated by their bosses. The pickers worry about picking enough to make the minimum weight so as to avoid losing their jobs and their housing. The higher one is positioned in the structure, the more control one has over time. The executives and managers can take breaks as they see fit. The administrative assistants and checkers can choose to take short breaks, given their supervisors' consent or absence. The field workers can take breaks only infrequently if they are willing to sacrifice pay, and even then they may be reprimanded. The lower one is located in the hierarchy, the less one is paid and the more structurally vulnerable one is. The executives and managers are relatively financially secure and have comfortable homes. The administrative staff and checkers are paid minimum wage and live as members of the rural working class in less comfortable housing. The pickers are paid piecemeal and live in poor conditions in the labor camp shacks. They are always aware that they are at risk of losing even this poor housing. Among the pickers, those in strawberries and blueberries make less money and are more likely to miss the minimum weight and be fired than those in apples. Although everyone on the farm works for and is paid by the same business, they do not share power or vulnerability evenly. The pay and working conditions of the pickers function as variables semicontrollable by the farm executives as partial buffers between market changes and the viability of the rest of the farm.

The ethnic-labor hierarchy seen here—white and Asian American U.S. citizen, Latino U.S. citizen or resident, undocumented mestizo Mexican, undocumented indigenous Mexican—is common in much of North American farming. The relative status of Triqui people below Mixtecs can be understood via a pecking order of perceived indigeneity. Many farmworkers and managers told me that the Triqui are more purely indigenous than other groups because Triqui is still their primary language and "they are more simple." Here, ethnicity serves as a camouflage for a social Darwinist perception of indigeneity versus civilization. The Anglo- and Japanese Americans inhabit the pole of civilization. The Triqui are positioned as the opposite: indigenous peasants, savages, simple children. The more civilized one is perceived to be, the better one's job. At the same time, the better one's job, the more "civilized" one is permitted (and perceived) to be. This hierarchy of civilization also correlates roughly with citizenship, from U.S. citizen to U.S. resident, Mexican citizen to undocumented Mexican immigrant. Yet this is only a small piece of the global hierarchy. The continuum of structural vulnerability can be understood as a zoom lens, moving through many such hierarchies. When the continuum is seen from farthest away, it becomes clear that the local family farm owners are relatively low on the global corporate agribusiness hierarchy. When looked at more closely, we see the hierarchy on this particular farm. In addition, perceptions of ethnicity change as the zoom lens is moved in and out. As mentioned above, many of the farm executives

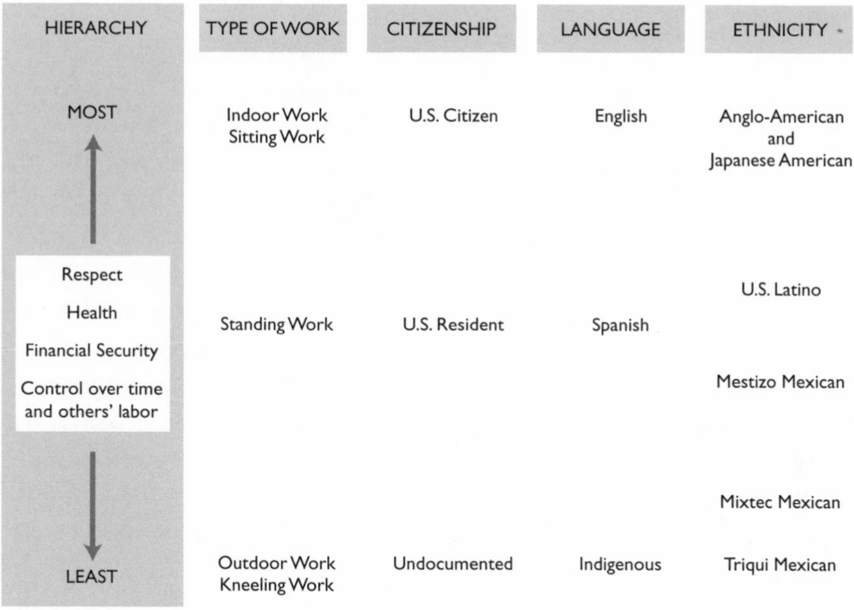

HIERARCHY
TYPE OF WORK
CITIZENSHIP
LANGUAGE
ETHNICITY
MOST
Indoor Work
Sitting Work
U.S. Citizen
English
Anglo-American and Japanese American
Respect
Health
Financial Security
Control over time and others' labor
U.S. Latino
Standing Work
U.S. Resident
Spanish
Mestizo Mexican
Mixtec Mexican
LEAST
Outdoor Work
Kneeling Work
Undocumented
Indigenous
Triqui Mexican

Conceptual diagram of hierarchies on the farm.

(as well as area residents) considered all migrant farmworkers "Mexican," whereas those in closer contact with the farmworkers came to distinguish between "regular Mexicans" and "Oaxacans," and those working in the fields themselves often differentiated among mestizo, Triqui, and Mixtec people.[16]

Laboring bodies are organized by ethnicity and citizenship into superimposed hierarchies of labor, respect, and suffering. The overdetermination of the adverse lot of the indigenous Mexican migrant berry picker fits Bourgois's concept "conjugated oppression."[17] On the Tanaka farm, class, race, and citizenship conspire to deny Triqui workers respect and deprive them of physical and mental health.

While class, race, and citizenship form the primary fault lines of power on the farm, gender hierarchies become visible when considering the individuals who appear to be out of place. The only people promoted above the position accorded their race and citizenship are male (e.g.,

Mateo, the only indigenous person promoted to supervisor). During my fieldwork, females were never promoted above their expected race-citizenship location in the hierarchy. In addition, this gender hierarchy is reinforced by education and language differences. Due to the assumed role dichotomy in San Miguel and in the United States between the private, domestic sphere for women and the public sphere for men, women have fewer opportunities for education. Most of the Triqui women in San Miguel have not moved beyond primary school because they are expected to fulfill domestic responsibilities. Thus many of the women do not speak more than a few words of Spanish. In contrast, most Triqui men finish secondary school in San Miguel and speak Spanish fluently. In addition, Triqui men in the United States are more likely than Triqui women to leave the home to work, thus offering further opportunities to perfect their Spanish and begin to learn English.[18]

As made clear by the ethnographic data above, this segregation is not conscious or willed on the part of the farm owners. Much the opposite. These inequalities are driven by larger structural forces as well as the anxieties they produce. The farm can be seen as a sort of "gray zone," related in some ways to that described by Primo Levi in the lagers of the Holocaust.[19] Levi's gray zone involved such severe conditions that any prisoner seeking his or her own survival was inherently complicit with a system of violence against others. Levi encouraged the use of his analysis, drawn from a horrific and violent setting, to understand everyday situations such as "a big industrial factory."[20] Similarly, Scheper-Hughes and Bourgois argue that wartime direct political violence and peacetime structural and symbolic violence mirror and produce one another through a violence continuum.[21] In the multilayered gray zone of contemporary U.S. agriculture, even ethical growers, in their fight for survival, are forced by an increasingly harsh market to participate in a system of labor that perpetuates suffering. This gray zone is seen most clearly when workers seek to impress their superiors in order to move up the ranks, for example, checkers cheating pickers out of pounds or minutes due to pressure from above.

At the same time, there are hints of "bad faith" on the farm, more with certain supervisors than others. The phrase "bad faith" was introduced by Jean-Paul Sartre to describe the ways in which individuals knowingly deceive themselves in order to avoid acknowledging realities disturbing to them.[22] Scheper-Hughes builds on this concept to indicate ways in which communities collectively engage in self-deception in the face of poverty and suffering.[23] She uses the concept of "collective bad faith" to analyze the practice in northeastern Brazil of giving tranquilizers to malnourished and starving children. Such collective bad faith is visible in the Skagit Valley when white area residents tell me they know what it is like for Mexican migrants to pick berries because they picked one summer as a child, despite the clearly and significantly different living and working conditions of the white teenage crews and the Mexican crews. Collective bad faith is visible also when indigenous languages are falsely demoted to "dialects," and impressively efficient, technical pickers are categorized as "unskilled."[24] Such forms of collective bad faith are fostered by official and unofficial policies and practices, such as barring pickers from farm English classes. It is further enabled by the spatial separation, layers of bureaucracy, and linguistic barriers shielding the growers from the more explicit mistreatment of the berry pickers. Collective bad faith is allowed to continue beyond the borders of the farm by the general hiddenness of migrant farmworkers. This is especially worrisome when seen in the perceptions and practices of those in service professions, such as the health care providers introduced in the following chapters.

FOUR "How the Poor Suffer"

EMBODYING THE VIOLENCE CONTINUUM

SOCIAL SUFFERING AND THE VIOLENCE CONTINUUM

During both of my summers of fieldwork on the Tanaka Brothers Farm, I picked berries once or twice a week and experienced several forms of pain for days afterward. I often felt sick to my stomach the night before picking, due to stress about picking the minimum weight. As I picked, my knees continually hurt; I tried different positions, sometimes squatting, sometimes kneeling, sometimes propped up on just one knee. Each time I stood up to take my berries to be weighed, it felt as if a warm liquid like my own blood was running down my pants and into my shoes. All day, I leaned forward to see the strawberries below the leaves, and my neck and back began to hurt by late morning. For two or three days after picking, I took ibuprofen and sometimes used the hot tub in a local private gym to ease the aches, all too aware of the inequality of having access to such amenities.

After the first week of picking on the farm, I asked two young female pickers how their knees and backs felt. One replied that she could no longer feel anything ("Mi cuerpo ya no puede sentir nada"), though her knees still hurt sometimes. The other said that her knees, back, and hips are always hurting ("Siempre me duelen"). Later that same afternoon, one of the young Triqui men I saw playing basketball every day the week before the harvest told me that he and his friends could no longer run because their bodies hurt so much ("Ya no corremos; no aguantamos"). In fact, even the vistas that were so sublime and beautiful to me had come to mean ugliness, pain, and work to the pickers. On multiple occasions, my Triqui companions responded with confusion to my exclamations about the area's beauty and explained that the fields were "pure work" *(puro trabajo).*

Knee, back, and hip pain are only a few of the ways in which the social context of migrant farmwork—especially living and working conditions—affects the bodies of my Triqui companions. These pains are examples of the structural violence of social hierarchies becoming embodied in the form of suffering and sickness. The shacks in which the Triqui pickers live, the grueling conditions in which they work, and the danger they face in the border desert function as mechanisms through which structural violence produces suffering. I use the word *suffering* to indicate not only physical sickness but also mental, existential, and interpersonal anguish.

Scheper-Hughes and Bourgois propose understanding violence as a continuum, including not only direct political violence but also structural, symbolic, and everyday violence.[1] They suggest that these wartime and peacetime expressions of violence potentiate, produce, conceal, and legitimate one another. Bourgois defines direct political violence as "targeted physical violence and terror administered by official authorities and those opposing [them]."[2] Structural violence is manifested as social inequalities and hierarchies, often along social categories of class, race, gender, and sexuality.[3] Symbolic violence, as defined by Bourdieu, is the internalization and legitimation of hierarchy, "exercised through cognition and misrecognition, knowledge and sentiment, with the unwitting consent of the dominated."[4] Scheper-Hughes uses the phrase "everyday violence" to describe the normalized micro-interactional expressions of violence on domestic, delinquent, and institutional levels that produce a common sense of violence and humiliation.[5] Bourgois poses this challenge to ethnographers: "to check the impulse to sanitize and instead to clarify the chains of causality that link structural, political, and symbolic violence in the production of an everyday violence that buttresses unequal power relations and distorts efforts at resistance."[6]

This chapter focuses ethnographic attention on "how the poor suffer," in this case the poorest of the poor on the farm, the Triqui strawberry pickers. Much of the suffering of Triqui migrant laborers can be understood as a direct embodiment of the violence continuum. During my fieldwork, many Triqui people experienced notable health problems affecting their ability to function in their work and families. I discuss in particular the experiences of three Triqui migrants whom I came to know well, Abelino, Crescencio, and Bernardo. While the suffering of Triqui berry pickers in general is determined by their position at the bottom of various hierarchies, each of these three vignettes serves to underscore the embodiment of a different expression of the violence continuum. Abelino's knee injury highlights the physical and mental suffering caused by the structural violence of segregated labor. Crescencio's headache brings to light the embodied effects of the verbal and symbolic violence of racist insult and stereotype. Finally, Bernardo's stomach pains underline the health effects of the direct political violence of military repression. At the same time, each case draws linkages between the embodiment of the primary form of violence and its interactions with the rest of the violence continuum.

ABELINO AND THE PAIN OF PICKING

The first Triqui picker whom I met when I visited the Skagit Valley was Abelino, a thirty-five-year-old father of four. He, his wife, Abelina, and their children lived together in a small shack near me in the labor camp farthest from the main road. During one conversation over homemade tacos in his shack, Abelino explained in Spanish why Triqui people have to leave their hometowns in Mexico.

Abelino working in the field. Photo by Seth M. Holmes.

> In Oaxaca, there's no work for us. There's no work. There's nothing. When there's no money, you don't know what to do. And shoes, you can't get any. A shoe like this *[pointing to his tennis shoes]* costs about 300 Mexican pesos. You have to work two weeks to buy a pair of shoes. A pair of pants costs 300. It's difficult. We come here and it is a little better, but you still suffer in the work. Moving to another place is also difficult. Coming here with the family and moving around to different places, we suffer. The children miss their classes and don't learn well. Because of this, we want to stay here only for a season with [legal immigration] permission and let the children study in Mexico. Do we have to migrate to survive? Yes, we do.

The economic situation in the Triqui Zone of Oaxaca is both depressed and depressing. To keep their homes and support their families in Oaxaca, they must leave to work. Oaxaca's economic depression is linked to discriminatory international policies—such as

NAFTA—originating in the United States as well as unequal economic practices with colonialist roots in Mexico. Abelino describes some of the ways in which the transitory nature of migration leads to suffering on many levels. Moving from place to place allows for the most earnings to be saved toward whichever goal each worker may have as well as to be sent back to family members in Oaxaca. At the same time, this ongoing movement leads to periods of homelessness, fear of apprehension and deportation, uprooting of connections and relationships outside of the migration circuit, and loss of productive studies and continuity for children. Moving from state to state also functionally disqualifies workers, including pregnant women and recent mothers, from social and health services for which they would otherwise be eligible.

Later that same night, Abelino explained the difficulty of entering the United States without official documents: "We have to migrate to survive. And we have to cross the border, suffering and walking two days and two nights, sometimes five days, to get here to work and support the American people. Because they don't work like we do. They just get rich working a light job like the shops, the offices, but they don't work in the field. We Mexicans from many Mexican states come here to maintain our families. We want to get permission to enter just for a harvest season and then return to our country."

Crossing the border from Mexico to the United States involves incredible financial, physical, and emotional suffering for Triqui migrants. Each migrant pays approximately $1,500 to $2,500 to various people along the way for rides and guidance. They walk hurriedly in physically impossible conditions, getting speared by cactus spines, attempting to avoid rattlesnakes, climbing and jumping over numerous barbed-wire fences—all the while using no flashlights in order to avoid being seen by the Border Patrol and vigilante groups. As a rule, they do not bring enough food or water because of the weight. Every step of the way carries a fearful awareness that at any moment one might be apprehended and deported by the Border Patrol, which would entail beginning the nightmarish trek all over again after figuring out a way to scrape together enough money for another attempt.

The suffering Abelino talked about most, however, related to picking berries on the farm. After arriving in the Skagit Valley, many Triqui people attempt to obtain various types of jobs, including in construction or in the farm's processing plant, but the only job they are offered is the harvest of berries. Early in my time on the farm, Abelino explained to me the experience of picking: "You pick with your hands, bent over, kneeling like this *[demonstrating with both knees fully bent and his head bowed forward]*. Your back hurts; you get knee pains and pain here *[touching his hip]*. When it rains, you get pretty mad and you have to keep picking. They don't give lunch breaks. You have to work every day like that to make anything. You suffer a lot in work." He explained that although picking blueberries in the autumn is not as physically strenuous as harvesting strawberries in the summer, one makes significantly less money.

One day in the middle of my first summer on the farm, like the other mornings I picked, I followed Abelino, his wife, and their oldest daughter as they led the way to the field we were to pick that morning. It was pitch black before the sun rose, and we wore heavy clothes in layers to take off as the sun came up. We walked through a line, and our picking cards for the day were marked with our beginning time, though, as we came to expect, the cards were marked as though we had arrived thirty minutes later. We were assigned rows next to each other and began picking into our individual buckets without saying a word. As usual, I was quickly left behind in the row, though I had learned to pick relatively quickly using both hands at once. We picked as fast as we could while squatting, alternating back and forth from right to left to pick both rows of berries next to us.

In the middle of one of the rows, while picking, Abelino experienced acute, intense pain in his right knee during one of the countless times he pivoted from the right to the left. At the end of the day, he told me about the incident. He said it felt like his foot would not move, and then the pain suddenly began. The pain was most intense on the inside of the knee just behind the kneecap. He also felt like there was something loose moving around within his knee. He attempted to keep working for the rest of the day in the vain hope that the pain would go away. He tried picking with his knees straightened while he bent at the hips, but this hurt almost as intensely and slowed him down significantly, and he almost missed the minimum weight. At the end of the day, as we approached our cars to drive back to the camp, Abelino told our supervisor about the incident. The supervisor said simply, "OK," and drove away in his white farm pickup without any follow-up. Unsure of what to do, Abelino tried to pick again the next day in great pain and once again barely picked the minimum. Abelino ended up seeing four doctors, a physical therapist, and a Triqui healer, as well as attempting to go through the bureaucracy of worker's compensation. In the end, his pain was diagnosed by a rehabilitation medicine physician as patellar tendonitis, or inflammation of the tendons behind the kneecap.

The social and political genesis of Abelino's knee pain could not have been clearer. His pain was caused unequivocally by the fact that he, as an undocumented Triqui man, had been excluded by both international market inequalities and local discriminatory practices from all but one narrow and particularly traumatic labor position. This occupation required him to bend over seven days a week, turning back and forth, in all kinds of weather, picking strawberries as fast as he possibly could. Tendonitis is understood biomedically to be inflammation caused by repetitive strain and stress on a particular tendon. The inflammation can be brought on over years of overwork and worsened by individual straining events. Abelino's position at the bottom of the farm's ethnicity-citizenship-labor hierarchy meant that he, like hundreds of other Triqui pickers with knee, back, and hip pain, was forced into the precise conditions ripe for the harvesting of chronic joint inflammation and deterioration. Furthermore, his suffering was compounded by the fact that he, like other Triqui people from Oaxaca, had been driven by the results of international economic policies and the expansion of multinational corporations to cross a mortally dangerous border and then live in fear and remain transient wherever he worked, despondently reproducing the same situation for his children, who could not stay in school to seek a better future. In this way, his body was victim to multiple layers of structural violence.

At the beginning of the following summer, Abelino told me he was still suffering from knee pain. Nonetheless, to improve the likelihood of survival of his family and to continue working toward the goal of putting a roof on his house in San Miguel, he again attempted to pick.

SUFFERING THE HIERARCHY

On the Tanaka farm, the hierarchies of perceived ethnicity and citizenship correlate closely with the labor and housing pecking order. On further inspection, it becomes clear that this whole complex maps onto a hierarchy of suffering. Attending to the body in an analysis of the violence continuum in U.S.-Mexico migration allows deeper understanding of the links among class, ethnicity, citizenship, health, and sickness. In many ways, employees of the berry farm in the Skagit Valley come to embody power differentials and prejudice. The working and living conditions, degree of respect received, and access to political power of each of the groups within the labor hierarchy lead to different forms of suffering from top to bottom. A focus on the embodiment of different expressions of violence lends clarity to the reciprocal importance of social forces to bodily suffering.

In general in U.S. agriculture, the more Mexican and the more "indigenous" one is perceived to be, the more psychologically stressful, physically strenuous, and dangerous one's job. Thus where a migrant body falls on the dual ethnic-labor hierarchy shapes how much and what kind of suffering must be endured. The farther down the ladder from Anglo-American U.S. citizen to undocumented indigenous Mexican one is positioned, the more degrading the treatment by supervisors, the more physically taxing the work, the more exposure to weather and pesticides, the more fear of the government, the less comfortable one's housing, and the less control over one's own time.

Of course, the people on every level of the hierarchy suffer. Yet suffering is also roughly cumulative from top to bottom. Some of the social and mental forms of suffering are described as anxieties over profitability and increasing competition by the farm executives, over farm profitability and disrespect from supervisors by the administrative assistants, and over racist insult from supervisors and familial economic survival by the berry pickers. On the more strictly physical level of suffering, this rough accumulation continues to hold. For example, the farm executives worry most about what are sometimes called the diseases of the upper middle class, like heart disease and breast cancer. The administrative assistants worry about these sicknesses, as well as repetitive stress injury like carpal tunnel syndrome. The strawberry pickers are at risk for heart disease and many cancers but worry most about pesticide poisoning, musculoskeletal injury, and chronic pain.

The Triqui people inhabit the bottom rung of the pecking order in the Skagit. They live in the coldest and wettest shacks in the most hidden labor camp with no insulation, no heat, and no wooden ceiling under the tin roof. They hold the most stressful, humiliating, and physically strenuous jobs working seven days a week without breaks while exposed to pesticides and weather. Accordingly, the Triqui pickers bear an unequal share of sickness and pain.

CRESCENCIO AND THE ANGUISH OF INSULT

After a full day of picking strawberries near the end of my first summer of fieldwork, I returned to my shack to find the local migrant clinic preparing a health fair in the labor camp. The health fair involved a retired Evangelical Christian missionary formerly stationed in South America arriving in a large RV that had been converted into a mobile dental clinic, as well as a dentist, a few nurses, a few health educators, and several medical students coming in their private cars. As the pickers showered, changed out of their berry-stained clothing, and did laundry, the nurses and health educators walked the dusty dirt road around the camp letting people know about the fair being set up on the basketball court. The fair began with the nurses and health educators rounding up the children who lived in the camp and demonstrating how they should brush and floss their teeth. After handing out toothbrushes and toothpaste to the children present, they brought out a large rectangular cake with brightly colored frosting, cut it into small pieces, and handed it out to the long line of excited children. Next, they showed a video in which a Mexican subsistence farming single mother contracted HIV from her boyfriend after her husband died. The nurse who led the question-and-answer session afterward made the point several times that "it is not just faggots *[jotos]* who get HIV; it is also women subsistence farmers *[campesinas]*, mothers, and girlfriends." The young men with whom I was standing snickered every time she said *joto.* The dozen medical students, all but two of whom spoke no Spanish, came from a nearby medical school and spent the three hours of the health fair alternately watching, chitchatting among themselves, and throwing used clothing up in the air above a bustling crowd of migrant workers.

As the health fair was winding down and the staff from the local migrant clinic packed up, a Triqui man approached me. Crescencio was living with his wife, two daughters aged five and eight, and a son aged twelve in a shack near mine in the camp. Having heard from the camp manager that I was a student doctor, he asked if I had any medicine for headaches. When I asked for more information, he explained that he had had a debilitating headache for almost seven years, approximately the same length of time he had been migrating for work. He described the headache as located on top of his head near the center, sometimes behind one or the other eye. The pain was so excruciating that he could no longer focus on anything until it dissipated. Like any good medical student, I asked far too many questions. I found out that the headache was not made better or worse by eating, resting, sitting, standing, exercising, drinking water, or taking Tylenol or ibuprofen. Crescencio patiently explained to me that every time a farm supervisor called him names on the job, made fun of him, or reprimanded him unfairly, he developed one of these severe headaches. The most common triggers included being called "stupid Oaxacan" or being told in a deprecating or angry manner to "hurry up" when he was already picking as fast as possible. He explained to me that he was concerned because whenever he developed the headaches, any unpleasant noise or annoyance could upset him, and thus he felt more prone to anger with his wife and children. His primary reason for seeking help with the headache was so that he would not get angry with his family. He wanted to take care of this problem before it could evolve into anything serious, specifically, violence against his wife or children.

After the first few seasons of migration to other states within Mexico, Crescencio went to see doctors at the government clinic in San Miguel who tried different pills and injections. Some of the medicines produced short-term relief, but the headaches kept coming back. After years of migrating within Mexico, Crescencio began coming to work on the Tanaka farm in Washington and the headaches continued. In the labor camp as well as back in Oaxaca when he returned in the winters, he met with a Triqui healer who performed the traditional reading of his future as well as a cleansing meant to draw bad spirits away from his body. These interventions alleviated the headaches for a time. After every biomedical or traditional treatment, however, the headaches returned when triggered by mistreatment on the job. The only treatment Crescencio had found that made his headache go away was drinking twenty to twenty-four beers. He told me matter-of-factly that when he drank this amount of beer, he could relax and the pain would be gone the next morning when he woke up. He had to use this remedy a few times in an average workweek.

Crescencio's headaches present a complicated cycle of linkages between suffering and the social and symbolic forces structuring his life. To start the series off, like Abelino and other Triqui migrants, Crescencio is victim to the social forces obliging him to live and work in damaging conditions at the bottom of a labor hierarchy. Next, some of the individuals positioned above him in the hierarchy insult him with racist slurs and impossible demands. In turn, the contempt with which Crescencio is treated leads to his excruciating headaches. These socially structured headaches lead him to get angry with his family and to get drunk, thus involuntarily embodying the stereotype of Mexican migrants as misogynists and alcoholics. This stereotype then serves to legitimate the ethnic-citizenship hierarchy on the farm as well as the racist treatment the migrant workers receive. This symbolic violence, embodied so precisely by Crescencio, works to make invisible the racism and xenophobia underlying the disrespect that he and other Mexican migrants are seen to deserve. Finally, this disrespect is added to the forces positioning migrant berry pickers at the bottom of the farm hierarchy.

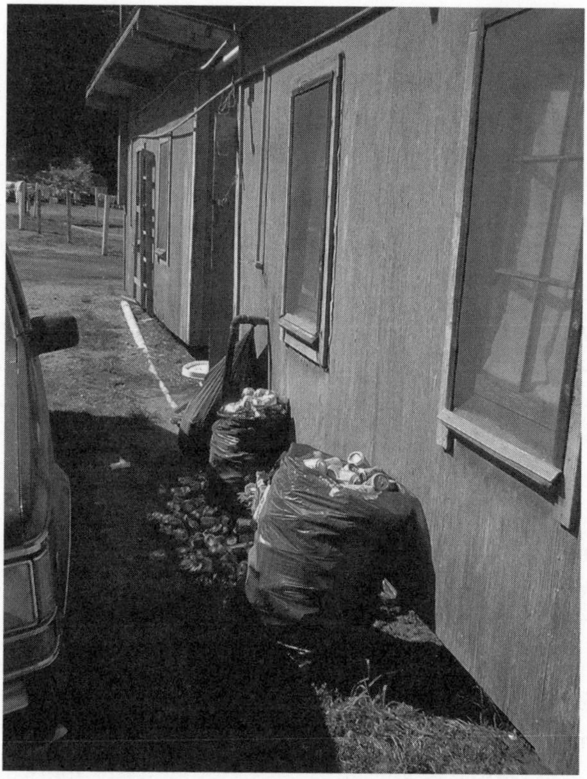

Self-medication: cans behind a *cabina* in the farm labor camp. Photo by Seth M. Holmes.

MIGRANT FARMWORK AND HEALTH DISPARITIES IN CONTEXT

Nationwide, migrant farmworkers are sicker than other groups. Consistent with the concept of structural vulnerability,[7] these health disparities fall along citizenship, ethnicity, and class lines. As mentioned in Chapter 2, the National Agricultural Worker Survey indicates that 81 percent of farmworkers are immigrants, 95 percent of whom were born in Mexico[8] and 52 percent of whom are undocumented.[9] Researchers estimate that there are one million indigenous Oaxacans in the United States, mostly Mixtec,

Zapotec, and Triqui.[10] The average age of agricultural workers is twenty-nine, and very few are over sixty.[11] However, health statistics for migrant farmworkers are inexact given the impossibility of an accurate census. Estimates of the migrant farm laborer population in the United States range from 750,000 to 12 million.[12] In addition, most morbidity and mortality data are skewed down due to undocumented workers' fear of reporting health problems, poor enforcement of labor and health policies in agriculture, and the fact that many Latin American migrants return to their home countries as they age or become disabled, leading to a "healthy worker bias."[13]

Despite a strong focus in public health on what is often called the "healthy Latino paradox," much research has shown that farmworkers bear a disproportionate share of sickness. The Latino paradox indicates that there are certain health conditions for which Latino populations overall fare better than other ethnic groups, despite having relatively lower socioeconomic status. One primary problem with this paradox is the definition of the metacategory "Latino." Much of the research into this paradox fails to differentiate between the American born and the foreign born, as well as between Spanish, South American, Central American, and Mexican, let alone indigenous, descent. Though the Triqui people I got to know did not consider themselves Latino, most public health and census data include all people who identify as having Latin American descent in one category, called Latino (or Hispanic in the case of the census). Recent research indicates that Latino children have twice the death and hospitalization rates from pedestrian injury than that of white children in the United States and that Latino adults have lower rates of screening for cancers.[14] Moreover, an Institute of Medicine report indicates that all nonwhite ethnic groups receive definitively lower-quality health care.[15] Though there has been little specific micropopulation research, it is likely that indigenous Oaxacans in the United States have worse health than other "Latinos" due to their relative paucity of social and cultural capital,[16] such as occupational, educational, and linguistic resources.

Beyond the Latino meta-ethnic group assigned them, Triqui strawberry pickers belong to the disadvantaged category of immigrants in the United States. Several studies show that the health status of immigrants declines with increasing time in the United States. Such health indicators as obesity, serum cholesterol, tobacco smoking, alcohol use, illicit drug use, mental illness, suicide, and death by homicide increase between first- and second-generation Mexican immigrants in this country.[17] Nutritional value of the diet of immigrants also decreases significantly during the first year in the United States.[18] Those immigrants who are undocumented have the additional negative health determinant of having to cross what one scholar has called the "most violent border in the world between two countries not at war with one another."[19] Undocumented status further increases "allostatic load"—understood biomedically as the accumulation of health risk associated with chronic stress—due to traumatic experiences crossing the border and fear of deportation.[20]

In addition, Mexican migrant farmworkers suffer poor health due to their class position. Agricultural workers have a fatality rate five times that of all workers.[21] Moreover, agricultural workers have increased rates of nonfatal injuries, musculoskeletal pain, heart disease, and many types of cancer.[22] There is also an increased risk of stillbirth and congenital birth defects in children born near farms.[23] Furthermore, research indicates that approximately one-third to one-half of agricultural workers report chronic symptoms associated with pesticide exposure such as headache, skin and eye irritation, and flu-like syndromes.[24]

To further specify class position, migrant and seasonal farmworkers suffer the poorest health status in the agriculture industry. The vast majority of these individuals and families live below the poverty line.[25] They have increased rates of many chronic conditions, such as malnutrition, anemia, hypertension, diabetes, dermatitis, fatigue, headaches, sleep disturbances, anxiety, memory problems, sterility, blood disorders, dental problems, and abnormalities in liver and kidney function.[26] Migrant farmworkers have increased pulmonary problems to such a degree that farmwork has an effect on lung health comparable to smoking.[27] They have increased incidence of acute sicknesses such as urinary tract and kidney infections, heat stroke, anthrax, ascariasis, encephalitis, leptospirosis, rabies, salmonellosis, tetanus, and coccidioidomycosis, most of which are believed to be caused in large part by poor living and working conditions and lack of sanitary bathrooms.[28] Tuberculosis prevalence, also related to poor living conditions, is six times higher among migrant workers than in the general U.S. population,[29] and HIV infection is three times more common than in the overall U.S. and Mexican populations.[30] Finally, children of migrant farmworkers show high rates of malnutrition, vision problems, dental problems, anemia, and blood lead poisoning.[31]

Despite worse health status and a resulting need for increased health and social services, migrant farmworkers have many obstacles to accessing these services. Farmworkers are entirely or partially excluded from worker's compensation benefits in all but fifteen states.[32] The Fair Labor Standards Act of 1938 guaranteed minimum wage, time and a half wage for overtime, and restricted child labor, but it did not apply to agricultural workers. Amendments in 1966 ostensibly extended eligibility to farmworkers but disqualified the majority by excluding those on small farms and those paid piece wages. These amendments restricted child farm labor such that any age child could work nonhazardous agricultural jobs but only children at least sixteen years old could work hazardous agricultural jobs. The 1974 amendments retained the previous exclusions. Most farmworkers were excluded also by the Social Security Act and its later amendments from benefits related to unemployment, which in any case are not available to undocumented immigrants. In addition, even though migrant housing conditions are addressed in the Housing Act of 1949 and the Occupational Safety and Health Act of 1970, living conditions in labor camps continue to fall below the requirements. Finally, agricultural workers were denied the right to collective bargaining under the Wagner Act of 1935. They have gained the right to bargain only in the state of California under the Agricultural Labor Relations Act of 1975 after strong organizing by and a heavy toll of violence against the United Farm Workers (UFW). While this win led to labor improvements, the agriculture system in California for workers on farms without UFW contracts remains extremely exploitative. Furthermore, we must remember that even existing provisions for farmworkers are violated regularly because of vast power differentials and threats by employers to have undocumented migrants deported if they report violations.

Although there is a federal Migrant Health Program, it is estimated that it serves only 13 percent of the intended population of migrant workers.[33]

Despite living well below the poverty line, fewer than one-third of migrant women qualify for Medicaid, primarily due to their nomadic interstate existence and their undocumented status.[34] Researchers estimate that less than 30 percent of migrant laborers have health insurance, in contrast to an estimated 84 percent of U.S. residents overall.[35] This disparity is likely to grow with the otherwise laudable health care reform of 2009 that promises—if fully implemented—to increase the rate of health insurance for U.S. citizens with no provisions for one of our most vulnerable populations, immigrant workers. Furthermore, it is estimated in California that less than 10 percent of indigenous Mexican farmworkers have health insurance, in contrast to 30 percent of their mestizo counterparts.[36] In part due to these obstacles, migrant laborers are less likely than other people to obtain preventive care, with 27 percent never receiving a routine physical exam, 25 percent never having a dental checkup, and 43 percent never receiving an eye exam.[37] In fact, many migrant workers in the United States go through significant hardships to return to Mexico for health care and cite economic, cultural, and linguistic reasons for this choice.[38] Importantly, these statistics directly contradict the popular American complaint that undocumented immigrants are the cause of the demise of the American health care system through overuse.

BERNARDO AND THE DAMAGE OF TORTURE

During my time on the farm in Washington State, I met one Triqui family who lived outside the labor camp in an apartment in town. The twenty-seven-year-old father in this family, Martin, had been able to gain U.S. residency through his father, Bernardo, who became a U.S. resident in the 1986 amnesty for farmworkers under the Bracero Program. Martin no longer works on the Tanaka farm but at a chicken packing plant, along with his wife. Bernardo was one of the first Triqui people to come to Washington. When he gained U.S. residency, he stopped working on the farm and moved back to Oaxaca. Each summer since the 1980s Bernardo has spent five months working in a fish processing plant in Alaska to support himself, his wife, and his sister.

This family is from San Pedro, a Triqui town in the mountains of Oaxaca near San Miguel, the hometown of the rest of the Triqui people I knew in Washington. While the whole Triqui Zone in Oaxaca is reputed to be violent, San Pedro is most notorious. It is also home to the Unified Movement for Triqui Liberation (MULT), which, at the time of my fieldwork, was in the process of transforming from a rebel movement to an official political party. The MULT was a relatively small movement, focused primarily in the small town of San Pedro without any clear link to other contemporary movements, such as the Zapatistas in Chiapas.

In the middle of winter, Martin called and invited me to go with him on a road trip to Oaxaca. We left two days later and drove straight to Oaxaca without stopping to sleep. There were five people in my Honda Civic hatchback for the three-thousand-mile trip in each direction: me, Martin, his four-year-old daughter, and his six-year-old and seven-year-old sons. The only stops we made were for oil changes in Arizona on the way down and the way back up, to buy food quickly once or twice daily, and to fix a flat tire once in rural Oaxaca. Otherwise, Martin and I took turns driving, napping, entertaining the children, and cleaning up after Martin's daughter got food poisoning, leading to diarrhea and vomiting on the drive south.

I spent my first week in the state of Oaxaca in Bernardo's house in the city of Juxtlahuaca. Though this family was originally from San Pedro, their land was on the edge of town, next to a mestizo village, and they were under frequent armed attack from their neighbors and frequently attacked those neighbors as well. The ongoing attacks were related primarily to landownership and political affiliations; most people in San Pedro support the MULT, whereas the neighboring town overall supported the Institutional Revolutionary Party (PRI), which had been in power in most of Mexico for over seventy years. Bernardo described the situation in broken Spanish, his second language.

> There have been many deaths. Oh! Many deaths! There was a fourteen-year-old girl there *[pointing toward the mountains where most Triqui people live]*, just a girl. They got her before she went up the hill. Many raped

> her. They raped her, many! Then she was killed, very violent, many knife cuts. Then a teacher was killed there, where we went *[pointing toward San Pedro].* Oh! The son of Miguel [one of the leaders of the MULT], remember? I gave him soda? I was here *[gesturing with his hand],* and you were there next to Martin. They shot his son. Then over there *[gesturing different directions with his hand]* and there and there. Oh, many deaths. Maybe eight, maybe ten in the last two months. Evil people, very evil. They kill between political parties.
>
> There is a lot of danger here. If you say something and don't realize someone heard you and they are hidden, all of a sudden, "pow!" or a knife, and you are dead. I can't go out at night, even if we need something. Not at night, no! A lot of danger; there is a lot of danger here. During the day is fine. I go to the market to see the doctor. But not at night. I have fear. A lot of danger, yes, yes.

Bernardo and Martin's family, along with many others, moved from San Pedro to the nearby small city of Juxtlahuaca to escape the violence. Many such land wars are still going on in La Mixteca region of Oaxaca. With the money Bernardo made migrating to the United States, the family was able to build a house in Juxtlahuaca and start a small store in one room of their house.

At night, after we drove back on the steep dirt roads from visiting San Pedro, Bernardo asked me if I knew of any good medicine for his stomach. He explained that his stomach had been hurting for eight years. He said, "My stomach does not like food any more. I don't have the desire *[ganas]* to eat. It hurts to eat." Before he goes to Alaska to work each spring, his doctor in Juxtlahuaca gives him a long series of "vitamin shots" and "shots to give [him] hunger" so that he has enough energy to work in the processing plant. When he returns from Alaska, he is weak and thin and receives another long series of the same shots to recover his strength in order to tend the family cornfields just outside Juxtlahuaca. The following description of his stomach pain was punctuated by frequent groans and moans.

> It gives me such a pain! Right here *[pointing to his lower abdomen],* such a pain, and it goes up. It jumps and jumps like chords jumping, like this, like this *[rapidly opening and closing his hands].* I wake up and my stomach hurts, ay! It gets hard like this bench is hard *[touching the wooden bench on*

> *which he sits].* So I mash my stomach with a soda bottle. I mash, mash, mash here, mash here *[pushing his fist slowly into his abdomen].* And it helps a little. But, ay! I can't stand it. I can't eat! Nothing! Each time I eat it hurts, but it hurts. But I hold out *[me aguanto].* I hold out until work is over.

Bernardo had lost weight over the past several years and felt weak each morning when he left at 5:00 to work the family cornfields before I woke up. His wife told me that he had to force himself to eat a tortilla and an egg before working in the fields.

When I asked him why his stomach hurt, he first explained that it was because he had worked so hard all his life.

> I have my pains because of so much work. Ay; so much work. I left for Veracruz to cut cane when I was eight. So much work all my life. Veracruz, Baja California, Washington, Oregon, California, Norte Carolina, ay! And now, 'laska. And here, the cornfield and the house, too. All my life I work a lot, and one gets tired, tired, and the body hurts. In 'laska, we work 16 hours, no! Seven days a week. No rest for 2 months. Then maybe 10 hours or 8 hours a day 7 days a week for 2 more months. Ay! So much work!

"So much working *[tanto trabajar]* wears out a body," he said with a weak smile. He continued, "All I have is from my work. I harvest the corn, cut the *zacate* [corn plants], bind it, all alone, alone. I am sixty-two or maybe eighty; I don't know.[39] This house, the land, it is all from my work. Who will feed me and my family if I don't work? No one. There is nothing here."

When I asked him why the pain started eight years ago, he added another important fact: "Also, the soldiers. You know what soldiers *[soldados]* are, right? Yes, the soldiers punched and kicked me many, many times. Punched like this *[making a fist and punching into the air]*, here in my stomach. Ah! But many beatings *[chingadazos]* until there was blood all over. Because of the Movement [MULT]. People said rumors against us and the soldiers, the blue soldiers, came and beat me up."

Eight years before, Bernardo was kidnapped and tortured by the Mexican federal police in charge of narcotics enforcement, whom he calls "the blue soldiers" because of the color of their uniforms. This branch of the Mexican military is funded by the U.S. Drug Enforcement Agency, officially in order to stop drug smuggling between Mexico and the United States. Bernardo was beaten several times by these soldiers and put in prison. There, despite several requests, he was denied medical help such that he resorted to drinking his own urine as a remedy to help his abdomen heal. Furthermore, he was refused food many of the days he was in captivity. The "blue soldiers" told him that he had been kidnapped under suspicion that he was part of the MULT, even though the movement had no links with the drug trade. After several months of petitions by Bernardo and his family, the mayor of Juxtlahuaca signed and stamped an official paper—which Bernardo proudly showed me—stating that Bernardo had done no wrong, and he was finally released from prison.

Like Abelino and Crescencio, Bernardo endures a form of suffering determined directly by social and political forces. The contemporary system of neoliberal corporate capitalism has built global inequalities, leading southern Mexico into a deepening economic depression. This poverty is one of the primary factors producing the local land wars as well as the survival-seeking out-migration of able-bodied workers. The political alliances of the Mexican military, with its ties to U.S. federal financing, have translated into a repression of the movements seeking redistribution of power and resources in a more equitable fashion. The political violence against suspected members of indigenous rights movements is not only embodied as sickness, as in Bernardo's case, but also reinforces the neoliberal economic project and thus deepens the poverty and suffering of millions of marginalized people. The logic behind this violence affirms that the poorest of the poor must not assert themselves or be allowed political economic power. The future of multinational commercial accumulation depends on it.

THE IMPOSSIBLY HEAVY STATUE

The day after Bernardo took me to visit San Pedro, I met one of his elderly Triqui neighbors. This elderly man told me an origin story of the Triqui people from San Pedro. Several times while in the Triqui Zone of Oaxaca, I heard different versions of this story.

> Pedro [or Miguel, if the person telling the story is from San Miguel] was a young Triqui man who lived long ago on fertile land in the center of Mexico. Pedro had one brother [either Miguel or Pedro, correlating with the other Triqui hometown] and one sister, Ana [correlating with the third Triqui hometown, Santa Ana]. When Pedro was just a teenager, the people *[la gente]* kicked his family out of the area. Pedro had to carry their statue of Jesus on the cross while his family walked out of town. They walked and walked, and the statue of Jesus became heavier and heavier until the family had to settle in the new spot where they found themselves and make a new home. After several years, the people kicked his family out of this area. Again, Pedro had to carry their statue of Jesus on the cross while they walked. Once again, the statue became very heavy, and they had to stop and make a new home. Yet again, the people kicked Pedro and his family out. This happened several times until Pedro reached these arid mountains in the clouds where it is difficult to grow any crops *[each speaker pointed to the mountains surrounding her or his hometown]* and the statue of Jesus became impossibly heavy. Pedro and his family settled here in these dry mountains, and he can still be heard laughing and celebrating during the patron saint festival every year.

This origin story parallels much of the history of the Triqui people, who have been violently pushed off of land in Oaxaca, forced by global markets to migrate, and disrespected in Mexico and the United States. At the same time, the Triqui people are identified by others and identify themselves as violent. Just after I left San Miguel to return to the United States, two of my Triqui friends were shot and killed while shooting and killing two other Triqui men. This incident occurred soon after an especially controversial Oaxaca state election in 2004 and was rumored to be related to political factions. A missionary couple I met near San Miguel told me about the husband being shot in the shoulder by Triqui people on one of their first visits to the area several years before. Several other people in the mountains of Oaxaca, including Bernardo, warned me to be careful because the Triqui Zone, they told me, was violent and dangerous.

This rumored and real physical violence perpetrated by Triqui people can be understood as another embodiment of the violence continuum. Following Michael Taussig's analysis of colonial violence in the Putamayo of South America, Triqui violence can be understood as a kind of mimesis, or reflection, of the violent displacement they have experienced numerous times.[40] In a similar manner, Frantz Fanon conceptualizes the interpersonal violence in colonial Algeria as something of a nearsighted mimesis.[41] Fanon identifies the violence perpetrated by a starving Algerian man against his Algerian neighbor, the shop owner who demands payment for the bread he is selling, as a misdirected reflection of the structural and political violence of the colonial regime. This individual sees his Algerian neighbor who owns the bread store as the person withholding food from him instead of seeing the colonial regime as the primary cause for his poverty and starvation. Similarly, Triqui violence between political parties and neighboring towns can be seen as a mirror image of the violence they have experienced at the hands of the Mexican military and the unequal global market. However, Taussig also points out that the violence of the colonist is produced by his own fears of the imagined violence of those he oppresses. In a similar way, the oppression of the Triqui people by the Mexican government is sometimes justified with the trope of Triqui violence.

The suffering of Triqui migrant laborers is an embodiment of multiple forms of violence. The political violence of land wars has pushed them to live in inhospitable climates without easy access to water for crops. The structural violence of global neoliberal capitalism forces them to leave home and family members, suffer through a long and deadly desert border crossing, and search for a means to survive in a new land. The structural violence of labor hierarchies in the United States organized around ethnicity and citizenship positions them at the bottom, with the most dangerous and backbreaking occupations and the worst accommodations. Due to their location at the bottom of the pecking order, the undocumented Triqui migrant workers endure disproportionate injury and sickness.

Abelino's knee pain is a direct result of structural violence, particularly as it drives him into jobs requiring repetitive, harmful movements that all but guarantee physical deterioration, inflammation, and pain. He is not given the option of other forms of work, like the "light jobs" in which he sees U.S. citizens engaged. National and local prejudices and stereotypes further shape the hierarchy of labor such that Triqui workers are often treated with disrespect and racist insult. For the vast majority, their undocumented status leads to fear of authority and fear of demanding the redress of wrongs. These external and internalized forms of symbolic violence not only shore up unequal labor hierarchies through normalization but also lead to various forms of suffering, such as Crescencio's intractable headaches. These headaches, in turn, lead back to the symbolic violence of stereotypes of Mexican migrant men as alcoholic and *machista.* Simultaneously, the Mexican military enacts violence in response to the fear of the economic elite at the prospect of disenfranchised people organizing for economic, health, education, and political rights. Bernardo's debilitating stomach pain began with the direct political violence of several well-placed fist and boot blows to his stomach and evolved through the structural violence requiring him to work long, difficult days in Alaska and Oaxaca in order for his family to survive.

Normalized everyday violence, akin to the institutional violence examined by Scheper-Hughes and Basaglia,[42] can be seen also in the interactions between Triqui migrants and their health care providers. In these relationships, insult is added to injury inadvertently through the bureaucratic dysfunction of health care and the lenses of perception used by well-meaning and idealistic health and social service professionals. Triqui experiences of health care—particularly those of Abelino, Crescencio, and Bernardo—are the subject of the next chapter.

FIVE "Doctors Don't Know Anything"

THE CLINICAL GAZE IN MIGRANT HEALTH

When I first arrived in San Miguel, I attempted to explain to the officials at *la presidencia* (the town hall) my reasons for being there. I said that I was hoping to live in town for several months to learn about the everyday life and health of the residents. The official in charge of legal issues *(el síndico)* explained that there was nowhere to stay, no hotel or guest house, but that I could work in the Centro de Salud (government clinic) in town since it was short-staffed. San Miguel has a small, federally funded clinic staffed alternately by a medical resident *(pasante)* and a nurse, often with a day or two in between when there is no staff. Every medical resident in Mexico is required to spend the year after graduating from medical school doing community service and is assigned a clinic. A new medical resident comes to the clinic each year, and most of the nurses are rotated by the federal government at least once a year. Thus there is minimal rapport between the village and the clinic staff. The

The village of San Miguel, Oaxaca. Photo by Seth M. Holmes.

síndico told me that the nurse, Josefina, and the doctor, Juan, were both from Oaxaca City and spoke only Spanish.

The síndico's suggestion that I help in the Centro de Salud made me nervous; I was concerned that I might be pigeonholed as only a medical practitioner instead of an anthropologist and that I might be mistaken for a fully trained physician. I told him that I would be interested in observing the physician and nurse in town and assisting when appropriate but that I was there primarily to learn from the people and that I could not practice medicine on my own. He looked disappointed and confused. When I repeated that I was there primarily to observe and learn from the Triqui people about their lives and health, he still seemed unconvinced that I could not fill a position at the clinic. I tried to explain that I had not finished my training as a physician and still needed to be supervised by a doctor with more experience. The síndico replied, "Ese médico no sabe nada" (That doctor doesn't know anything).

This harsh statement took me aback. I wondered whether it was due to a difference in illness explanatory models between an indigenous Triqui person and an urban allopathic physician, an appropriate judgment of the lack of knowledge of a pasante not yet finished with his training, or the result of a lack of knowledge or bedside manner on the part of this particular médico. I assumed, irrespective of the primary reason, that the account was specific to Juan and the situation in the Centro in San Miguel.

However, as I continued my fieldwork in Washington, California, and Arizona and returned to San Miguel during the tenure of a new pasante, I heard "Los médicos no saben nada" (Doctors don't know anything) in several contexts. I found this refrain quite disconcerting. I had assumed that the physicians working with the Triqui people in migrant clinics or government-funded clinics in Oaxaca would be appreciated, partly because they had forgone prestige, state-of-the-art facilities, and higher salaries in order to work with this population. In addition, I was in the midst of demanding training to become not only an anthropologist but also a physician, and I wanted to work in the future in both capacities with Latin American migrant laborers. Why did the Triqui people think that the physicians working with them did not know anything? What was wrong with the doctor-patient relationship? Why was it so unhelpful in its present form? Could it be changed to be more helpful for my Triqui companions? What were the economic, social, and symbolic structures impeding such change? And how might anthropology speak to clinical medicine and public health? These questions form the impetus for this chapter.

In the previous chapter, I described the illness narratives of Abelino, Crescencio, and Bernardo, considering the effects of the different expressions of violence at work in migrant farm labor. Here I continue the histories of Abelino's knee, Crescencio's headache, and Bernardo's stomach pain as these individuals interact as patients with health professionals in Washington, California, and Oaxaca. Using these illness narratives as well as interviews with clinicians and observations of clinical encounters, this chapter explores both the structural factors affecting migrant health care and the lenses through which health professionals perceive their migrant patients.

THE CLINICAL GAZE

As an anthropologist and a physician, I am concerned both with theorizing social categories and their relationships with bodies and with the possibility that suffering might be alleviated in a more respectful, egalitarian, and effective manner. My dual training has been at once stimulating and disorienting. The lenses through which cultural anthropologists and physicians are trained to see the world are significantly different, and at times contradictory. I have found the critical social analyses of anthropology incredibly important at the same time that I have valued the grounded human concerns of clinical medicine. Others at the margins of clinical medicine and anthropological analysis have offered valuable insights and methodologies. Well known are Kleinman's writings on illness narratives and the explanatory models of patients as well as Farmer's essays on pragmatic solidarity and structural violence.[1] Kleinman's work focuses on the ways patients somatize social realities and on the importance of clinicians listening to their patient's understandings of illness. Farmer's work drives home the importance of structural determinants of sickness and calls for more equal distribution of biomedical resources.[2] This chapter takes the analyses of Kleinman on the perceptions and explanatory models of patients and of Farmer on the effects of structural violence on patients and turns them on their heads by focusing on the health professionals rather than the patients. After accompanying my Triqui friends to migrant clinics, hospitals, and traditional healers in the United States and Mexico, I have become interested also in the ways in which social and economic structures affect health professionals, the lenses through which they perceive and respond to their patients, and the care they are ultimately able to offer.

One of the most important analyses of the perceptions of medical professionals in the clinical encounter is Michel Foucault's *The Birth of the Clinic*.[3] Foucault describes what he calls "the gaze." He explains that the clinical encounter changed drastically from the eighteenth to the nineteenth century: "This new structure is indicated . . . by the minute but decisive change, whereby the question: 'What is the matter with you?', with which the eighteenth-century dialogue between doctor and patient began . . ., was replaced by that other question: 'Where does it hurt?', in which we recognize the operation of the clinic and the principle of its entire discourse."[4]

Around the time of the advent of the dissection of cadavers, the conception of disease transformed from an entity affecting the whole person to an anatomically localized lesion. It was no longer considered necessary for doctors to listen to patients describe their experience of the illness—their symptoms—in order to diagnose and treat. Instead, physicians began to focus on the isolated, diseased organs, treating the patient increasingly as a body, a series of anatomical objects, and ignoring the social and personal realities of the patient, the person. In the paradigm of the clinical gaze, physicians examine and talk about the patient's diseases, while the patient remains largely silent. In many ways, this can be seen as the advent of modern positivist science in which human, social, and historical contexts are considered irrelevant.

Since the change described by Foucault, many medical scholars have critiqued clinical medicine's objectification of patients. The aphorism, "Ask not what disease the patient has; ask what patient has the disease," has been attributed to the nineteenth-century Canadian physician Sir William Osler.[5] In the mid-1990s, Tom Boyce, a pediatrician and sociobiologist, wrote similarly, "For me, there is a growing unease that, in our headlong efforts to bring into focus finer and more discriminating views of the lesions lying *beneath* disease, we will have missed the opportunity to envision the person or the patient that lies *beyond* the disease."[6] Boyce describes the clinical gaze as the "myopic vision" that sees through the patient to focus on the pathology, the organ, the lesion.

Others discuss the consequences of the paradigm of the gaze for health professionals themselves. Stefan Hirschauer describes the ways surgery transforms everyone involved—patient, surgeon, nurse—into tools.[7] The rituals surrounding surgery depersonalize not only the patient but also the health professionals. Yet he implies that this temporary, ritualistic depersonalization protects the personhood of everyone involved. Similarly, Joseph Lella and Dorothy Pawluch describe the dehumanizing experience of medical students in the objectification of cadavers.[8] As the students objectify the human bodies they dissect, they experience their own dehumanization.

The clinical gaze is taught not only in the anatomy lab and the operating room but also in the models of doctoring presented to students. Holmes and Maya Ponte, both anthropologists and physicians, explain that the structure of the written and verbal medical student patient presentation transforms patients and their human, social, and bodily reality into generalized cases of a medical disease at the same time that it protects the students from uncertainty.[9] Melvin Konner, an anthropologist and physician, writes of his experiences as a medical student in *Becoming a Doctor*.[10] For the most part, he writes, resident and attending physicians model survival skills and patient objectification instead of an interpersonal relationship with the patient. In the conclusion, Konner specifies that the doctor-patient relationship is not one of "I-Thou," as Martin Buber would have it, but rather one of "We-You."[11] This is meant to show the primacy of interactions among physicians and trainees; they form a medical team, a "Doctor-Doctor" relationship. Only after the team exists as a relational entity is there a relationship with the patient. This can be seen also in Foucault's description of Charcot and the Salpêtrière Clinic.[12] Charcot displayed female patients in front of psychiatry trainees in order to teach about hysteria. He spoke about the patients, had them touched and prodded (including their pubic areas), and had them taken away if their poses became too sexual. In this way, the Doctor-Doctor relationship of Charcot and his trainees led to the objectification of the women such that they were hidden if they showed too recognizable a sign of their personhood.

More recently, Beverly Ann Davenport has analyzed one of the homeless clinics that have become a notable part of the training of medical students. This is a space of struggle between two medical paradigms, "witnessing" and the medical gaze.[13] Witnessing, or treating patients as whole persons, Davenport writes, is taught by physician-educators in this clinic as conscious resistance to the medical gaze. Physicians attempt to enact this humanizing model, all the while practicing within a system characterized by the biotechnical. At some points they model witnessing to their students, while at others they enact a myopic gaze on pathology.

I am especially interested here in discovering how the analyses of the medical gaze by Foucault and others apply to the field of migrant health in the twenty-first century. What are the characteristics of the medical gaze in a contemporary migrant clinic? How do they relate to the relatively recent movement to make medical education "biopsychosocial" and culturally competent? How do they relate to larger social, economic, and political structures? What might be an alternative model for the migrant clinic? I explore these questions through the interactions of Abelino, Crescencio, and Bernardo with the health care system.

ABELINO'S KNEE: STRUCTURE AND GAZE IN MIGRANT HEALTH CARE

Two days after Abelino's knee accident, the crop manager canceled picking in the morning because of a heavy, cold downpour. Abelino and I went to an urgent care clinic. Abelino ended up seeing several doctors and a physical therapist over the next several months, usually without a Spanish translator and never a translator proficient in Triqui. During these months, he limped around camp, taking care of his kids while his wife and eldest daughter continued to pick in the fields.

The urgent care doctor listened briefly to Abelino's description of what happened and examined his swollen right knee. He ordered an X-ray, which showed that no bones had broken but could not show anything of the soft tissue, tendons, bursa, meniscuses. The report from the X-ray concluded, rather simplistically, "normal right knee." The doctor explained that Abelino should not work picking berries, emphasizing rest to let his knee recover. This physician was not sure if the knee pain was due to a ligament sprain or a meniscus tear and planned for further evaluation once the pain had subsided. Abelino asked for an injection, a common method of medication administration in Mexico, and the doctor refused. Instead, he gave Abelino a referral to physical therapy, an anti-inflammatory medicine, and instructions on icing his knee regularly. This urgent care physician also filled out the paperwork to open a worker's compensation claim for Abelino with the State of Washington

Department of Labor and Industries (LNI). Two days later, Abelino went in to see the physical therapist, who performed his own evaluation of the knee. At this point, Abelino described his knee pain as a 7 on a scale with 10 being the worst pain imaginable. The physical therapist gave Abelino knee exercises to do at home and recommended a consultation with an orthopedic specialist.

The next week, when Abelino and I went to the clinic for his appointment, the original urgent care doctor was not on duty, so we saw one of his partners. This physician looked at Abelino's chart, listened briefly to Abelino tell him what had happened, and told Abelino that he could work "light duty," provided he did not bend, walk, or stand for long periods. This doctor filled out a form to this effect and gave it to Abelino to take to the Tanaka farm. The doctor explained the cause of injury in the chart as "while picking, twisted his right knee." This description is not only vague; it also linguistically makes Abelino the subject whose action produced the problem: *he* twisted the direct object, his knee. Although Abelino has chronic gastritis such that he cannot eat traditional spicy Triqui food and although the physician did not ask Abelino about any stomach symptoms, this physician wrote in the chart, "[Patient] also specifically states he has no GI upset from taking NSAID." Nonsteroidal anti-inflammatory drugs (NSAIDs), such as ibuprofen, aggravate gastritis, and there is a relative contraindication to their use in the context of gastrointestinal problems. No future health professional working with Abelino double checked this assertion. The physician gave Abelino a brace and instructed him to wear it. Abelino later told me that the brace made the pain worse, so he wore it twice only. That afternoon, Abelino went to the farm office to ask for lighter work. The bilingual receptionist, Samantha, told him in a frustrated tone, "No, because no *[No, porque no],*" and did not let him talk with anyone else.

In the meantime, Abelino consulted a Triqui healer. This elderly monolingual man who worked during the day picking strawberries saw Abelino at night in his labor camp shack. I sat in on the consultation, and Abelino translated the words I could not understand. The healer shuffled and rearranged a deck of Mexican cards several times in order to understand the source of the pain. He let Abelino know that the spirit of a person Abelino had seen die had attached to him. In order to get rid of the spirit and heal his patient, the Triqui healer covered several raw eggs in rum and rubbed them over Abelino's body, especially around his knee. The rum-covered eggs might be able to entice the spirit to attach to them instead, he explained. Next, he left the shack and threw the eggs into the distance, luring the spirit away from Abelino's knee.

Over the next few weeks, as Abelino rested, his knee pain subsided somewhat, to 5 out of 10 on the pain scale. He was able to walk with a limp, but it still brought excruciating pain if he tried to bend or squat. Since Abelino was not given the option of lighter work, he attempted to return to picking strawberries to help support his family. The swelling immediately increased, and the intense pain returned, so Abelino stopped working again after two days.

Nineteen days after the injury, LNI opened a claim for Abelino that would pay his medical bills and two-thirds of his salary while he was unable to work. The medical and worker's compensation coverage would end when Abelino's knee had improved enough for him to go back to his job or the problem was deemed chronic without improvement. The LNI file states that he returned to work on "lite duty until reinjured knee." It is unclear how LNI understood Abelino's return to strawberry picking as "lite duty." The urgent care physician recognized this was an incorrect representation and wrote in the medical chart that there was "apparently no light duty work" at the Tanaka farm, without checking this assertion. The LNI file also states, "He indicated he does not speak English. I asked him if he speak Spanish, he said yes (I think)." However, LNI did not order or authorize a Spanish interpreter for his medical appointments for another two weeks. Three months after this note, LNI put an alert in Abelino's file that all communication should be sent to Abelino in Spanish. The vast majority of letters that were sent after that time, however, were in English only.

The Tanaka farm told LNI that Abelino made $7.16 an hour and that he did not receive any other benefits. This report undervalued Abelino's pay considerably since he routinely picked well above the minimum and received housing as part of his benefits. The farm sent a copy of Abelino's working hours and pay for the month *beginning* with his knee injury, a month in which he worked only two days and picked very slowly. This incorrect information was used by LNI to calculate how much Abelino worked *before* his injury and, therefore, his benefits. A pro bono social worker from a local nonprofit phoned LNI to find out what was needed and helped Abelino fax copies of his checks from the month prior to his injury to rectify the hours, though LNI never recalculated Abelino's benefits. LNI sent Abelino a letter written in English two months after the injury and one month after they calculated his worker's compensation, asking him to review their calculations and let them know if he received housing or any other benefits. Unable to read the letter, Abelino did not respond. Once I saw the letter, I called LNI to request that his wage be recalculated to include his housing. This request was entered into his file and never acted on.

The urgent care doctor requested an orthopedic consult, which reaffirmed the recommendation of light duty work. He also ordered an MRI scan, which showed normal bone structure with abnormal swelling in the soft tissues in front of, below, and internal to the patellar tendon. The MRI report concluded that there was "no instability" in the knee, though it did not specify what precisely this meant. After a few weeks of seeing Abelino without significant improvement, the urgent care doctor ordered the physical therapy discontinued and successfully passed his patient off to a rehabilitation medicine specialist.

The rehabilitation medicine physician initially did not want to take on an LNI patient because of the extra paperwork involved but eventually agreed. This physician restarted Abelino's physical therapy since it seemed to help and told Abelino that he must work hard picking strawberries in order to make his knee better. She did not seem to be aware that his attempt to return to work had caused more pain and swelling. In addition, she seemed to think his last name was his first name and repeatedly addressed him in this way. She asked me to translate that he had been "picking incorrectly and hurt his knee because he did not know how to bend over," though in the midst of her busy schedule she had not asked how he picked or bent over. She wrote in her chart, which was riddled with typos, that "he is a somewhat poor historian, however, secondary to the language," though it could have been equally true to say she was a poor interviewer due to language barriers. Nonetheless, she did not request a translator for Abelino's future appointments. She concluded the appointment, handing him a prescription for strong NSAIDs. Like the previous physicians, she did not ask Abelino if he had contraindicating stomach problems.

After a few months, LNI arranged a meeting for Abelino with administrators from the Tanaka farm and a consultant to determine what kind of work agreement might be reached. Abelino and I went to the farm's front office for the meeting. When Samantha came into the room twenty minutes late, she greeted us warmly. The other farm official was still meeting with the LNI consultant in another room and called to say that they were running late. Samantha replied, "No problem, take your time." I wondered why the consultant was meeting with the farm administrators without Abelino. Samantha turned to Abelino and said in Spanish that it was cold outside. Abelino replied that it was really cold in the labor camps. I explained that the morning frost on the inside of the tin roofs melted every morning as a cold indoor rain on the inhabitant's face and belongings as soon as the sun rose. I also mentioned that most of the families in our camp had to leave their gas stoves on all night to keep the inside from freezing. Samantha said in Spanish, "Yeah, yeah, it's so cold! I live on a *ranchito,* and I have two geese and four cats and two horses and two dogs. And every morning the water for the horses is frozen and I have to go out in my slippers with hot water and give water to the horses and the other animals and when I come back in it's so cold it's hard to use my hands!" I remember feeling surprised and offended that Samantha seemed unaware of the fact that hundreds of people on the farm lived and slept without insulation or heat in the below-freezing temperatures while she complained about her hands getting cold temporarily in the morning. Abelino responded, "Oh, so you have a rancho?" Samantha, "No, no, it's just a couple acres—it's a ranchito." Much like the "contest of suffering" in California's Proposition 187, described by James Quesada,[14] Samantha diminished the ongoing suffering of the Triqui migrants by giving precedence to her own temporary suffering.

Once the LNI consultant and the Tanaka farm administrator arrived, the consultant explained to Abelino, with Samantha translating, that she would help him get light duty work on the farm. Abelino explained that he needed to move to California with his family a month later, when the picking season in Washington ended. He told her that what he really wanted was for the farm to guarantee him a light duty job for the next season the following summer. The consultant explained that if Abelino left the state of Washington, LNI would no longer cover his medical bills related to the work injury and would no longer help him get light duty work. He restated his request for light duty work for the next season; she restated that his file would be closed if he left the state. The farm official sat silent, the meeting ended, and everyone shook hands.

Soon thereafter, the LNI consultant filed a form recommending that Abelino be given the job of "General Laborer" with "light duty work," including a "variety of farm activities during the four seasons in which work varies." The activities specified by the consultant included "hoeing by hand," "trimming raspberry plants," "hand harvest of berries," "machine harvest of berries," and "other general laborer duties as needed." According to this form, "hand harvest of berries" was "light duty work." There was no mention in the report that picking berries involves repeatedly bending at the knees, precisely what had caused and later exacerbated Abelino's knee pain. Though Abelino's care had been transferred to the rehabilitation medicine physician, LNI sent the report to the original urgent care doctor whom Abelino had not seen in months. This urgent care physician signed his agreement to the report.

In the next medical appointment, again without a translator, the rehabilitation medicine doctor injected Abelino's knee in several places with locally active steroids. This significantly reduced the pain and swelling in the knee, though Abelino still experienced significant pain later when the physical therapist had him squat or bend. His pain now averaged a 3 or 4 out of 10 on the pain scale. This improvement prompted the physical therapist to point out the irony that the treatment initially requested by Abelino and refused by the physicians had turned out to be most effective. The physical therapist also told me he was concerned that the rehabilitation medicine physician appeared to disbelieve Abelino's indication of pain and instead looked only at the X-ray and MRI. This physician paid most attention to these radiological tests and the findings of her brief physical examination—which are entered in the medical chart officially under the heading "Objective"—and discounted Abelino's descriptions of his own symptoms—which are supposed to go in the medical chart under "Subjective."[15] The separation of "Subjective" (what the patient observes and experiences) from "Objective" (what the physician observes or tests in the body) in the medical chart becomes a permanent record of the clinical gaze. This physician continued to tell Abelino that he must go back to work in order to get better, despite his indications that bending and squatting still caused intense pain.

The filing of the employment plan by the consultant prompted LNI to attempt to send Abelino back to work. This also involved sending the rehabilitation physician a form for a final evaluation. This physician responded on the form that Abelino could return to full duty work. Justifying her decision, she quoted directly from the MRI report that there was "no instability" in Abelino's knee. This effectively and immediately closed Abelino's LNI claim, his minimal worker's compensation checks, and the coverage of his medical care. Without fully understanding the LNI process and her direct role in terminating Abelino's benefits, this physician explained to me in private that Abelino described an improvement in his knee after the injections, not because he really got better, but rather because "the picking season is over and therefore he can no longer have worker's comp."

After going to Oregon and California for the winter and spring, Abelino returned to the Tanaka farm in summer. He attempted to pick berries for two days, but the intense pain and swelling in his right knee returned. Abelino appealed, with the help of a bilingual physician at the migrant clinic, to reopen his claim. The physician at the migrant clinic indicated that Abelino's knee was now more swollen and his range of motion was decreased since the year before when his claim was closed. LNI set up two independent medical evaluations. These evaluations summarized the previous MRI findings incorrectly in their report to LNI as "entirely normal." The section of the report titled "Socioeconomic History" indicated only "married with eight dependents, has six years of schooling, no military service, no tobacco, alcohol, or medications, including prescribed medications," with no mention of his living or working conditions. They concluded that his knee was "probably not worse" and ordered another MRI, stating that the decision to close the claim should be based on the findings of this MRI. In this way, the biotechnical scan read by a radiologist who would never meet or examine Abelino would trump the physician's as well as the patient's accountings of what happened. The radiologist's MRI report stated that the knee swelling "had not worsened," that Abelino might have degenerative arthritis, and that—though radiologists are not trained or certified in occupational medicine—"the claim can be closed." On the basis of this report, LNI denied Abelino's appeal. The letter sent to Abelino said in English that his claim would remain closed and concluded, "Best wishes with your further health, employment and safety." Years later, Abelino still tells me that he has knee pain and that "doctors don't know anything" (los médicos no saben nada).

After considering in some detail the course of Abelino's interactions with health care institutions, this common statement makes more sense. Several assumptions were made along the way, from the absence of stomach problems to his first return to work being "light duty," from his ability to read English to his being paid as an hourly worker, from his incorrect picking as the cause of his injury to his faking of the pain, from the importance of "Objective" biotechnical tests to the disqualification of his words and experiences. Several of these assumptions were made into fact via their inscription in charts and reports that were later picked up and incorporated by other officials. Some of the actions of the health professionals might be considered bad medical practice (such as giving a contraindicated medication without first asking thoroughly), though all are likely the outcome of an impossibly hectic, understaffed, underfunded, and impersonal health care system.

This ethnographic vignette brings into relief three important aspects of the clinical gaze in the field of migrant health to which I return below. First, as might be expected in Foucault's paradigm of the clinical gaze, physicians in migrant health—as in other biomedical spaces—value their own observations and biotechnical testing of the patient's body over the words of the patient. Abelino's descriptions of his social and employment history receive little attention, though international market asymmetries and local discriminatory practices placed him in the labor position that caused his injury in the first place. Similarly, his descriptions of his bodily experiences are considered suspect. In the end, simplistic interpretations of the radiological studies, inscribed as truth in the medical record, functioned to justify the physician's decision to send Abelino back to picking and LNI's decision to close his file. Second, physicians in migrant health—as in other clinical sites—may inadvertently blame their patients for their suffering. Lacking the time to fully explore the problem and unable to see the transnational and local structures affecting Abelino's body, the rehabilitation medicine specialist indicated that Abelino's pain was the result of his behavior; that is, he was "picking incorrectly." Third, structural violence victimizes not only the poor and the patient but also, though in a different fashion, the professional, the physician. As can be seen in this vignette, the physicians worked in busy, hectic environments with only partial information about the patient and the institutional process. They had to fill out multiple bureaucratic forms, perform an examination and an interview, and formulate and enact a plan within a ten- to fifteen-minute appointment. The pressures of the current neoliberal capitalist system of health care and its financing force health professionals into a double bind. Either they spend the time and energy necessary to listen to and fully treat the patient and put their job and clinic in economic jeopardy, or they move at a frenetic pace to keep their practice afloat and only partially attend to the patient in their presence.

THE FIELD OF MIGRANT HEALTH

Before moving on to the health care experiences of Crescencio and Bernardo, I want to explore the general social and cultural context in which clinicians in the field of migrant health work. On Thanksgiving,

1960, CBS News broadcast a program titled "Harvest of Shame." This show was part of a national movement to raise awareness about the poor living and working conditions of what became known by governmental agencies as "migrant and seasonal farmworkers." At this time, most migrant farmworkers were white people known as "dust bowl migrants" from the Midwest and black people from the East coast.

Largely in response to this movement and the discussions it provoked, Congress passed the Migrant Health Act in 1962, which modified the Public Health Service Act to create the Migrant Health Program, providing grants for medical and social services to migrant farmworkers. Since the act's passage, there has been controversy over the changing ethnic makeup of farmworkers and whether or not to include Latin Americans in the definition of migrant and seasonal farmworkers. However, the terms *farmworker* and *migrant worker* currently connote almost exclusively people of Latin American descent. The Migrant Health Program currently provides grants to over four hundred migrant health clinics in forty-two states. "Migrant health" has become increasingly recognized as a field within health care since the beginning of this program. This field is generally understood today to apply to Mexican and Central American migrant workers. In 1984 the Migrant Clinicians Network was established to link and educate clinicians who work with these populations.[16] The Network currently has over two thousand members nationwide.

In each of the three major sites of my fieldwork, there was one primary medical institution that my Triqui companions visited for health-related issues. In the Skagit Valley of Washington, there is a federally funded migrant health clinic with six physicians, one nurse-practitioner/midwife, two dentists, two health educators, six nurses, and several administrative staff members. The physicians were an idealistic white woman who graduated from a top medical school; a white woman who grew up in South America, the daughter of Christian medical missionaries and a graduate of another top medical school; a white male mountaineer who enjoyed living close to the North Cascade Mountains; a woman of Central American descent who grew up in the region; and a retired white monolingual English-speaking man working on a locums (daily) basis. The nurses were primarily Latina women from the area as well as a black woman who moved to the area to be close to her family. The migrant clinic charges are based on a sliding scale, with most undocumented Mexican farmworkers earning well under the lowest threshold, thus having a $15 copay for each visit. In the past, the clinic was open two nights a week after 5:00 P.M. Recently, the clinic schedule was changed from being open two nights a week until 7:00 P.M. to now being open one night a week until 9:00 P.M. This schedule change, as well as the mission of the clinic to treat all the local poor instead of solely migrant farmworkers, has led to a correlated decrease in the percentage of patients involved in farmwork. On any given day, one is just as likely to see poor white area residents as poor Mexican migrant workers in the clinic's waiting room.

In the Central Valley of California, there is one primary federally funded migrant health clinic that my Triqui companions visited. This clinic had four physicians, eight nurses, one dentist, and several administrative staff members. Most of the clinic staff were Latinos who grew up in the Central Valley. One physician was from South America and was required to work at a federally qualified community health center until his immigration documents were finalized. The clinic charges are based on a sliding scale, with the lowest copay set at $30. The patients of this clinic are a mixture of Latino U.S-citizen area residents and Mexican and Central American migrant workers. Because the copay was twice as high, my Triqui companions went to the clinic in California less often than the one in Washington.

As noted previously, in San Miguel there was one federal Centro de Salud staffed alternately by the visiting medical resident and the visiting nurse, often with no staff for a day or two in between. Both the resident and the nurse were from Oaxaca City and spoke only Spanish. Several Triqui families from the border areas of their towns have moved to larger, primarily mestizo cities in the state of Oaxaca due to the border violence related to land claims. In each of these cities, there is one federal clinic as well as several private physicians with their own practices. The other two major Triqui towns had been downgraded by the federal government from being county seats and, therefore, had lost the funding for their clinics. My Triqui friends explained that there had been too much political organizing in the other Triqui towns, and the Oaxacan state government had responded by demoting those towns such that they now fell under the political jurisdiction of nearby primarily mestizo county seats. In addition to clinics, my Triqui companions sought help from traditional Triqui healers. As seen in the health care experiences of Abelino described above, traditional healing practices are performed not only in Oaxaca but also among Triqui migrant farmworkers in the United States.[17] Notably, the monolingual Triqui-speaking elderly father of the town síndico is a traditional healer in San Miguel. In addition, Crescencio is an apprentice healer who is not yet widely recognized.

STRUCTURAL FACTORS AFFECTING MIGRANT HEALTH CLINICIANS

Biomedical professionals in the field of migrant health work under demanding and difficult circumstances. Most clinics serving migrant farmworkers are nonprofits with unreliable and changing sources of funding, and many lack certain expensive medicines and medical instruments. Physicians and nurses in these clinics perform many extra duties, from requesting free medicines for their patients to filling out paperwork for discounted perinatal care for expectant mothers. These clinicians often feel hopeless as they witness the systematic deterioration of young, healthy people who come to the United States to work on farms. Dr. Samuelson, the physician and mountaineer in the migrant clinic in the Skagit Valley, spoke about the frustration of seeing his patients' bodies deteriorate over time.

> I see an awful lot of people just wearing out. They have been used and abused and worked physically harder than anybody should be expected to work for that number of years. Then they come out with this nagging back pain. You work it up, and it's not getting better, and you don't think there is any malingering going on. It gets to the point where you just have to give them an MRI scan, and their back is toast. In their early forties they have the arthritis of a seventy-year-old, and they're not

> getting better . . . . They're told, "Sorry, go back to doing what you're doing," and they're stuck. They're screwed, in a word, and it's tragic.

Several clinicians also pointed out the difficulties caused by racism in the clinic waiting room. Physicians and nurses spoke of white patients telling them such things as, "I can't come at that time because I don't want to be in the waiting room with those people," meaning Mexican migrant workers. Some white patients complained about the smell of the farmworkers after picking, and some complained that the farmworkers always brought their children with them.

Only approximately 5 percent of undocumented migrants nationwide have health insurance, and most do not qualify for Medicaid or Medicare due to their immigration status.[18] This means not only that many clinics are reimbursed for few of the services they provide but also that there are many obstacles to providing high-quality care. The low level of reimbursements means that such clinics must repeatedly apply for grants from various public and private sources in order to stay afloat. Given the uneven levels of funding, clinic administrators must cut important programs from time to time when funding is low or when the priorities of funders change. To compensate for the shortfalls, the physicians and nurses spend a lot of time and energy trying to obtain samples or donations of medicines needed by their patients. Dr. Goldenson, the South American physician in the migrant clinic in California, told me about a patient of his who got valley fever (coccidiomycosis) from working the fields of the Central Valley. This potentially fatal lung infection is caused by breathing in soil and is therefore a significant concern among farmworkers. Dr. Goldenson had two migrant farmworker patients with valley fever over the previous three years. Both will require suppression therapy with an expensive antifungal antibiotic for the rest of their lives. Dr. Goldenson described one patient's progress.

> He's not doing as well. . . . But at least he's surviving. Basically, he's going to need $1,000 a month of Diflucan for life. Of course this guy cannot afford even $100 a month. So far, we were able to get MediCal to cover it, although every month I have to go through reapprovals. . . . Quite often I have spent more time trying to get samples. I'm calling

friends or looking for special programs. It's a lot of work, but you feel good about it, because these are people who really appreciate that.

The need to make enough money to survive and the lack of flexibility in farmwork schedules make it difficult for migrant farmworkers to take time off to go to the clinic during the day. This encourages the workers to wait until they are very sick before going to the clinic and forces them to miss appointments on days when picking goes later than expected. Clinicians told me on several occasions how difficult it was to treat migrant workers effectively given that they do not make use of preventive services and often miss appointments. Continuity of care is also very difficult to ensure because most migrant workers move to different towns every few months. This means that a new source of discounted or free medicines must be found by the clinicians in each new town. Dr. McCaffree, a thirty-something female physician in the Skagit migrant clinic who grew up in a missionary family in South America, told me, "Most [migrants] don't have any insurance, so that's even harder, 'cause you start them on a medication and you know they're just going to be off it again wherever they go next." The migratory nature of farmworkers' lives also means that their medical records are extremely patchy. Each clinic has at least one medical record for each patient that covers only the seasons during which she or he lived in that area. Many clinics have more than one record for each patient due to confusion over whether the record should be alphabetized by maternal last name, paternal last name, or spouse's last name as well as direct mistranscription of names in Spanish. In addition, some undocumented patients give nicknames or false names for fear of their information being turned over to the Border Patrol.

Language differences complicate the field of migrant health on several levels. Most clinicians are bilingual in English and Spanish; however, some, like the locums doctor in the Skagit Valley, need a translator when they see Spanish-speaking patients. Often clinicians with poor Spanish-language skills do not have time to get a translator and instead conduct the appointment in English, which the patient cannot understand, or with an untrained interpreter—for example, the child I observed translate during her mother's gynecological exam. One Triqui patient I know gave premature birth to a baby girl. The nurses wrote, "Patient refuses breast pump," though they did not have a translator with them when they had the interaction that brought them to this conclusion. The hospital social worker who pointed this out to me said, "I can only imagine what she thought they were saying as they gestured toward her breasts with the electric machine." The nurse-practitioner/midwife in the Skagit Valley told me about the ways in which language differences and lack of time and personnel lead to poor care: "There are a lot of staff who don't want to be bothered getting a trained interpreter. People grab me and say, 'Oh, could you be an interpreter?' This person has a right to get a real interpreter and not a five-minute discussion with me when I am running from patient to patient. It's just reluctance. It's just that one more step. It's racism. It's being overworked because our system is a total train wreck right now." "Are you sure you want to be a doctor?" she asked.

Very few migrant clinics offer services in languages other than Spanish or English. The hospital in the Skagit Valley, where my Triqui friends went when they needed inpatient services, offers Mixtec translation through a local nonprofit language service. However, a Mixtec translator is often called when hospital staff find out a patient is from Oaxaca, even if the patient speaks only Triqui. In addition, several clinicians indicated that it is especially hard to communicate with Oaxacan women. Fewer Triqui women have attended school in San Miguel than Triqui men, and as a result some do not speak Spanish. In addition, clinicians complain that Oaxacan women speak quietly and do not look them in the eyes.

Sometimes, assumptions about language and lack of interpretation have even more dire consequences. One Triqui man, Adolfo Ruiz-Alvarez, was held in an Oregon state mental hospital and medicated for over two years after being interviewed only in Spanish and then charged with trespassing and public indecency.[19] According to my Triqui companions, because Mr. Ruiz-Alvarez could not communicate in Spanish, which it was assumed was his native language, he was thought to be crazy. When I heard about this case, I remembered that several times while homeless in California during my fieldwork I could have been charged with public indecency for relieving myself in a public park after the toilets were locked at sundown. My Triqui companions also described the case of a Mixtec man, Santiago Ventura Morales, who was charged with murder without Mixtec translation. Mr. Ventura Morales was held in an Oregon state prison for four years before a nonprofit agency advocating for indigenous Mexicans provided interpretive services that led to his case being overturned.[20]

Clinicians in the field of migrant health work in difficult environments that require extra time and work procuring medicines, dealing with the racism of their patients, and working in several languages, all the while lacking reliable resources. Despite feeling overworked, powerless, and sometimes hopeless, they also feel a commitment to work with this population. Many described Latin American migrant farmworkers as deserving high-quality care, and most described feeling a calling, a vocation, to provide quality health care to this population. As Dr. Goldenson put it, "It's a very difficult problem. We have a bad insurance crisis and health care crisis. I mean, citizens cannot really afford health care. And the migrant workers, I truly believe they should have at least the same access as the others. I mean, this work that they are doing is something that nobody else is willing to do. That's the truth. That's probably the only reason why we are able to go to the supermarket and buy fruit for a fair price. So this is a group of people that really deserves our attention."

CRESCENCIO'S HEADACHE: STRUCTURE AND GAZE IN MIGRANT HEALTH CARE

The last chapter left Crescencio describing his headaches to me after the health fair in our labor camp. He said he developed these excruciating headaches after being called racist names and treated unfairly on the job and explained that he wanted treatment before he might become agitated or violent with his family. He explained that he had seen several physicians in the United States and Mexico as well as a traditional Triqui healer, but none of their therapies had been effective over the long term. He asked me if I had any medicines I could give him. Not knowing what else to do, I suggested Crescencio go to the local migrant clinic to see if they could try something new for his problem. I remembered the algorithm for headache diagnosis and treatment that I had learned in medical school and wondered if the doctors in the migrant clinic might use something similar, moving through trials of medications for tension, cluster, and migraine headaches. A week later, Crescencio told me that he had seen one of the doctors in the clinic but that she didn't give him any medicines. He said that she had referred him for therapy and asked me what that meant. I described paying someone to sit with you, ask you questions, and listen to your answers in order to help you work through your feelings and thoughts and help you decrease your unhealthy use of substances. At the same time, I knew he barely had money to go to the clinic the first time, and it was unlikely he would spend $15 a session for psychotherapy or substance abuse therapy (though that would seem a bargain to others).

After several weeks of trying to make an appointment with the doctor who saw him at the migrant clinic, I was able to ask her about Crescencio's headache. She thought for a minute and then looked at Crescencio's chart to refresh her memory. She told me that she met with him once briefly over a month ago. She had asked him to cut back on his drinking and then return to see her for further evaluation. However, he ended up returning at a different time and seeing a different doctor, the locums physician who spoke only English. After looking at her chart note and the notes from the locums physician, she told me about Crescencio's situation from her perspective.

> Well, yes, he thinks that he is the victim and thinks that the alcohol or the headache makes him beat his wife . . . but really he is the perpetrator and everyone else is the victim. And until he owns his problem, he can't really change.
>
> I'm on the CPS [Child Protective Services] subcommittee, and so I've learned a lot about domestic violence. What we've seen is that nothing really works, none of these migraine medicines or anything, but to put people in jail because then they see a show of force. That's the only thing

> that works because then they have to own the problem as theirs and they start to change. It's a complex psychosocial problem, a patterned behavior. Probably his dad treated him this way, beat him, and was alcoholic, and now that's what he does. It's a classic case of domestic abuse.
>
> He came to see me once, and I told him to come back two weeks later after not drinking. But he didn't come back two weeks later. Instead, he came back a month later and saw one of our locums. Apparently, he told the doc something about when people at work tell him what to do, it makes him mad, and that's what gives him a headache.
>
> Obviously he has issues. He needs to learn how to deal with authority. We referred him to therapy. Do you know if he's going to therapy?

As in Abelino's health care experiences, this doctor was pressed for time and made assumptions without fully exploring the patient's psychosocial realities. In Crescencio's case, the physician made the assumption that his description of feeling agitated and angry indicated that he had already beaten his wife and continued to beat her. Without enough time to pay full attention to the patient's concerns and focus on the headache and its source, she focused primarily on assumed intimate partner violence. While paying attention to the possibility of such violence is of utmost importance, this focus may have led to a short-circuiting of the treatment possibilities for Crescencio. Without being able to explore all the possible therapies for severe headeaches, the physician retrospectively advocated incarcerating people like Crescencio.

After reading in the chart that Crescencio's headaches were due to mistreatment from supervisors on the farm, the physicians recommended therapy to help him overcome his "issues" with authority and treat his substance use. Without the lenses to see that Crescencio's suffering was determined by multiple levels of social inequality and disrespect, they inadvertently blamed the headache on the patient's psychological makeup. In the end, their primary interventions were twofold. First, they told him to stop drinking cold turkey, even though drinking was the only effective intervention he had found after years of active searching. Unfortunately, though perhaps expectedly, he was not able to stop drinking. Second, the physicians referred him to therapy, without the patient understanding what this meant. Therapy performed in order to help a patient accept poor treatment from supervisors may be helpful to the patient in developing coping mechanisms in the midst of a difficult situation. Substance abuse therapy may help a patient reduce the harm of substance use and develop healthier behaviors. At the same time, therapy may also promote the patient's acceptance of his place in a labor hierarchy that may include the disrespect and racist insults that Crescencio experienced. In this way, the migrant clinic's interventions were not only ineffective but also inadvertently complicit with the social determinants of suffering, serving to reinforce the social structures producing Crescencio's labor position and headache in the first place.

Crescencio's headache is a result most distally of the international economic inequalities forcing him to migrate and become a farmworker in the first place and more proximally of the racialized mistreatment he endures in the farm's ethnicity and citizenship hierarchy. These socially produced headaches lead Crescencio to become agitated and angry with his family and to drink, thus embodying the stereotype of Mexican migrants as alcoholic and potentially violent. The racialized mistreatment that produces his headaches is then justified through the embodied stereotypes that were produced in part by that mistreatment in the first place. Finally, due to powerful economic structures affecting the migrant clinic as well as limited lenses of perception in biomedicine, this justifying symbolic violence is subtly reinforced throughout Crescencio's health care experiences.

THE GAZE OF MIGRANT HEALTH CLINICIANS: WASHINGTON AND CALIFORNIA

The importance of perception in social interactions cannot be overstated. Social scientists have shown the significance of social perception in such diverse contexts as the effects of representations of "the poor" in international development,[21] the results of symbolic linkages between gender hierarchies and human cells in medical science,[22] and the consequences of class-related meanings of smell.[23] The French sociologist Pierre

Bourdieu states that "being is being perceived."[24] In other words, human beings are defined through perception by others. This perception or identification[25] determines the actions of other people toward an individual. These actions, in turn, shape the actions of this individual herself insofar as she acts in response to others and insofar as her potential actions were produced or constrained by the actions of others. In addition, these perceptions and actions affect the material conditions in which this individual lives insofar as those conditions are continually produced by social actions on larger political-economic and smaller intimate scales.

The experiences of suffering and sickness of Triqui migrant farmworkers are shaped significantly by responses from medical professionals in the field of migrant health. Understanding these medical responses to Triqui suffering requires an analysis of the lenses through which these health professionals perceive the suffering of their Triqui patients. As the ethnographic data indicate, these perceptions range from positive to neutral, negative to outright racist.

Several medical professionals working in migrant clinics said that migrant farmworkers are a group deserving assistance and are enjoyable to work with. The medical director of the migrant clinic in the Skagit Valley told me that the migrant workers who cross into the United States are "the stars" of Mexico. The midwife in the same clinic told me that they are "the best and the bravest" of Mexico because they have successfully crossed the border and found work in the United States. Dr. McCaffree told me she was continually "amazed by how they keep going" and how they "seem happy and content despite their difficult lots in life." Several clinicians told me that Mexican farmworkers complain less than white patients about their sicknesses and use fewer public resources such as clinic services, welfare, and worker's compensation. Multiple times, physicians and nurses told me that the migrant farmworkers were more respectful and their children better behaved than the white patients in their clinic and that the indigenous Oaxacan people were especially respectful.

However, clinicians also had complaints about their farmworker patients. One of the nurses in the Skagit Valley told me, "They don't really take care of themselves," explaining that they needed to be educated about how "to take care of their bodies." Dr. Goldenson complained to me that Mexican migrants "don't think they need medicines." As an example, he said they often misunderstand the results of untreated diabetes and come to the conclusion that diabetes treatments, like insulin, cause the disease's sequelae, like blindness and nerve problems. Several physicians also complained about the practices of Mexican patients in relation to traditional healers and so-called culture-bound syndromes such as *susto*.[26] Some clinicians blamed the poor health outcomes of their patients on these beliefs and practices. Johanna, the midwife at the Skagit migrant clinic, told me that she had invented a cure for *sustos* that she considered a great success. The cure involved chamomile tea and rest from household chores. She went on to explain other difficulties she encountered while working with Mexican migrant farmworkers.

> One of the most interesting aspects of working with a Spanish-speaking patient is just this real disinclination to want to be specific and quantify. It's just enormous. I don't know if you've tried to get a history out of somebody, but if you ask somebody, "How long has this been bothering you?" or "Where does it hurt?" or "What can you tell me about your problem?" what you are going to get is one big basket full of vague stuff. Let's say you are having a stomachache and, for example, I ask you what is going on and you say, "Well, it started on Monday, and it feels like this, and I have these associated symptoms." You and I would be on the same wavelength, and that would be very helpful to me. I would be so grateful that you could exactly explain what is going on. In Mexican people, almost to the person, no matter how long you have known them, you are going to get something that is very vague, like, "A while ago, it kind of hurts here, it feels like vaguely aching," typically minimizing the symptoms. It's just really hard to get a good history and there are a lot of ideas that I have.

Johanna said she thinks this problem relates to a lack of good health care in Mexico and a religious shame about sickness being related to personal sin or moral failing. At the same time, this communication problem could very well relate more to misunderstandings across class differences than across nationalities or ethnicities. As a crude example, the Mexican physicians and nurses I know would respond to these questions in much the same ways I would because of their education and professional background, unrelated to the language they speak or their nationality.

Most clinicians indicated that the primary health problems of migrant farmworkers included diabetes, body pain from work, work-related injuries, and dental problems. The medical director of the migrant clinic in Washington stated that in response to her question, "Are you okay?" many of her migrant patients often reply, "Well, it all hurts, but that's just the way it is." A retired dentist told me that Mexican people wait a long time to go into the dental clinic so that the problems are often so serious that he has to extract their teeth. He explained also that working with Mexican patients was difficult due to what he perceived as ethnic bodily differences: "It's genetics. Their bone structure's just different; it's like you're trying to pull the tooth out of granite. You pray it'll lift. Your right arm gets about three times the size of your left. You'll see that in a lot of Mexican people, you know, big jaws or real heavy bone structure. Northern Europeans have much lighter features." On the other hand, the physicians in the migrant clinics told me that the dental problems of migrant workers were the result of being given juice too often in their baby bottles.

Johanna, the midwife, told me that she sees a lot of domestic violence perpetrated by the men against their wives. Her theory was that much of this violence comes from men's deep disappointment about unmet expectations in the United States. Some of the nurses in the same clinic, however, told me that there is very little domestic violence among migrant farmworkers. Dr. McCaffree added that she sees a high rate of unwed pregnancy and a high rate of depression. The depression, she told me, is masked as alcoholism in the men and as vague aches and pains in the women. All the other clinicians told me that the migrant workers had lower rates of substance abuse than their U.S. citizen patients. At the same time, Dr. McCaffree's nurse explained that she sees a lower incidence of depression among the migrant patients than the white patients. In addition, there is often a misunderstanding about marriage between health professionals and their Triqui patients. The vast majority of Triqui people engage in traditional marriage practices, which involve the male paying a bridewealth of approximately $1,500 in San Miguel or $2,500 in the United States to the family of his fiancée. Most couples do not have an officially recognized church or state wedding. The legal status of this partnering, then, is complicated because the couples do not fill out government marriage forms. Yet for the Triqui people, these are recognized as marriages. Thus many of the "unwed pregnancies" cited by Dr. McCaffree are likely not as simply categorized.[27]

In addition to the common invalidation of Triqui marriage by health professionals, another intercultural and legal problem surrounding Triqui marriage relates to the ages of the couple. Triqui males routinely marry between the ages of sixteen and twenty, and their female partners are often between the ages of fourteen and eighteen. According to Triqui people and migrant health clinicians in Washington and California, the following is a common occurrence. A Triqui couple goes to the hospital for the wife to give birth to her first child. During the patient interview, the nurses or social workers use simple definitions to determine that the couple is not legally married and then go on to discover that the woman is under seventeen and the man is seventeen or older. The hospital staff then make contact with law enforcement agencies, which is required by law in some states. The woman is placed in the custody of a relative or the court, and the man is convicted of the felony of statutory rape. He is then put in prison (for up to ten years in some states).[28] In 2009 the mainstream English-language media in the United States misrepresented traditional Triqui bridewealth practices in Greenfield, California. Despite the nuanced and contextual statements released by the local chief of police, the mainstream media ran the following ethnocentric story title, "Man Sells Daughter for Money, Beer, and Meat."[29] In fact, it appears that the money, alcohol, and meat was the agreed-upon bridewealth that would allow the wife's family to throw a traditional wedding party. Despite the similarities to mainstream white Protestant marriage traditions that include an expensive wedding party (involving money, beer, and meat), this sensationalist story and the related legal battle were covered nationwide by such news outlets as CNN and the *Los Angeles Times.* Despite this kind of potential misunderstanding, the nursing staff chose not to report the Triqui couples I observed through their first child's birth, though they had undergone a traditional marriage and the ages were as described above. After coming to know the Triqui couples giving birth, the nursing staff considered the story described above a cruel misunderstanding.

The medical director of the clinic in the Skagit Valley told me that a large percentage of worker's compensation claims by white or Mexican people are just "trying to work the system." She went on to explain that many migrants in Texas and California move to Washington because they have heard or experienced that the public health plan is good. On a similar note, several of the welfare agents in Madera, California—including the one who owned the slum apartment in which we lived—told me that there are signs all over Oaxaca telling people to go to Madera because they can get welfare there. Over the course of my fieldwork, however, I never heard a single migrant mention welfare or health plans as a reason for their migration. In all my travels through Oaxaca, I never once saw a sign advertising welfare in the United States, much less specifically in Madera, California. In fact, the vast majority of my Triqui companions did not qualify for health and welfare programs in most states because they moved too frequently or were undocumented. Some Triqui families applied for and received basic short-term perinatal nutritional support, though this support proved minimal and the process time-consuming.

One of the physicians in the Skagit clinic told me that Mexican people in the United States misuse the health care system by trying to get multiple opinions on their sicknesses and the appropriate treatments. Dr. Samuelson, the physician at the same clinic who sees the most work-related injury cases, contradicted this in certain ways. He performs many of the independent medical exams of Spanish speakers for worker's compensation in the area. He explained that the language barrier often causes problems with testing the reliability of the patient. In addition, he explained that migrant patients have a different mind-set about pain, and "this is not allowed in the [worker's compensation] industry." He explained that when migrant patients pull away during certain aspects of worker's compensation tests, "it is interpreted as faking pain, while in reality it is fear of pain." "So," he continued, "I will go through the same exam and get completely different results. But the suspicions of malingering have already been raised." For the few undocumented migrants who file worker's compensation claims due to work injuries, this suspicion leads to problems in their permanent files. Thus, Dr. Samuelson explained, it is often necessary for migrant patients to see numerous physicians in order to find one who might treat them with sensitivity.

The health professionals with whom I interacted often noticed other differences between the Oaxacans and the mestizo Mexican migrant farmworkers. Several physicians and nurses pointed out that their Oaxacan patients are poorer than their other patients. Dr. McCaffree told me, "They seem a lot poorer, and so they don't have access [to heatlh care]. . . . Their clothes are a little bit dirtier. They tend to be a lot thinner and not much obesity and clothes that don't get changed a lot." On many occasions, clinicians told me that the health status of Oaxacans is worse than that of other groups. One told me, "They're just sicker and have more body pains." This reflects the health disparities literature discussed earlier in the book.

Clinicians in the field of migrant health in Washington and California hold a variety of beliefs about their Mexican migrant patients. They consider them respectful, tough, and deserving of quality health care. At the same time, many clinicians see the migrant workers as frustrating to work with due to their traditional health practices and vague medical histories. Some clinicians make ethnocentric assumptions about their patients, such as regarding the reality of their marriages. Different clinicians hold contradictory views regarding the prevalence of substance abuse, depression, and the use of worker's compensation services in this population. However, these health professionals seem to agree in blaming certain health conditions, such as dental problems, on their patients' bodily makeup and cultural behavior.

BERNARDO'S STOMACHACHE: STRUCTURE AND GAZE IN MIGRANT HEALTH CARE

Bernardo was experiencing a chronic, constant stomachache that made it painful for him to eat, thus causing him to feel weak and slowly lose weight. Every year before he left Oaxaca to work in a fish processing plant in Alaska, he went through several weeks of injections that he explained made him stronger and gave him an appetite. When he arrived home from Alaska weaker and thinner, he underwent this same series of injections again. He attributed the pain to a lifetime of strenuous migrant work as well as to being beaten by the (U.S.-funded) Mexican military as a suspected member of an indigenous rights movement.

During one season in which he picked berries on the Tanaka farm, Bernardo went to the local hospital to be seen for his stomach pain. He requested medicines to decrease his pain and increase his appetite. Although Bernardo is an elderly Triqui person and speaks very little Spanish, he was seen by an English-speaking physician while his daughter-in-law translated. His daughter-in-law is a Mixtec woman who speaks no Triqui and little English. She did her best translating from Spanish to English. In the chart, the physician defined Bernardo as a "Hispanic" male "who speaks only in Spanish, apparently broken Spanish at that, which is difficult for the Spanish interpreter to understands *[sic]*." Later, the physician indicated his impression: "I must say the history was obtained through an interpreter, and my impression is that the patient tended to perseverate on unrelated things from the questions that were asked, but these were usually not translated to me." With this misunderstood multilayered linguistic barrier, the physician concluded that "he apparently has no past medical history. No medical history." The extent of the social history is summed up in two sentences: "He lives locally. Works as a common laborer." After misunderstanding the translation of Bernardo being beaten, the physician charted simply that Bernardo "is an old boxer and wonders if possibly the blunt trauma to his abdomen could contribute to his present condition."

Due to the temporal and linguistic limitations of the medical interview, the physician was unclear about the location and quality of the pain. Bernardo was admitted to the hospital overnight for "chest pain" in order to rule out a heart attack. He was given an exercise test, after which the technician noted that "he has superb exercise capacity" and "this is a low risk heart scan." Bernardo repeatedly explained that he needed medicines to decrease his pain and increase his hunger. He also explained that he needed to be at work on the farm by 3:30 in the afternoon. After undergoing the exercise test, Bernardo refused to give a third sample of blood and undergo ultrasound evaluation because he had to get back to work.

Bernardo was required to sign an "Against Medical Advice" form before leaving the hospital and was later sent a bill for over $3,000.

Bernardo's hospital experience exemplifies many of the problems caused by lack of time and lack of skilled interpreters, both due in large part to a health care financing system built on maximizing profit instead of patient care. As a result of these structural limitations, the physician assumed Bernardo was a "Hispanic" Spanish speaker, recorded a very limited social history that ignored his migratory status, and determined that ruling out a heart attack was the only important plan. Bernardo's repeated requests for treatments for stomach pain and for lack of appetite were not acted on. Most poignant and horrifying was the bad faith translation of military torture into Bernardo's categorization in the permanent record as "an old boxer."

During my most recent visit to Oaxaca, I stayed again with Bernardo in Juxtlahuaca and visited the private physician who gives him the injections that Bernardo indicated were the only remedy that helped his pain and weight loss. I interviewed the physician at night while his clinic was closed temporarily due to an electricity blackout. He told me that Bernardo had a peptic acid problem such as gastritis or an ulcer. He suggested that this gastrointestinal problem was due to eating "too much hot chili, too much fat, and many condiments." He continued, "[Indigenous people] also don't eat at the right time but wait a long time in between meals." The physician gives Bernardo a pill to decrease his peptic acid levels. He explained that there were better pills for this, but they were too expensive for Bernardo. He recommended that Bernardo drink milk and eat yogurt to help protect his stomach lining. The doctor also gives injections of vitamin B-12 in order to treat what he considers neuropathy (nerve pain). He explained that this neuropathy was due to the fact that indigenous people "bend over too much at work and bend too much in their sleep."

Like many of the U.S. clinicians, this physician was not able to see Bernardo's social and occupational context and instead blamed his suffering on his assumed behaviors and culture. Either the physician was not able to perform a sufficiently extensive intake interview to know about Bernardo's experience of torture or he did not connect this history to the chronic pain. Rather, the practice of biomedicine depoliticizes sickness, functioning in part to erase the structural determinants of suffering such as the political history of military torture and the economic inequalities leading to a lifetime of migrant hard labor.

THE GAZE OF MIGRANT HEALTH CLINICIANS: SAN MIGUEL, OAXACA

While Bernardo received medical care in a mestizo town due to being displaced by ongoing "land wars," most Triqui people in the state of Oaxaca receive health care through the federally funded Centro de Salud in their home village. Over the course of my fieldwork, I lived in the Triqui village of San Miguel full-time for five months and returned for several shorter visits. During this time, I observed and interviewed the doctors and nurses in the Centro in the middle of town. The Centro consists of a small entryway that doubles as a waiting room and has six chairs, a small examination room, a small room for sick patients to stay overnight on one of two beds (though I never saw this room used), a small bathroom for clinic staff with a flush toilet and a shower, a small kitchen for clinic staff with a gas stove, and a small bedroom for clinic staff. The bathroom receives water from a large black barrel on the roof. The barrel is supplied with water by the mothers in town who are poor enough to be part of the federal Oportunidades program, formerly known as Progresa.[30] This program provides regular, small amounts of money, disbursed through the Centro, for food and school clothing for children. Centro staff require that the women who are enrolled in this program bring a bucket of water in exchange for their disbursements, though this was not a requirement of the federal program. According to the sign on the door, the Centro was open officially seven days a week for drop-in care from 8:00 A.M. to 2:00 P.M. and from 4:00 P.M. to 6:00 P.M., as well as twenty-four hours a day, seven days a week, for emergency care. However, at least half the times I went to the clinic, almost always during drop-in hours, the clinic doors were locked and no one answered to my knocks.

In the waiting area of the Centro hang three large posters for everyone to see. One is a map of the small town with each family's house hand-

Market day in the center of San Miguel, where the Centro de Salud is located. Photo by Seth M. Holmes.

drawn and marked for the presence of such sicknesses as tuberculosis, diabetes, miscarriage, and malnutrition. One poster is titled, "10 Rights of Patients,"[31] among them, "Receive dignified and respectful attention; Decide freely about your medical attention; Decide whether or not to give your consent for risky procedures; Be treated with confidentiality; Receive medical attention in the case of urgency." Of note, the first poster's public announcement of sicknesses directly counteracts the claim of the second poster to the right to "confidentiality." The last poster is titled, "Ten Commandments of the Good Patient,"[32] and includes such things as "Have confidence in your doctor and take the treatments they prescribe; Know that the Health Center is yours and you should take care of it; Ask the doctor how to make it so you do not have more children; Be respectful with the doctors and nurses; Keep yourself and your house clean." The ethnographic vignettes below demonstrate how these contradictory views of the physician-patient relationship—from the surveillance biopower of the first poster to the individualized patient rights of the second to the patron-client sick role of the third—compete with each other in everyday clinical interactions in San Miguel.

The doctors and nurses I met at the Centro perceived Triqui people in several different ways. For example, the Centro had recently prepared a summary report on the health of the town of San Miguel. The nurse who prepared it listed "lack of family planning by the families" and "not accepting the taking of cervical cytology [Pap smears]" as the two most important health problems. I asked the nurse to explain these problems further, and she explained simply, "They don't give in to it [Pap smears] easily." The report listed "culture and customs" as the reasons for these two problems. It listed 33.6 percent illiteracy as a less important problem and charged that this was "due to the fact that fathers of families prefer that their children dedicate themselves to the fields than to finishing their primary education. . . . Sometimes the father of the family takes the children to the states of Culiacán, Sinaloa, Hermosillo, Ensenada, U.S.A. *[sic]*." A third problem listed in the report was "housing," with the explanation that "promiscuity exists in this population because in some houses, three families live together." The nurse wrote that this crowded housing was due to "customs of the population." For the problem of "pollution," the nurse blamed "burning garbage" and "not always using latrines." In all these examples, Triqui behavior and culture were blamed for health problems and social structures were ignored. In what sense is refusing a Pap smear a more important health problem than the high rates of childhood death due to poverty-related malnutrition and diarrhea? In what sense is it valid to state that parents prefer that their children work instead of making it clear that parents are practically forced to have their children work in order for the children to survive in the midst of international and domestic economic inequalities? As I read the section on overcrowded housing, I wondered again why the nurse listed "customs" instead of poverty, neoliberal corporate capitalism, or social and economic inequalities as the underlying cause.

Every week as I observed interactions in the Centro, the nurse or doctor present told at least one Triqui mother that her child was malnourished. They routinely said things like, "If you feed them more tacos and less

Sabritas [brand chips], we wouldn't have this problem," though I never heard them check to see if the family bought chips at all or had money to buy Sabritas. On one such occasion, the nurse castigated a Triqui mother, "Oh, woman, woman! What are we going to do?! Your girl is one year and seven months old and weighs what a girl of six months should weigh! Woman!" In the midst of these interactions, the nurses and physicians use *tú,* the informal version of "you," while the patients respond with *usted,* the formal version. The Centro is required by government policy to weigh and measure all children categorized as malnourished each month until they are considered well nourished. However, the nutrition categories are based on averages as norms, and the malnutrition index is based only on weight and height. This index was developed in Mexico City in a primarily middle-class, mestizo population with a different diet and a higher average body mass and height. In front of several Triqui people in the waiting room of the Centro, one of the nurses explained to me that this index did not work well with indigenous people, though it was still required by the health department. Here a medical index developed among one ethnic group and class is applied normatively to another group in such a way that the patients are defined as abnormal, monitored, and, at times, shamed for their assumed behaviors. This practice is an example of structural medical racism and classism at work.

After the nurse explained to me in Spanish the problems with the nutrition index, she went on to tell me in front of the people in the waiting room, "I don't like it here, and I want to leave." She said that she would stay if the Triqui people paid more attention to her and thanked her. During this conversation, she saw the patients in the waiting room without taking them into the examination room for privacy. One of them had flu-like symptoms—aches and pains and a significant fever. The nurse explained to me that the Centro was not stocked with very many kinds of medicines, and she had to give this patient a pain pill "because that's all I have." After she saw these patients, she told those waiting outside that she was closing because she had papers to fill out. Much like the other doctors and nurses I observed, she closed and locked the front doors, pulled the blinds, and turned on music, despite the fact that the schedule on the front door indicated that the clinic was open for drop-in visits for the next two hours. She did not respond the few times I heard knocking at the door of the clinic.

She took me into the kitchen in the back of the building and made us a tripe mole lunch. She continued to describe her experiences living in the village.

> I talked with a friend of mine who is a psychologist, and she told me to find something I like here and to focus on it. I've looked a lot and haven't found anything I like. I don't like the land, or the climate; the people even worse! The people here are lazy, dirty, ignorant, mean gossipers. I used to work in another town where the people were clean. Yes, there was running water there, but still the people were clean and combed their hair! Here, the women just pee wherever they want to. No wonder they have respiratory illnesses here if they pee everywhere and then the wind blows dust around. I told a woman to comb her daughter's hair so that she would look pretty, and the woman said, "No, that is not good; we are Triqui."
>
> The people here are traitors, don't trust them, Set'. They might kill you because you say hello to someone and don't remember to say hello to someone else. I used to work in a town where the climate and the people were warm. Now I am with cold people. Why would I want a friendship with an indigenous person? I don't need anything from them.
>
> I used to think the indigenous people were so poor and fucked and poor. Now, I know they are just lazy and dirty. I used to want to give my life to help them even if they didn't pay me and even if they didn't thank me. Now I won't give my time or even a peso for a *pueblo* [indigenous town]. Not even one peso! That is bad, huh? But I won't give a minute or a peso for an indigenous person. They don't deserve me, and they don't deserve my friendship.
>
> Do you know why Mexico has a very big debt and doesn't build roads or anything? It all goes to the pueblos so they can have medicines. It all goes to the pueblos.
>
> And furthermore, they don't know how to cook! Sometimes, when I give seminars about nutrition, I ask them to bring pumpkin or squash and meat, and I try to teach them to make tamales, but they don't want them, and they don't bring the food to cook with. I tell them to make more rellenos or *masitas* or mole, and they don't even know how to make it! All these plants out here—from radish to mustard greens—they boil the leaves and eat them. That's their whole world!

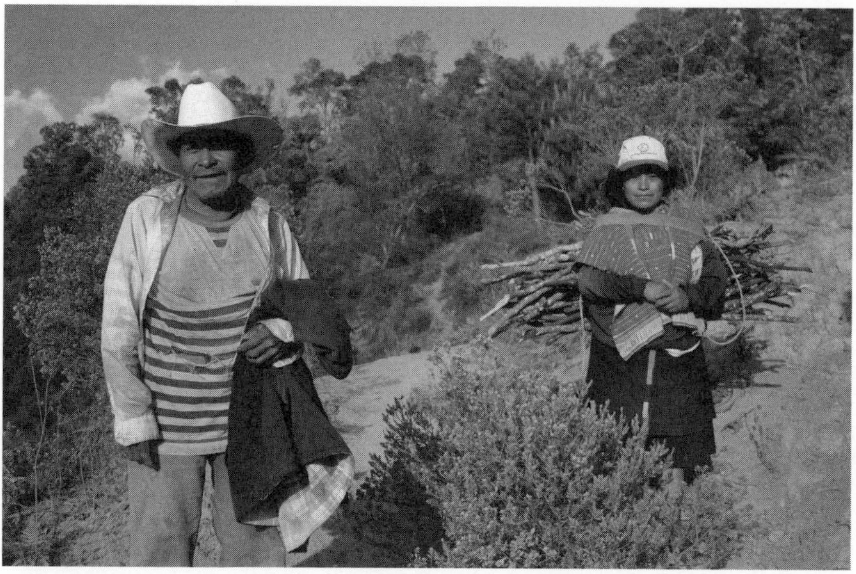

Samuel's sister carrying firewood, returning to San Miguel with Samuel's father after cutting firewood for the day. Photo by Seth M. Holmes.

As we finished lunch, the nurse told me that she has found one older Triqui woman who is very nice to her, tries to get her to learn Triqui, and cooks for her sometimes.

The nurse's comments show a lack of awareness of social context similar to that described among clinicians in the United States. However, they have more antagonistic affective overtones that may be due to the fact that the federal government makes this nurse leave her home and friends in Oaxaca City for several days each week for work. In addition, with regard to cleanliness, she fails to acknowledge how much work goes into bathing in San Miguel. In this mountain village, one must hike to the bottom of a long, steep hill and carry ten to fifteen buckets of water home from the well each day. This water is used for cooking, for the animals, for drinking, for washing plates and silverware, and for bathing. In addition, one must hike several miles into the communally owned forest, cut firewood with a machete, and carry it back home. One must also hike to a nearby river and wash one of the few changes of clothes one owns.

Next, the wood is used to make a fire big enough to cook meals, simmer corn in order to make masa and tortillas, sanitize drinking water by boiling, and prepare water warm enough to bathe in the cold air of the mountain village. Next, the bather has to find a location somewhat private enough without dirtying the inside of the house and without making so much mud that the bath is in vain. While in San Miguel, I helped the family with whom I lived harvest and plant corn and take the oxen and goats to pasture each day. For all the above reasons, despite becoming sweaty and muddy from this work, I bathed at most once a week. On the other hand, Centro staff members are able to bathe every day in the shower's running water that is carried regularly by the poorest women of San Miguel.

When I returned to San Miguel on one of my later visits, the nurse was no longer there; she had been asked to leave by the town leaders "because she took too much vacation." The new nurse was a friendly woman, also from Oaxaca City. I met her for the first time with a Triqui friend, Nicolas, whom I had met on the Tanaka farm in Washington. Nicolas asked for her help preparing the health documents needed to apply for residency in the United States. She replied, "Well, I don't know if you really work hard [in the United States] like you say, but I'll see what I can do." While Nicolas was present, the nurse explained that she was an Evangelical Christian. She told me that the Triqui people are mostly Catholic and that "here Catholic means that they pray to images of wood and iron and steel and who knows what else. We just pray wherever we are to the God who is alive, the God who made the wind and the sun. Catholic means you can do whatever you want. You can drink and have lovers and have lots of fiestas, celebrate birthdays and other days all the time."

She went on to tell me, "The customs of the Triquis are virgin; they haven't been changed by anything. They are still the same as they have always been. Some of the Triqui pueblos are pueblos without laws; they just have customs." She then asked me, "So, you are thinking of crossing the border? For them *[motioning with her hand toward the Triqui pueblo]*, it is just another adventure, like a lot of their lives are an adventure. You should take some snake antivenom, though." Like Samantha in relation to Abelino's knee, this nurse discounted the suffering of the Triqui migrants, specifically by referring to the difficult and dangerous border crossing as simply "an adventure." In addition, she echoed the social Darwinist understandings of indigenous simplicity heard on the Tanaka farm.

The nurse went on to tell me (in front of Nicolas) that a baby had died in San Miguel a week ago. She explained that the mother of the baby told the nurse she had brought the baby to the Centro and that the doctor thought the baby had a cold and gave her some pills. The nurse added, "Babies can't swallow pills anyway." Several times as the baby continued to get worse the mother tried to find the doctor, but he did not answer the door of the clinic. She took the baby to the nearby mestizo town, Tlaxiaco, and the baby died in the hospital from complications of a lung infection. "If we were working in a *ciudad* [city], instead of a pueblo, he would be in jail. If we were both there and gave only *pastillitas* [little pills], we would both be in jail."

A few days later, the nurse returned to Oaxaca City for the weekend and the doctor returned to San Miguel. The doctor complained to me that the Triqui people do not come to the clinic enough. To illustrate his point he said, "There was a mother who took her baby all the way to Tlaxiaco last week instead of bringing him to me, and the baby died because it took so long to get there." He then complained about how the Triqui people gossip and start rumors about him not being in the Centro.

The clinicians in San Miguel work in the difficult environment of a clinic that lacks medicines and medical instruments. They are required by the federal government to travel several hours away from their friends and family for several days each week to work in a town where the people speak a different language. Like the clinicians in Washington and California, they lack awareness of the social forces impinging on the health and well-being of their patients. Instead, they tend to blame the sicknesses of their patients on assumptions about their culture and behaviors. They are given and required to employ ethnocentric metrics, such as the malnutrition index. Because of the relative lack of political power of their patients, they are given impunity for what could be considered malpractice. Finally, they perceive their patients through racist metaphors of dirtiness, violence, and laziness that lead them to understand them as not deserving care.

ACONTEXTUAL MEDICINE AND APOLITICAL CULTURAL COMPETENCY

As would be expected in the paradigm of the clinical gaze, the clinicians I spoke to see the individual Triqui bodies in their offices, yet they are unable to engage the social context that produces suffering. It was only infrequently (e.g., Dr. Samuelson and Dr. Goldenson) that I heard a health professional point out the context in which the person lives: conditions in the labor camp, working conditions, or international economic and immigration policies. Yet these larger political, economic, and social forces are the fundamental causes of their patients' suffering. At the same time, the health care professionals cannot be blamed for their acontextuality. They, too, are affected by social, economic, and political structures. Much of their blindness to social and political context is caused by the difficult, hectic, and emotionally exhausting circumstances in which they work. It is caused also by the way medical science is thought and taught in the contemporary world. Most of these individuals have chosen their positions in migrant clinics because they want to help. They have a great deal of compassion and a sense of calling to this work. Yet the lenses they have been given through which to understand their patients have been narrowly focused, individualistic, and asocial.

Physicians in the United States and Mexico are not trained to see the social determinants of health problems, or to hear them when communicated by their patients. This acontextuality is seen when the sections of medical charts reporting social history entirely exclude social realities and when torture is reported as boxing. They are trained, instead, to give most heed to the "Objective" information provided by their own physical examinations and, more so, biotechnical blood and radiological tests.[33] Thus it is unavoidable that they would fall into the trap of using a narrow lens that functions to decontextualize sickness, transporting it from the realm of politics, power, and inequality to the realm of the individual body. The most upstream determinants of suffering are left unacknowledged, unaddressed, and untreated. Much like the "anti-politics machine" of development agencies described by Ferguson,[34] biomedicine effectively depoliticizes suffering, blaming sickness not on political economic and social structures but rather on individual behaviors, assumed cultural practices, and perceived ethnic body differences.

Beyond this acontextual gaze, physicians in North America today are also taught to see behavioral factors in health—such as lifestyle, diet, habits, and addictions. Behavioral health education has been added as part of a laudable move to broaden medical education within the paradigm of biopsychosocial health first described by George Engel in 1977. However, without being trained to consider the global political-economic structures and local hierarchies that shape the suffering of their patients, health professionals are equipped to see only biological and behavioral determinants of sickness. Symbolically, they are limited to understanding the genesis of sickness as located in the patients: their bodies (the genetics mentioned by the dentist), their behavior (the incorrect bending assumed by the rehabilitation medicine physician), or their culture (the customs invoked by the nurse in San Miguel). Thus well-meaning clinicians inadvertently add insult to injury, subtly blaming their patients for their suffering.

Largely in response to social science critiques of the limited gaze of biomedicine in a multicultural world, biomedical institutions have adopted training in cultural competency.[35] In many ways, the field of cultural competency seeks to broaden the clinical gaze in order to avoid ethnocentric assumptions and ineffective interventions. Most mainstream cultural competence training focuses on lists of stereotypical traits of ethnic groups.[36] This focus suggests that the culture of the patient is the problem that needs to be understood and the barrier that should be overcome in order to provide effective health care.[37] In the formulations of cultural competency, the culture of biomedicine and the structural determinants of health and health care are left largely unexamined. However, the ethnographic data above contradict this focus by showing that it is often the structure and the culture of biomedicine that function as barriers to effective care. As suggested by Jonathan Metzl, medical educators should exchange mainstream cultural competency for training in social analysis and "structural competency."[38]

Without appreciating the continuum of violence located in ethnic and citizenship hierarchies and international policies that place their patients in injurious conditions in the first place, clinicians often blame the sickness on the patient—the assumed incorrect manner of bending while picking, the presumed trouble with authority, or the expected inappropriate diet. The way one stands while picking berries, if indeed incorrect in some unhealthy way, is only a proximal ingredient of one's suffering. Ironically, the progressive move to include behavioral health in medical education without the correlate inclusion of social context may be exactly what leads clinicians to blame, even criminalize, the victims of social suffering.[39] Even those health professionals who are acutely aware of the social determinants of health may resort to biological and behavioral explanations as a defense mechanism against that which they experience as hopeless. Thus the victim of prejudice and economic and historical inequalities is blamed for her predicament. She is blamed for the bad jobs and the poor health she has, even though these are outcomes of the social structures by which she is situated.

The reality of migrant health, however, is even more complicated and potentially dangerous. The difficult circumstances and limited gaze of the migrant clinic make it impossible for even the most idealistic clinicians to provide effective treatment. Not only are these physicians unable to recommend appropriate interventions; they often prescribe ineffective treatments with unintended harmful results. Some of these treatments—such as returning a patient with an injured knee to full duty work—can be directly harmful to their patients. Even the interventions of well-meaning physicians—for example, pain-relieving injections and referrals to therapy in order to, among other things, accept potentially cruel treatment from supervisors—may function inadvertently to shore up the unequal social formations causing sickness in the first place. These treatments unintentionally depoliticize suffering, thereby buttressing the very structures of oppression causing sickness. The violence enacted by social hierarchies extends from the farm to the migrant clinic and back again, despite the impressive values and intentions of those in both institutions. The structure of health care must be changed to offer quality care to all patients instead of seeking private profit and cost-savings. The contemporary biobehavioral clinical gaze must be transformed to recognize the social, political, and economic determinants of sickness and health, to include structural competency. In the meanwhile, it is no wonder that my Triqui companions conclude that los médicos no saben nada.

SIX

"Because They're Lower to the Ground"

NATURALIZING SOCIAL SUFFERING

THE HIDDENNESS OF MIGRANT BODIES

"There are no migrants here; why are you looking here? I haven't heard of any. If you want migrants, you'll have to go to the other side of the mountains in eastern Washington. There are lots who pick apples around Yakima, I think. But there aren't any over here." A regional public health officer in Washington State advised me thus in fall 2002 as I explored the possibilities of ethnographic fieldwork in Skagit County.

The Skagit Valley is an active node in the transnational circuits[1] of thousands of Mexican migrant laborers, including my Triqui companions from the Mexican state of Oaxaca. So how can thousands of people, the very people who make the valley's famous agriculture possible, be overlooked? How can postcards of the annual tulip festival erase the workers who care for and harvest the tulip fields? The public gaze—especially that of the wealthy public who shop at elite grocery stores and live in exclusive neighborhoods—is trained away and spatially distanced from the migrant farmworkers.[2] A white resident of the Skagit Valley with whom I became friends during my first summer on the Tanaka Brothers Farm explained to me, "For the world in which I live and the people I live with and surround myself with, the thing that frightens me most is that [Mexican migrant workers] don't exist. They're totally off our radar. They just don't exist. It's more likely we would get involved with a child in Acapulco in an orphanage because it is more glitzy or, I don't know, less scary than finding out that there are people five miles away that I could be interested in."

In many of the rare instances that this gaze focuses on Mexican migrants in the United States, anti-immigrant and racist rhetoric along with hate crimes result.[3] Here, as in many places where diasporic laborers struggle to survive,[4] the hiddenness of migrant bodies is just one factor that enables their continued mistreatment and suffering.

In order to work consciously to bring about the amelioration of social suffering, people must first be aware of the inequalities that cause suffering. This applies not only to the white residents in the Skagit Valley and Central California but also to the migrant workers themselves. In addition, these hierarchies must be recognized as historically and socially constructed and, thus, changeable. Conversely, the perception of inequities as normal, deserved, and natural permits the reproduction of such destructive social formations as well as indifference to them.[5] It is vitally important, in this case, to understand how the ongoing mistreatment and suffering of migrant laborers has become taken for granted, normalized, and naturalized by all involved. This is a critical first step toward working for respect, equality, and health in the context of U.S.-Mexico migration.

SYMBOLIC VIOLENCE

Pierre Bourdieu's concept of symbolic violence has proven especially helpful for my understanding of the ways in which the order of inequalities described thus far has become unquestioned and unchallenged, even by those most oppressed.[6] Symbolic violence is the naturalization, including internalization, of social asymmetries. Bourdieu explains that we experience the world through *doxa* (mental schemata) and *habitus* (historically accreted bodily comportments) that are issued forth from that very social world and, therefore, make the social order—including its hierarchies—appear natural. Thus we misrecognize oppression as natural because it fits our mental and bodily schemata through which we perceive it. Bourdieu writes, "The effect of symbolic domination (whether ethnic, gender, cultural or linguistic, etc.) is exerted not in the pure logic of knowing consciousness but through the schemes of perception, appreciation and action that are constitutive of habitus and which, below the level of the decisions of consciousness and the controls of the will, set up a cognitive relationship that is profoundly obscure to itself."[7] In other words, symbolic violence acts within the process of perception, hidden from the conscious mind. Whereas Sartre's concept of bad faith inheres a sense of consciousness in that individuals knowingly deceive themselves in order to avoid realities that disturb them, the activity of symbolic violence is hidden precisely because it works through the very categories and lenses of perception.

Continuing with his metaphor of the social world as a "game," Bourdieu describes *illusio* as "investment in the game." All social actors in a given field must "buy into," via some degree of *illusion,* the rules of the game. One of the primary rules of the social world is that the actor's "being is a being-perceived, condemned to be defined as it 'really' is by the perception of others."[8] Taking this into account, the victims of symbolic violence, by definition, unknowingly consent to their own domination by inhabiting the game in the first place. In Bourdieu's book *Masculine Domination* we see that both the dominated and the dominant are victims of symbolic violence, although quite differently. Here, both men and women perceive themselves and the other as part of a world "naturally" made up of such dichotomous schemata as "high/low, male/female, white/black, etc."[9] Thus social actors have no other option than to perceive themselves and their world through schemata produced by asymmetric power relations. The asymmetries comprising the social world are thus made invisible, taken for granted, normal for all involved.[10]

CITIZENSHIP, CULTURE, AND DIFFERENCE

Many of the words used to refer to Mexican migrant workers by other area residents function to exclude them from the assumed "us"—based on a symbolic assertion that they are out of their proper place. As discussed further in the conclusion, the word *migrant* carries assumptions of moving between one bounded "sending" community to a separate "receiving" community. Given that *migrant* is used almost exclusively to describe a person residing and working outside his or her hometown, the word connotes the person being out of place in the current location and belonging elsewhere. Other commonly used words like *Mexican, foreigner,* and *Oaxacan* imply that the referent is from, pertains to, and *belongs* somewhere else. Interestingly, the usage of these words by most white area residents has very little to do with official citizenship, in other words, whether one is legally a Mexican or an American. Thus, J. R., one of the white residents of Central California whom I came to know, did not think twice when he referred to the Latino mayor of a nearby town as a "foreigner," even though in order to qualify to run for election as mayor he must be a U.S. citizen. Furthermore, the mayor to whom he referred, unlike himself, was a California native. This usage belies an unspoken fear of the ethnic Other such as in J. R.'s elaboration, "The first thing you run into when you have some foreigner running your community, he doesn't know nothing about politics or nothing. The only thing he wants to do is take over."

I came to know J. R. and his wife, Janet, through their nephew, who was one of my close childhood friends growing up. J. R. moved to Central California with his family from the Midwest as a poor "Okie," to harvest crops in the 1940s. His family lived in tents and picked grapes for a dozen years before moving into other types of work. When I met J. R., he had recently retired from his job as a mechanic at a large aeronautical company located in California and spent most of his time taking care of their yard and antique cars. Janet grew up in a middle-class white family in Fresno, California. She worked as a supervisor for one of the public transit systems in the region. Over the course of several meetings, they served me soda and fruit and I tape recorded our conversations.

Many white residents of the Skagit Valley and Central California labeled U.S. citizen Latinos "Mexicans" in a deprecating manner. Janet told me, "One of these days, California will be 75 percent Mexicans." The dichotomy between "Mexican" and "American" and the assumption that "American" means only someone who is ethnically white became clear later in the same conversation when she complained, "It drives me nuts when I go to the grocery store and they have [ethnic clothing] on . . . it's like, 'Why don't you start dressing like an American?!'"

The underlying fear of difference was clarified when J.R. explained, "Entertainment in my day in [Central California] was busting a Mexican up." I asked, "Just because?" He clarified, "You know, knock him out if you caught him on the street, because sooner or later he was going to do you that way. . . . Just beat the hell out of one of them. Catch him out alone and stomp him, man, real good. Just because he's a Mex." "But you see," he continued, "he was an endangerment to us. He was taking farmworkers' jobs." Janet corrected him that white people stopped being willing to pick in the fields in California before the farmers had to recruit Mexicans. J.R. agreed to this and concluded, "Plus, he was different than me."

This distaste for difference was clarified in this conversation when J.R. responded to Janet's musings about potential solutions to interracial tensions. He countered, "Why would it ever change? It's because they're not hungry. So, he's going to stay Mex. That's just the way it is. Too much free welfare. You get your person hungry, and he'll blend; he'll blend then. But until then, why should he change his name, you know like Gonzales instead of Smith? He'll stay Gonzales, and he'll be getting all that free stuff. There's the biggest problem, the welfare. . . . He's a burden to me because he doesn't want to change."

Here, difference—"staying Mex"—is blamed on the assumed receiving of welfare, "getting all that free stuff." In a separate interview, Janet made a similar criticism: "We let those Mexican people come here. When they get to feeling like, 'Gee, we don't want to pick cotton, we don't want to pick this,' we let them on our welfare." However, none of the Mexican migrants I knew qualified for or had ever received welfare. Thus the people J.R. and Janet imagine on welfare are conflations of Mexicans and American Latinos. In this way, their words indicate that U.S. citizen Latinos are out of place, are not American, and do not belong here. In another conversation, J.R. said, "That's why the Mexicans are having problems and now your Hmongs are having problems is they don't want to change. They want to keep their culture. You've got to get people blended right away. People have to mix. If you don't mix and you're alienated over there, guess what? You're different." Not only is difference considered a problem, but it is equated with "staying Mex" instead of "blending" into what is understood to be (*white*) American.

J.R. reiterated the assumption of "acculturation" in both popular imagery and public health literature. This concept suggests the progressive erasure of difference via movement from the "ethnic" culture to the "mainstream" culture. Linda Hunt and others explain problematic suppositions in the model of acculturation in the public health literature: "Thus, the ethnic culture is understood to lie in contrast to the advantages and pitfalls of Western culture, with the acculturating individual proceeding away from tradition and toward modernity."[11] And Matthew Gutmann criticizes the same literature: "Discussion . . . is frequently based on an implicit standard of differences when compared with the 'normal.'"[12] However, the public health literature, as well as J.R.'s statements, strangely avoids any definition of the "normal" or the "mainstream." Guttman posits that the unmarked, assumed mainstream toward which immigrants acculturate is the white, American middle class. Thus the concept of acculturation conflates citizenship, race, class, and habitus (including clothing style) while erasing history and international politics. "Hybridization" is offered as an alternative by scholars in diaspora studies,[13] who remind us that the practices of immigrants are simultaneously maintained and transformed through ongoing contact with other people and places.

Another alternative is offered by my Triqui companions, who do not want to stay in the United States long term or become American citizens. Instead, Samuel and my other Triqui friends want to obtain legal permission to work in the United States seasonally while remaining Mexican citizens. They tend to see the entire transnational migration circuit linking San Miguel, the Skagit Valley, and Central California as their spatially extended community.[14] At the same time, they conceive of San Miguel as their primary home and desire to be located as much as possible with their nuclear and extended family there. However, they want permission to work seasonally in the United States so that they and their families can survive without having to cross the dangerous desert. Some of my Triqui friends have attempted to migrate for work to the primarily mestizo town of Tlaxiaco near San Miguel, but the wage they are offered there is much lower. The wage they are offered increases with the distance from San Miguel, receiving slightly more in Oaxaca City, more in Mexico City, more in Baja California, and even more in the United States. Thus, ironically, in order to afford to live as much time as possible in their hometown, my Triqui friends migrate as far away as possible. Most work toward a specific goal—enough money to finish construction on their houses, pay for a year of food and school uniforms, or offer bridewealth to the family of the woman they want to marry—and plan to return to San Miguel as soon as possible after its realization. The experience of my Triqui companions highlights another deep irony in contemporary U.S.-Mexico migration, namely, the more dangerous and expensive crossing the border is made by "closing the border" through militarization and the building of physical walls, the longer Samuel and my other Triqui friends stay in the United States.

RACE, PLACE, AND EXCLUSION

Local residents perceive migrant laborers differently, depending on their own social location and proximity to the inner workings of U.S. agriculture. The white residents I came to know in the Skagit Valley and Central California usually considered anyone of Latin American descent, regardless of citizenship, "Mexican." Those involved in agriculture, yet relatively removed from Mexican migrant workers—such as the executives and crop managers on the Tanaka farm—tended to recognize a difference among U.S. Latinos (whom they usually call "Hispanics"), mestizo Mexicans ("regular Mexicans" or "traditional Mexicans"), and indigenous Mexicans from the state of Oaxaca (called simply "Oaxacans"). Those who worked directly with Mexican migrant workers, such as the Latino crew bosses on the Tanaka farm, tended to distinguish among

U.S. Latinos ("Tejanos" or "Chicanos"), mestizo Mexicans ("Mexicanos"), Mixtecs, and Triquis. A realistic understanding of the many ways in which social inequalities are reproduced and the social suffering of migrant laborers is normalized requires recollection of this multilayered landscape of social categories.[15]

In one of the largest public high schools in the Skagit Valley, dozens of students started a gang called "WAM," which stood for "Whites Against Mexicans." This gang painted "WAM" on walls, wrote it on their notebooks and cell phones, brought firearms to school, threatened other students, and provoked fights. The school administration responded by giving detention or expelling anyone found with "WAM" written anywhere on them or their possessions. In response to WAM, another group of students started a weekly event called "WAMsketball" to ease tensions and promote positive interethnic relations. Similar to the usage in Central California, "Mexican" in both these instances did not denote primarily someone of Mexican citizenship or origin but rather someone different, someone to be looked down on. One of the teachers in the school explained, "There are plenty of kids in the high school who are proud to be Mexican and flaunt that. Some kids in the high school think they bring it on themselves because they don't just make the choice to be like the white kids." She gave examples of the way students flaunted being Mexican: the kinds of jeans they wore and the ways they arranged their hair. She went on to say that it was not just racially white students who were part of WAM but also Samoan, Russian (who are considered a separate ethnic group in the Skagit Valley), Asian American, and Latino students. These practices and perceptions offer a lens onto competing understandings of race—what it means to be "white" or "Mexican"—in this rural American valley.

Junior, who self-identifies and is identified by other students as Latino, regularly plays WAMsketball on the white team or serves as referee. He explained, "It's an attitude thing. It's like the Mexicans have the attitude in high school." His white friend John, who was active in WAM in the beginning and later joined WAMsketball, attempted to explain Junior's ethnicity: "I know Junior, he is Mexican, but not really. *[Speaking to Junior]* You can't be Mexican . . . because if you are Mexican, white people can't talk to you at our school." Despite the immediate context of violence recently engendered by WAM, Junior responded, "Mexicans are the ones who are like gangsters; that is what a Mexican is." He continued, "When you say someone is Hispanic, it is like saying you have respect for that person. But if you call them Mexican, it is like saying, 'You are a dirty Mexican.'"

In *Purity and Danger,* Mary Douglas explains that dirt is simply matter out of place: "Dirt is essentially disorder. . . . It exists in the eye of the beholder. . . . In chasing dirt, in papering, decorating, tidying, we are not governed by anxiety to escape disease, but are positively re-ordering our environment, making it conform to an idea."[16] Much like sand is considered "clean" when it is on a beach or in a sandbox but "dirty" when it is inside a house or on a child's hands, those considered Mexican, and therefore out of their proper place, are often referred to as dirty. Area residents and local newspapers used metaphors of "cleaning up the neighborhood" to indicate a project that functionally displaced those considered Mexican from their area by shutting down a labor camp, a day laborer pickup spot, and an apartment building occupied primarily by Mexican migrants or U.S. Latinos.

Although in one breath J. R. complained that "[Mexicans] dress better than I do," in another he called them "dirty" and "filthy." For example, he described a local farm labor camp in Central California: "So, what [the Mexicans] had done was they'd blamed the farmer for their filthiness; blamed him! Says he's running a slave labor camp out there with substandard housing flats. No plumbing; you know, none of this. . . . The toilet was broke off its plumbing; it hadn't been cleaned or swept since they moved in; beer cans everywhere. There he was drinking beer when he should've been cleaning his house. Filthy-ass Mexicans for you now."

When I asked for clarification, J. R. acknowledged that he had not seen the camp firsthand but heard about it through one of the local news channels. He continued, contrasting his childhood as an immigrant "Okie" in California with the Mexicans:

> When we lived in tents, that floor was just as this one *[pointing to his spotless white tile kitchen floor]* and the kids were clean. My mother always said, "Soap is cheap." And there wasn't no cockroaches in our house. No, because we kept things clean. But these wetbacks—what I still call them;

> now they're "migrants"—they come into a beautiful settlement and they tear it up drunk, drinking, and then they want another one. Now, there's a town out here called Dos Palos. They had a beautiful setup there, you know, work camps. It was an old airport left over from World War II. They took a bulldozer to that sucker because the Mexicans were complaining how filthy it was. It was; it was filthy. But it was *them.* All you could see in there was fast-food wrappers, fast-food cups. They'd stop off here at the old Taco Bell and whatever and buy their food and go on eating and then drink *cervezas, mucho cervezas,* oh, just keep it coming.

J.R. again acknowledged that his description of this work camp came from what he heard on one local news station. Another area resident I met during my preliminary trips to Central California, who identified herself as half Latina and half Native American, complained to me, "Those Mexicans are dirty. They are dirty and selfish. They're taking over like cockroaches!" As an example, she told me of Mexican migrants bathing in the nearby river and leaving trash on the riverbank. Thinking back now on her complaints, I remember again the week I ate and bathed in public parks while sleeping homeless out of cars waiting to find a slum apartment in Madera that would rent to people without credit histories.

As pointed out by George Orwell in *The Road to Wigan Pier,* the everyday living and working conditions of "the lower classes [lead them to] smell."[17] In a material sense, picking strawberries is a dirtier occupation than working in an office building. The Tanaka Brothers Farm labor camp shacks in Washington were surrounded by dirt roads that alternated between deep mud when it rained and fine dust in the sunshine. It was extremely difficult to keep anything clean; every day I wiped down the inside of my shack as it became quickly covered in light brown dust.

At the same time that U.S. Latinos and mestizo Mexicans are symbolically excluded from the category "American" they enact another linguistic category that excludes indigenous Mexicans. When used by these speakers, the words *Mexican* or *Mexicano* denote mestizo Mexicans only. Despite their Mexican citizenship, Mixtec and Triqui Mexicans are called simply "Oaxacan," "Oaxaqueño," or, more deprecatingly, "Oaxaco" or "indio." At times, U.S. Latinos referred to mestizo Mexicans as "regular Mexicans," differentiating them from indigenous Mexicans, who become understood as the opposite—"irregular"—in some way. Interestingly, several U.S. Latino crew bosses on the Tanaka farm described Mixtec and Triqui people but not mestizo Mexicans as "dirty." Samantha, the bilingual white receptionist on the farm, described Oaxacan people as "dirtier than regular Mexicans." These symbolic dichotomies are some of the many factors enabling white U.S. citizens and, in turn, Latino U.S. citizens and mestizo Mexicans, to become indifferent to the suffering of those considered different, Other, or out of place.

Mary Weismantel argues that categories of race are unnecessary without racism.[18] In other words, racial categories come to be used only in the context of exclusion. She argues against entirely biological understandings of race on one pole and immaterially constructivist critiques on the other. Weismantel and Stephen Eisenman posit that contemporary biological conceptions of race erase the body: "The science of genetics disdains the natural history of the human body after conception: its daily interactions with the world and other organisms are an afterthought, unimportant in the face of a biological destiny predetermined by a genetic code that is insubstantial and invisible."[19] At the same time, they argue against an "anti-essentialism [that] easily shades into anti-materialism."[20] Based on fieldwork in the Andes, Weismantel and Eisenman describe indigenous conceptions in which "race accumulates within the body, in its extremities and its orifices, its organs and its impulses, as a result of a life lived within a particular human community at a specific moment in time."[21] In this understanding, one's race may be altered over time as one's bodily shape and smell change as a result of daily bodily practices. As an example, the authors describe how smell relates to what it means to be indigenous and white (including mestizo) in Ecuador. Here, indigenous people are recognized not simply by the color of their eyes or skin but rather by the "dirty" smells that indicate their poverty and their residence with animals on subsistence farms. In contrast, whiteness involves the purchase and use of imported products that produce bodies that smell and look like they have had no interaction with other living things. They explain that whiteness is "a set of economic and political privileges passed down from generation to generation"[22] that then affects the appearance, shape, and smell of the body. This embodied and contingent understanding of race applies well to the context of U.S.-Mexico migration, in which people are perceived to occupy different racial categories depending on the social location of the perceiver; people are understood to be "flaunting" their Mexicanness based on how they dress and wear their hair; the violence of white gangs is erased through the act of translation of a "Mexican" style of dress into being a "gangster"; and poor and nonwhite people are considered "dirty" only in contexts in which they are considered out of place and excluded.

BLAMED FOR SUFFERING

At every level of the ethnicity-citizenship hierarchy on the Tanaka farm, each group of people believes those below them deserve their plight. White residents of the Skagit Valley and Central California regularly told me that Mexicans are not educated because they are "lazy." Several white residents explained to me that "Mexicans" have bad jobs because they "don't try to learn English." During one of our conversations on the Tanaka farm, Samantha claimed that "they don't have bank accounts because they don't know how; they are like kids." In Central California, Janet told me, "I get kind of pissed off about the Mexicans because they seem like they don't try to learn English, you know, and they are in our country, why don't they learn it?" Later in the same interview, Janet explained:

> In the morning, I get up, get ready for work, and turn on the TV to see the news. You can learn how to speak English. It's "number one," and they hold up a number one. Every day it's something different that's like, "thank you," "thank you." They'll repeat it, and then they'll hold the word up and show it to you. There's things on TV, and if people really wanted to—I know they're out in the field, but still—I think that if they wanted to, they could learn something, as far as to make it.

Janet acknowledges that Mexican farmworkers are in the fields and unable to watch the program she describes on TV, but she leaves out other aspects of the social and material context of learning English. All my Triqui companions told me they wanted to learn English, and several attempted to do so during my fieldwork. Abelino tried to study English in the evening classes hosted on the Tanaka farm but was told the classes were not open to people who live in the labor camps. Next, he signed up for an English as a Second Language (ESL) course at the local community college. He completed one semester and then had to quit because the next-level course took place in the early evening, when Abelino would be finishing his work or taking his family to the local church that gave away free food at that time.

Repeating the commonly held myth of a classless, individualistic society, J.R. concluded one interview, "You can do anything you want in this country. Anyone can be anything they want to. There is no excuse in this country. There are no barriers. Nothing holds you back except for you. You have no one to blame if you don't become the best you could except for you." This trope, reminiscent of Horatio Alger's myth of the poor young man succeeding based on his hard work alone, erases the ethnicity-citizenship hierarchy that shapes the material lives of those working in American agriculture. In a similarly acontextual manner, many white U.S. citizens blame the country of Mexico or "Mexican political corruption" for the poverty in rural Mexico that is impelling people to migrate in order to survive. However, this narrative eschews the power of the economic interests in the United States that pushed for NAFTA, effectively producing poverty by banning Mexico from protecting indigenous small corn producers while allowing American corn subsidies for large corporate agribusiness.

Within Mexico, mestizo Mexicans often blamed Triqui people for their own suffering. Luz María, one of the mestiza nuns in San Miguel, explained her understanding of why Triqui people are poor:

> They are not capable of making sources of work. Many do not know how to live. In everything, in hygiene and cleaning the house and preparing food, keeping animals and doing economics. Someone could make a *tortillería* [tortilla factory] that would be open a few hours a day, and people could sell their corn to them, or there could be a pharmacy so people don't have to go to Tlaxiaco or a big grocery store—though that would be difficult because you would have to pay someone to stay watch in order to keep your earnings from being stolen away. They don't work very hard, and they don't know how to work very hard.

On the contrary: during my fieldwork I observed several small stores in San Miguel struggling to survive despite the economic depression of the town. In addition, when Luz María stated that Triqui people "don't work very hard," I could not help but wonder how picking bent over seven days a week did not qualify. When I asked Luz María how Triqui people are different from mestizo Mexicans, she stated simply, "They are violent." At one point, this nun admitted that Triqui people carry guns "because of generations of being kicked out of places and defending themselves." Like many of the indigenous towns of Oaxaca, San Miguel had experienced several consecutive battles with many fatalities over landownership with nearby, encroaching larger towns. Luz María told me in Spanish, "The land conflicts are over just a meter or two. Probably *[a lo mejor]*, these Triquis wanted the line another meter over there and the Mixtecs from Santa Marta wanted another meter this way." She minimized the causes of violence, implicitly backing up her claim that Triqui people are inherently violent and that they brought the violence on themselves unnecessarily. Juana, one of the nurses in San Miguel, similarly warned me about the violence of the Triqui people and told me that I should think twice before helping any of them in any way.

"Want" is a common metaphor through which migrant workers are blamed for their plight. For example, John Tanaka, president of the Tanaka Brothers Farm, told me that the pickers "are not going to take a lunch break. They're just not going to do it. They don't want a lunch break." The next summer, Scott, the apple crop manager, told me almost exactly the same thing, claiming that pickers *wanted* to work all day without a lunch break. In response to pickers' complaints about the confusing pay scale, John Tanaka whispered to me, "They don't want to understand."

In addition, Mexican migrant workers are regularly blamed for the suffering of those considered American. J. R. considered them "a burden on [him] because [they] won't change" and because he believes they collect welfare. When I asked a neighbor of the migrant camp in which I lived in the Skagit Valley, named Phil, what he thought of his migrant laborer neighbors, he replied, "I lost my job because of them!" He explained that he had worked for a local white farmer for over ten years but was replaced because that farmer could hire two migrant workers for what he was being paid. His mother then reminded him that he hated that job, and Phil agreed. Phil had been a truck driver, delivering potatoes from a local farm throughout several western states. Now he works at the local fire station, being trained as a firefighter. Interestingly, he blamed the Mexican migrants, excused the farmer who actually made the hiring decisions, and kept silent about the pressures from the international market. Regarding the farmer, Phil stated simply, "I understand where he is coming from; he wants to run his farm efficiently."

NORMALIZATION

For many white residents of the Skagit Valley and Central California, the suffering of migrant laborers is understood as normal, though for different and sometimes contradictory reasons. First, and perhaps most important, people simply get used to seeing the conditions in which migrant workers live and work. Although the migrant camps are hidden from view for the vast majority of Skagit Valley residents, those who live near the camps walk, bike, and drive past the camps every day. Several of these people told me that they were troubled by the conditions of the camps when they first moved to the area but got used to them and now pass by without a second thought.

Second, many people justify the living conditions of migrant workers based on what they assume is normal for them. John Tanaka echoed what many people told me—that the camps were acceptable because they were much better than the housing the pickers had in Mexico. None of the people making this claim, however, had visited the pickers' hometowns or asked about their housing in Mexico. Nonetheless, this justification assumes as acceptable the original economic inequalities that leave Triqui people in meager housing in Oaxaca. Ironically, several other people in the Skagit Valley justified the living conditions of migrant farmworkers with the opposite assumption, that the housing the pickers had in Mexico or California was much better than the camps. The owner of the closest grocery store to the camps, where many pickers walked to buy food, told me that the camps were fine because "They all have pools and big houses in Mexico and California and are just here for the summer." A neighbor of the labor camp where I lived in the Skagit reasoned, "Well, they all have cars, so they don't need anything."

A few people in the Skagit Valley described beliefs in economic mobility and ethnic succession. John Tanaka mentioned several times over the course of my fieldwork that "once any particular group of people go through a three-generation move, they'll no longer be in agriculture." He based this assertion on his understanding that Japanese Americans had "worked [their] way up" the economic ladder in the United States since they arrived. Several other people told me that they hoped the pickers would "work their way up" in society. These statements recognize that picking fruit on a farm is an undesirable and difficult occupation at the same time that they subtly justify the related working conditions as a temporary step along the rags-to-riches mythology of American success.[23]

Finally, the segregation of the farm aids normalization in various ways. Shelly, the supervisor of the checkers who reprimanded white teenagers if they interacted with the Mexican pickers, explained to me that white teens should not get to know pickers because this would bias the weighing of berries. This active segregation certainly led to, among other things, an everyday violence that dehumanized the Mexican pickers. White teenage checkers regularly carried on conversations without any sign of acknowledgment as Mexican pickers brought their berries to be weighed. They continued their stories and jokes as they weighed the berries and marked the picker's card as though the picker were not present. While Shelly told me that having teenage checkers work on the farm brings "community value," it also fosters the sense that ethnic labor hierarchies are normal and acceptable.

NATURALIZATION

When I asked a mestiza Mexican social worker why Triqui people have only berry picking jobs, she explained, "Oaxacans like to work bent over *[A los Oaxaqueños les gusta trabajar agachados]*." Then she explained that mestizo Mexicans, whom she called "Mexicanos," get too many pains if they work in the fields. In response to the same question, Mateo, the one Mixtec crew boss, told me that the Triqui people are "tough brutes, raring to go for work [*bruto para trabajar*]." He said that when he first came to the Tanaka farm ten years ago, all the pickers were mestizo, from northern Mexico. The Mixtec people who began to migrate to the farm picked faster, and over time the mestizo Mexicans stopped coming. Now, Mateo told me, the Triqui people are the fast, "brutish" pickers, and fewer and fewer Mixtecs are coming to the farm to pick.

Later, I asked Scott, the farm's apple crop manager, why I had not seen any Triqui people harvesting apples, the contract field job with the highest pay. He explained, "The O'xacans are too short to reach the apples, they're too slow. . . . They have to use ladders a lot more than some of the other guys. The other guys just use the ladders to pick the very top of the tree, where the O'xacans are having to, you know, halfway. . . . And, besides, they don't like ladders, anyway."

Ironically, later that week one of Scott's crew bosses told me that her crew's fastest picker was Triqui. Scott continued the above conversation by explaining that Oaxacans are perfect for picking berries "because they're lower to the ground." In response to my questions about why Triqui people have different jobs from mestizo Mexicans, several other people stated simply, "They're short." The sentiment that Mexicans should pick berries was echoed by U.S. Senator George Murphy from California during a Senate debate on immigration in the 1960s; he stated that Mexicans should be farmworkers because they are "built lower to the ground so it's easier for them to stoop."[24]

Perceptions of bodily difference along ethnoracial lines serve as the lenses through which symbolic violence is enacted such that each category of body is understood to *deserve* its relative social position. Because of what are considered their "natural characteristics," indigenous Oaxacan bodies are understood to *belong* picking berries as opposed to other jobs. On the other hand, other ethnicities have bodies that do not fit well in the picker category and belong doing other forms of work.

When I asked Scott about the potential negative health effects of pesticides, he replied:

> The laws are so tight that there's no way anybody should be able to get sick from pesticides. I mean, it's that strict. . . . There are a few people out there that are a lot more sensitive, and they show it once in a while. It's not that we did anything wrong, or a neighbor did anything wrong, they're just a lot more sensitive to it, and you're always going to find those people. I've been working with pesticides for twenty, twenty-five years. The laws are a lot stricter and the pesticides are softer. Go out and spray and eat it the same day! The chemistry has changed and really advanced. Some of it you can see: pesticide residue. Some of it that people claim is residue is actually dirt, dust.

Here it is not simply ethnic body differences but also individual body differences that deflect blame from the farm for the responsibility for pesticide exposure and its health effects.[25]

INTERNALIZATION

At the same time that symbolic violence is enacted from without in the above ways, the concept inheres a sense of internalization and subtle complicity of the dominated. One does not perceive only others, but also oneself, as belonging in ordained social locations.

During my second day picking strawberries, a tractor with long metal extensions spraying something in the air drove through the field while we picked. I asked Mateo what it was. "Do you really want to know? You sure you want the truth?" he asked. I nodded. "Dangerous insecticides," he said, shaking his head. Later in the summer, I noticed danger signs (in English only) posted on several large canisters surrounding one of the hand washing and outhouse stations at the edge of the field. Strawberry pickers worked everyday without gloves as the visible pesticide residue dissolved in the mixture of strawberry juice that stained their hands dark maroon. If they ate anything, they ate it in the fields while picking, without washing their hands so as not to take time away from work and fail to pick the minimum weight. Our only education about pesticides came from a short warning cassette tape in monotone Spanish played inaudibly in one corner of a huge warehouse full of over one hundred

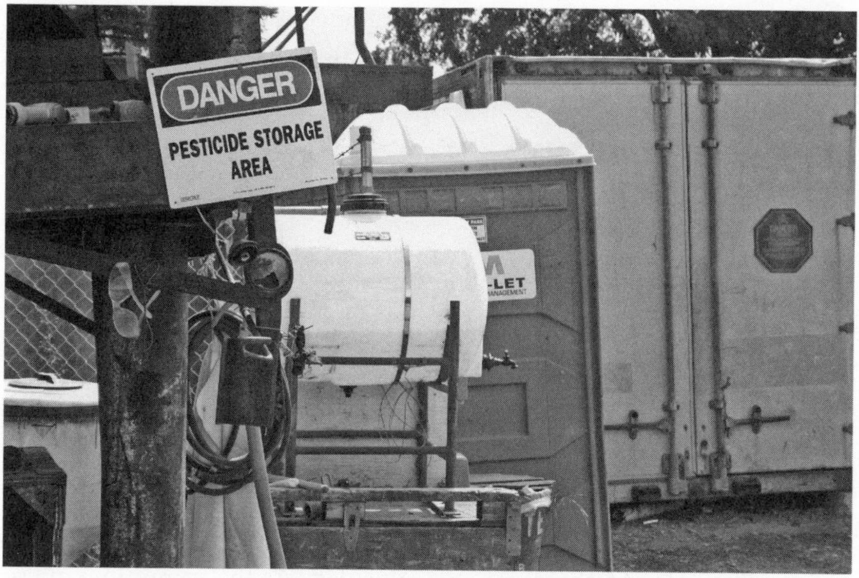

Danger: pesticide storage area. Photo by Seth M. Holmes.

workers and their children during one of the picker orientations. After the tape, the farm administrator in charge of the orientation asked if we had any questions. After a brief silence, he was satisfied and moved on to explain where we should sign the forms we were given, all of which were printed in English. One of the forms stated in English that we agreed not to organize.

The same week the spraying described above occurred, I received a video I had ordered from the United Farm Workers about the health dangers of pesticides. Several Triqui pickers watched it with me in the shack where Samuel's family lived. Afterward, I asked them what they thought. One told me matter-of-factly, "Pesticides affect only white Americans *[gabachos]* because your bodies are delicate and weak." Another said, "We Triquis are strong and *aguantamos* [hold out, bear, endure]." The others nodded. These ideas were reflected several times over the course of my fieldwork. One of the Triqui people with whom I traveled to Oaxaca bragged to me that there were many Triqui people in the military in Mexico because "we endure *[aguantamos]*." Here Triqui people internalized their class position through ethnic pride in perceived bodily differences that ironically aids in the naturalization and therefore reproduction of the very structures of their oppression.

BODY POSITION IN LABOR

In addition, perceptions of body position impute a hierarchy of humanness on the farm. The interpretations of class and body position offered by Strauss and Scheper-Hughes and Brandes[26] prove helpful. The dual meaning of the word *position* as both a post of employment and a stance of the body hints at one phenomenon. Occupations performed seated behind a desk are symbolically linked to the mind, such that they are more prestigious in a society that subjugates body to mind. Jobs executed standing or walking are seen as more closely linked to the body, less intellectual, and therefore less esteemed. At the same time, these standing bodies are understood as humans of solid standing. This basic respect is seen in the phrases "upstanding citizen," "upright character," and "standing up for oneself." Finally, the jobs at the bottom of the hierarchy that require bodies to kneel in the dirt or bend over in the bushes are the least respected. Like animals, these workers are seen "on all fours."

This general analysis applies well to the Skagit, where those with the most power and prestige hold desk jobs, where midlevel supervisors stand and walk, and where the lowest-level workers—bent over all day—are derided as perros and burros. Mateo, the only indigenous Oaxacan on the farm who was promoted to supervisor, explained to me that he hopes to continue studying English and being promoted until he can "work with his mind instead of his body." He explained the superiority of desk jobs over manual labor in the following way: "The body will not always give *[no siempre va a dar]*, and I think it will tire *[cansar]*. Your mind might tire after years, but not like the body, not enough to give you a sickness *[no tanto para darte una enfermedad]*." During a strike my second summer on the farm, the pickers complained that they felt treated like they were "lower" than other workers because they picked. Scott dismissed this

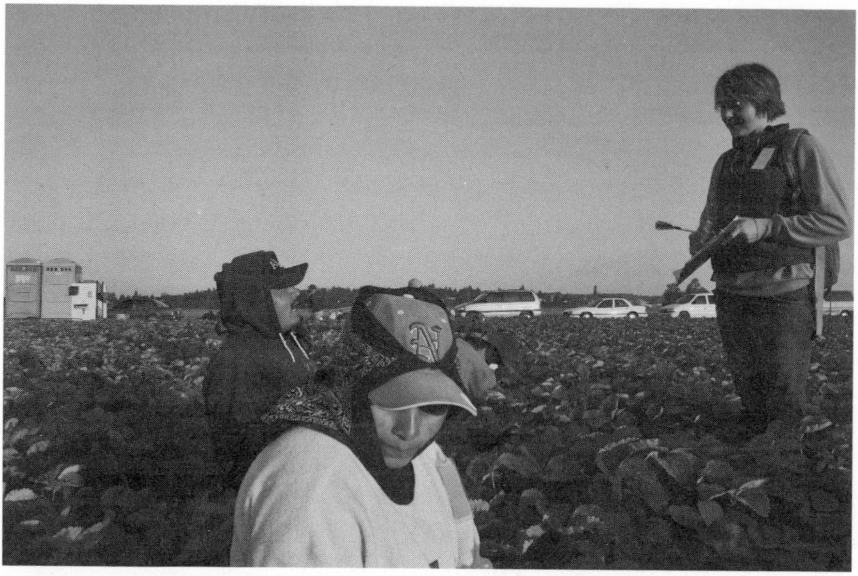

A checker stands while pickers kneel in the strawberry field. Photo by Seth M. Holmes.

complaint, explaining to me, "I almost got the feeling that they thought that they were lower just because they were a picker, which, to me, that's one of the most important jobs on the farm." While the job of the pickers is clearly important to the harvest, my ethnographic research indicates that this role is not routinely treated with respect or prestige.

Over the course of my fieldwork on the farm, berry pickers were treated as subhumans on several occasions. During one Northwest rainstorm, several Triqui women waited outside the farm office to ask a question about their paychecks. They huddled together in the mud, under the overhang of the roof. When Shelly arrived, she said in English, "What are you doing standing in my flowers? Shoo! Shoo! Get, get!," waving her hands as if to scare away an unwanted pack of dogs.

In essence, the migrant body is made to betray itself. Specifically, because of perceptions of ethnic difference and body position in labor, the migrant body is seen as belonging in its position in the very agricultural labor hierarchy that then leads to its deterioration. These mechanisms of rendering inequality invisible are potentiated by internalization into Triqui forms of pride. The structural violence inherent to segregated labor on the farm is so effectively erased precisely because its disappearance takes place at the level of the body, and is thus understood to be natural.

RESISTANCES AND REFUSALS

Though powerful, the normalization and naturalization of these social hierarchies and health disparities are incomplete. Very rarely, I caught glimpses of spaces in which people did not entirely accept their own social location and instead offered insightful critiques.

The bank through which the Tanaka farm paid the pickers had a policy that berry pickers had to wait in a separate line at the bank on paydays and let all the other customers go first. Every Friday, there was a long line of Mexican migrant workers spreading out into the parking lot, waiting up to several hours, watching as each white customer who came to the door was escorted to the front of the line. Though I was paid by the farm as a berry picker each week, the bank personnel repeatedly tried to escort me to the front of the line when I arrived on payday with my Triqui companions. While this practice implicitly teaches white and Triqui people the social hierarchy present in the valley, a few white area residents told me that this was not fair, and at least one asked the bank to change its policy. In a minor way, I saw this awareness of inequality also when neighbors of the farm camp admitted that sometimes they felt "guilty" or "bad" when they drove by the camp on their way home. Even more rarely, people in the United States and Mexico employed some degree of broader social analysis. The owner of a small bed-and-breakfast near one of the migrant camps in the Skagit Valley explained many of the international forces constraining farmers in the area. He clarified this statement by saying that if the state of Washington were to raise the minimum wage too far, growers might choose to mechanize, costing thousands of picking jobs and making the situation worse for migrant laborers. He rightfully concluded, "It's very complex."

In San Miguel, Pepsi is delivered weekly by a large semi driving through the dirt roads of town, whereas Mexican Rey sodas are sold in small, Triqui-owned *tiendas.* Some families are beginning to buy huge flats of Pepsi bottles for fiestas like baptisms or weddings, instead of buying Rey from their neighbors. However, there is a common rumor in town among all age groups that Pepsi and Coca-Cola are made with human blood. I asked Samuel's niece, one of the family members with whom I lived in San Miguel, to explain how the blood was made into soda. She explained that people are ground up, alive and screaming, into a bloody pulp in the factories of these companies and put into their drinks. Although some of her friends drink Pepsi, she did not want to drink human blood and therefore drank only Rey sodas at fiestas.

Using a "hermeneutic of generosity,"[27] there are many ways in which multinational corporations thrive while grinding up living human beings, especially those who are poor and marginalized. They produce unhealthy products in environmentally unsustainable ways in factories that often have poor working conditions, market them primarily to the global poor and form large conglomerations of soda brands that are all sold cheaply, functionally driving smaller producers out of business. This rumor, then, critiques and leads to practical resistance to unequal and harmful economic structures. Nonetheless, Pepsi and Coca-Cola continue to grow, most smaller companies close, and there is a developing trend to drink Pepsi in San Miguel.

THE STRIKE AND THE MEMO

One morning late in my second summer on the Tanaka farm, the strawberry pickers walked out of the field on strike. The strike was not planned ahead of time. Rather, after learning that the pay per weight was being lowered and that several people were being fired because they had not picked the minimum weight the day before, a few Triqui pickers began to whistle. More and more people joined in whistling until everyone walked out of the field. Afterward, my Triqui friends explained to me that whistling—which I had heard and wondered about while picking

Strawberry picker strike, Tanaka Brothers Farm. Photo by Rob Mercatante.

blueberries in the midst of a cold rain the summer before—communicates discontent. In the days leading up to the strike, the pickers were becoming increasingly anxious because the berries had become progressively fewer and smaller as the summer wore on, and it was therefore becoming more and more difficult to make the minimum weight. The strawberries become fewer and smaller later in the summer primarily because each of the fields has already been picked earlier in the summer and also because the plants simply produce progressively fewer berries at the end of the season. In this context, firing several people who had not been able to pick the minimum the day before was seen as unreasonable and lowering the pay per weight was considered entirely unjust.

With the help of Jaime, the social worker who introduced me to Triqui families on my first visit to the Skagit, the pickers created a document listing over twenty grievances about the working conditions, from low pay to explicit racist statements from supervisors, from lack of lunch breaks to unfair promotions of mestizo and Latino workers

Strawberry pickers on strike reading the list of grievances. Photo by Rob Mercatante.

over indigenous pickers. Over the next few days, several executives and a dozen pickers held meetings to discuss the grievances, with Jaime and I translating between English and Spanish. The executives became visibly surprised and upset at the descriptions of explicit racist treatment and differential promotions on the farm. They promptly instructed all the crop managers to pass along the message to treat all workers with respect. More important to my Triqui companions, thirty-minute lunch breaks and slightly higher pay were instituted. The pickers considered this a success. They called the document a *contrato* (contract) and each of the dozen picker representatives signed it according to Triqui legal tradition. Samuel's uncle, one of the picker representatives, passed the signed contrato to John Tanaka for the farm executives to sign as well. According to Triqui legal practices, the contrato would become a binding agreement between the signatories. John Tanaka re-printed the grievances, signed the paper, and filed it as a "memo." The following summer, the lunch breaks and higher pay were silently rescinded, though some of my Triqui friends feel that they continued to be treated with more respect.

The strike, the temporary nature of its results, and the conversion of the contrato into a memo highlight the complicated nature of power and resistance on the farm. The executives demand that all workers are treated with respect at the same time that their real anxieties over farm survival prohibit them from effectively addressing the primary, economic concerns of the pickers in a lasting way. The increasingly harsh market in which the farm operates coerces these growers to remain complicit with a system of labor segregation harmful to the pickers.

SOCIAL CHANGE AND SOCIAL REPRODUCTION

Though there are small signs of awareness of unequal social structures and their detrimental effects, the ethnic-citizenship hierarchy in U.S. agriculture and its correlated hierarchy of suffering are largely unquestioned and unchallenged by all those involved. The normalization and naturalization of farm hierarchies, which foster their reproduction, take place on many levels through various symbolic and physical means. The ethnic-citizenship segregation itself as well as language and social network differences allow certain individuals to become insulting and racist with relative impunity while others attempt to be ethical and respectful. For example, Shelly's racist attitudes toward indigenous Oaxacans and her actions enforcing farm segregation appear to be invisible to the ethical farm executives, perhaps because she is married to Rob Tanaka. The explicitly racist treatment of indigenous pickers, conducted in Spanish, by Betty's mother, who is a crew boss, go unnoticed by the farm executives and crop managers largely because they occur in a language other than English.

The working and living conditions of migrant farmworkers are hidden from public view and justified by assumptions about what kinds of housing and jobs different people deserve. Metaphors of dirt and terms of reference exclude them from the category "American" and belie a supposition that they are out of place in the United States. Migrant laborers are blamed for their own suffering, often using the metaphor of "want," as well as for the suffering of those categorized as "American." Finally, and perhaps most effectively, Triqui people are understood to deserve their location in the social hierarchy because of what are perceived to be their natural, ethnic, bodily characteristics. This naturalization of oppression and racism is particularly efficient and unquestioned because it is invisibly effected at the level of the body. In order for there to be an effective, broad coalition of people working to change the unhealthy inequalities in U.S. agriculture, we must first see such hierarchies as socially and historically constructed and malleable. Only then might we be able to imagine symbolic, economic, political and interpersonal means of working toward equality and dismantling the structures that produce social suffering.

SEVEN Conclusion

CHANGE, PRAGMATIC SOLIDARITY, AND BEYOND

POSSIBILITIES FOR HOPE AND CHANGE

Early in my fieldwork, I began to notice the segregation of workers in U.S. agriculture into a hierarchy of perceived ethnicity and citizenship. I observed economic inequalities and social hierarchies producing displacement, migration, sickness, and suffering, including among my Triqui companions Abelino, Crescencio, and Bernardo. As my fieldwork progressed, I became discouraged by what appeared to be a depressing situation without any possibility for change.

I noticed several ways in which social and health inequalities had become considered normal, natural, and justified. Naturalization occurred via the racialization of bodies and the perception that certain categories of ethnic bodies belonged in certain occupational positions. The normalization of social inequalities occurred through the hiddenness of certain classes of bodies as well as through the subtle meanings of body position.

At the same time, Bourdieu's concept of symbolic violence incorporates a measure of internalization, which could be seen in Triqui conceptions of pride that may partially function to justify their position in the occupational hierarchy. In addition, the medical gaze of clinicians in the field of migrant health did not allow them to see social inequalities or how these inequalities produced sickness. Instead, they often inadvertently blamed the suffering of their patients on the patients themselves—their behavior, culture, or racialized biology—and consequently recommended interventions inadvertently complicit with the harmful social structure. The naturalization of social and health inequalities was especially effective because it took place at the level of the self-evidently natural, the body. The structural nature of these inequalities is illuminated by the fact that even idealistic and ethical farmers and clinicians operate within a gray zone that neutralizes and sometimes even reverses their efforts at ethical action. The importance of political economic structures was highlighted further by the lack of choice experienced by my Triqui companions as they made the mortally dangerous yet necessary trek through the border desert.

This multiply determined structure of inequalities seemed to explain everything and made it especially difficult for me to imagine social, economic, political, and health change. Whether hope is based in the unknown, the unnameable as described by Crapanzano,[1] or the practice of leveraging knowledge for symbolic, political, and material change as described by Miyazaki,[2] the harmful and overdetermined social and symbolic structures at work in U.S.-Mexico migration seemed to leave little room for hope.

Pierre Bourdieu, whose concepts inform much of the analysis in this book, is often described as a theorist of social reproduction. Scholars use his theories to analyze the ways in which social and symbolic structures lead to the reproduction of the whole social system, including its inequalities and hierarchies. While his theoretical framework is often understood as an overdetermined, all-explaining metanarrative of reproduction with no possibility for change, there are several places in which Bourdieu focuses explicitly on the potential for transformation. The possibility of social change can be seen especially in his concepts of habitus and symbolic violence. For Bourdieu, habitus indicates the historically accreted dispositions and habits of the body. In other words, the bodily comportments of one's habitus are issued forth and added in layers by the social world over time. Thus one's habitus can change over time if one's position in a particular social world or that dimension of the social world itself, which Bourdieu calls a *field,* changes. In addition, something new and unpredictable is produced inevitably when one's habitus comes in contact with a field it does not match. If one's habitus has developed in a particular social position or social world and one later occupies a new position or a new field, this encounter will bring about transformation. Those who study im/migration should be especially aware of this site for potential change.

The concept of symbolic violence is another important location for change according to Bourdieu. In "Gender and Symbolic Violence," he argues against the possibility of social change solely through the "immediate effect of the 'raising of consciousness.'"[3] This directly contradicts a common expectation in public health and medicine that education alone will bring about direct health-related—including behavioral—change. Rather, Bourdieu argues that social change occurs "through a radical transformation of the social conditions of production of the dispositions." In the same section, he writes "a relation of domination . . . depends profoundly, *for its perpetuation or transformation,* on the perpetuation or transformation of the structures of which those dispositions are the product (and in particular on the structure of a market in symbolic goods . . .)."[4] Bourdieu indicates that there are strong mutual relationships among social structures, the bodily dispositions produced by them, and the symbolic structures reinforcing them. These relationships perpetuate or transform power-imbued social relations. Changes on the level of social structures (e.g., immigration and labor policy) will produce new embodied dispositions and symbols (metaphors, stereotypes, meanings, connotations—such as "illegal" vs. "legal" and "unskilled" vs. "skilled") at the same time that changes in symbols will lead to transformations in bodily actions and, therefore, in the social structures themselves (e.g., votes and the resultant policies). With this fuller picture of Bourdieu's theories, there may be room for hope—in Crapanzano's or Miyazaki's senses—related to the feed-forward loop of transformation through social structures, bodily dispositions, and symbolic meanings.

Many scholars, from Bourdieu to Foucault to Gramsci, have asked what the role of the scholar should be in the world. Considering Gramsci's proposal of the organic intellectual[5] and Bourdieu's multidirectional understanding of structure and symbol may lead us to consider the denaturalization of social suffering. If we social scientists are to research, theorize, and confront socially structured suffering, we must join with others in a broad effort to denaturalize social inequalities, uncovering linkages between symbolic violence and suffering.[6] In this way, the lenses of perception as well as the social inequalities they reinforce can be recognized, challenged, and transformed. This book endeavors to denaturalize ethnic and citizenship inequalities in agricultural labor, health disparities in the clinic, and biologized and racialized inequities in society at large. Exploration of the ways in which symbolic violence regarding Mexican migrant laborers legitimates and reinforces the fatal conditions of the U.S.-Mexico border will be crucial to challenging the further militarization of the borderlands. And in order to imagine more effective and contextual health care, we will need to explore how greater social structural analysis can be incorporated in medical training. More broadly, we social scientists must turn our attention to understanding and theorizing the ways in which certain classes of people come to be written off, forgotten, or understood to deserve their particular forms of suffering. Ethnography—with its thick description and nuanced analysis—is an especially important methodology for understanding the multilayered meanings and vertical slices of power that make up social and cultural life, including its inequalities and justifications.[7] As C. Wright Mills has been quoted as saying, "Theorists and methodologists—get to work!"

IM/MIGRATION STUDIES, BINARIES, AND MEANINGS

There are several terms in immigration studies that can misrepresent and justify social and health inequalities. To begin, the words *migrant, migrant worker,* and *farmworker* are used to denote the primarily undocumented Mexican people who work harvesting fruit and vegetables in the United States.[8] As discussed earlier, many people who use the words *immigration* and *migration* assume freely chosen movement between distinct and disconnected places and communities. For my Triqui companions, however, migration is an experience of forced movement for survival that involves what might be called a complex transnational circuit of people and capital.[9] The relatives of a young Triqui girl, whether in person in California or via telephone from Oaxaca, weigh in on the decision of whether to permit her to marry. The few houses with gas stoves instead of wood fires and the several houses with concrete floors instead of dirt floors in the hometown of my Triqui companions have been built with monetary remittances from relatives in the United States. There are important, everyday interconnections among places and people in the Triqui experience of migration.

Many who write of "immigration" and "migration" assume (and politicians often demand) "assimilation" or "acculturation," the slow erasure of difference through the adoption of mainstream cultural practices by im/migrants. Furthermore, scholars in diaspora studies[10] remind us that identities and practices of those who immigrate are "hybridized," both maintained and transformed through their interactions with other people and places. For example, some young Triqui men are beginning to propose government-sanctioned church weddings to the women they want to marry instead of the traditional bridewealth practices in order to avoid the potential misunderstandings and legal ramifications described in chapter 5. While it would be ethnocentric to demand assimilation, it would be unrealistic to assume that the culture of migrants is entirely unaffected by the conditions in which they move.

Many of the terms used to refer to migrant workers hold strong class- and race-based connotations. "Farmworker" should precisely apply to everyone who works on a farm. However, the owners, managers, checkers, administrative assistants, crop supervisors, crew bosses, and field bosses are never called farmworkers in practice. On the farm, in farm-related research, and in common usage, they are instead referred to by their job titles. "Farmworker" applies only to those workers who harvest fruit and vegetables by hand. Though in the past this term applied to white and black U.S. citizen pickers, often from the Midwest "dust bowl," this term is used currently to denote only migrant pickers from Latin America. Notably, this phrase is not used to refer to the white teenage berry picking crews on the Tanaka farm, though they engage in exactly the same work as their Mexican counterparts. These workers are instead represented by the terms "the white crew" or "the teen crew."

In addition, the term "migrant," as well as its derivatives "migrant worker" and "migrant laborer," seems linguistically to apply to anyone who migrates and works, anyone who moves among different locations or different nations as they work. However, wealthy people who migrate for work, like the businesspeople described by Aihwa Ong,[11] or the architects from Mexico City who designed the new UCSF research campus, are never represented by these terms. They are called "international businesspeople," sometimes "diasporic people," or sometimes simply by their job title and hometown, such as "architects from Mexico City." Thus "migrant" carries distinct lower-class connotations. In addition, lower-class people who migrate from Canada or Europe to work on farms or in factories are not called "migrants." They are usually called something akin to "temporary workers from Canada" or simply "factory workers from Canada." Thus "migrant" also has strong ethnic connotations. In common current usage in the United States, "migrants" are only poor, Latin American laborers. On a related note, migrant farmworkers are often referred to as "unskilled labor." However, we must interrogate this categorization, as well as this use of the concept of skill and who gets to decide which kinds of skills count. After many days of trying as hard as I could—having attempted multiple body positions and psychological maneuvers—to pick as fast as I possibly could, I inevitably fell significantly behind the Mexican migrant strawberry pickers around me. In this context, I recognized quickly that I was an unskilled laborer and that my Mexican companions were quite skilled, with precise techniques for picking quickly and sustaining this pace. The use of these terms involves inequalities in respect based on class and ethnicity. Instead of being given respect for their specific work title and their home country, they are merged into one category of lower-class Latin American people.[12]

Many in the news media refer to undocumented migrants as "illegal aliens." First, the word *illegal* is an adjective modifying the migrant, as though it were a characteristic of her or him as a person. Yet, as the division chief of the Border Patrol in Washington State pointed out to me, these migrants are more hardworking and law-abiding than most U.S. citizens. He stated that they drive the speed limit, they pay their taxes, they work very hard, and they avoid any activities that would draw attention from the police. In fact, the division chief explained to me that Social Security in the United States would have gone bankrupt years ago if it were not for the undocumented workers paying taxes into it without collecting from it. He went on to say that every once in a while, there is a Mexican migrant who commits a crime, just like there are U.S. citizens who commit crimes, and these undocumented migrants are sought and deported. Otherwise, he said, he is not interested in prosecuting people who are working hard on U.S. farms. The only illegal thing they did was cross the border without the appropriate documentation. This, in his estimation, does not make them wholly "illegal."[13] He prefers the term "undocumented," which is more precise and less a trigger of anti-immigrant fear. Second, the word *alien* connotes extreme difference, unbridgeable alterity, and often triggers fear.

In addition, there are clear inconsistencies in the dichotomies commonly employed in immigration studies: "refugee" versus "migrant," "political" versus "economic," "forced" versus "voluntary."[14] The terms *refugee, political migrant,* and *forced migrant* are related. In order for one to be considered a refugee and receive asylum privileges in the United States, one must prove, among other things, that he or she was forced to migrate for political reasons. Thus the opposing terms in the dichotomies above function as characteristics justifying exclusion from legal refugee status and the economic and political rights it brings. The Triqui people I work with are all considered "voluntary" "economic migrants" within traditional migration studies and U.S. government discourse. However, as the ethnographic data show clearly, their migration is in fact forced, and there is no valid separation between the political and the economic forces impelling them. In order to survive, Triqui people are forced to leave their homes, cross a potentially fatal border, and work in an inhospitable environment. The economic and political conditions forcing them to migrate are caused directly by international policies and military actions that lead to global, regional, and local inequalities and suffering.

Finally, the dichotomy "language"/"dialect" must be questioned. The word *dialect* precisely indicates a minor variety of a major language, usually limited geographically to one area. A dialect is not considered a language itself but rather a derivative of one. Triqui and other Latin American native languages are commonly referred to as dialects. The apple crop manager on the Tanaka farm believed this implication about indigenous languages so much that he told me, "Oaxacans speak different dialects of Spanish. If I listen really closely and pay attention, I can understand it." However, linguistically, Mixtec and Triqui are entirely unrelated to Spanish. They are not Romance languages. They are both their own languages, they are tonal languages, and they show a distant past relation to each other but not to Spanish. They are related much like Spanish and English or English and Latin are related. Instead of understanding them as languages that were spoken in the area long before the Spanish conquest, calling them dialects implies that they developed as derivatives of the real language, Spanish. This misrepresentation supports the prevalent attitude that indigenous Mexicans are less important, even less *Mexican,* than mestizo Mexicans.

THE WAR OF POSITION THROUGH WORDS

In *The Prison Notebooks,* Antonio Gramsci describes his concept of hegemony, the phenomenon of one group or class of people, primarily the capital-owning class, coming to control the economic and symbolic means of production.[15] Very briefly, hegemony exists with consent from the dominated classes, though it is not in their own economic or social interest. However, Gramsci indicates that hegemony and its requisite consent are never total.[16] There are always struggles over economic structures—ownership, redistribution, regulation—as well as symbolic structures—representations and meanings. Gramsci differentiates between two primary means for achieving control of a society. The first is an all-out military "war of manoeuvre," and the second is a subtler "war of position."[17] "War of position," in Gramsci's terms, refers to the ongoing struggle over meanings and cultural forms, which in turn affect political and economic structures.

For example, the meanings attached to Latin American migrant workers with the use of terms like "illegal aliens" have produced fear and correlated justification of legislated exclusion from health care, education, and other services. The wording of California's Proposition 187 provides a perfect example: "[Californians] have suffered and are suffering personal injury and damage caused by the criminal conduct of illegal aliens in this state."[18] Quesada states that the language of this so-called Save Our State initiative successfully promoted division and fear, validating the suffering of (white) Californians while erasing that of Mexican migrant laborers.[19] These representations have led to real legal and material hardships for those against whom they were directed. While anti-immigrant organizations have utilized the tactics above, others (including social scientists) have attempted to portray the humanity as well as the indispensable, difficult, and skilled work of migrant farmworkers.

In the United States and most other postindustrial nations, military wars of force are not officially permitted (though the militarization and criminalization of the inner city and the borderlands, among other phenomena, could be considered precisely wars of force). In these societies, struggles related to hegemony occur primarily through wars of position. In order to bring about political and material change regarding such issues as immigrant rights and worker rights, then, we must engage in struggles over the manners in which immigrant workers are represented and perceived.[20] These representations and perceptions lead to associated legal and economic inclusions, exclusions, liberations, and violence. While acting at this level of discourse and perception has real, material and social effects, it is only one level on which strategic action is necessary. To be effective, as suggested by Gramsci and Bourdieu, an academic critique of the symbolic order must be accompanied by other forms of solidarity on material and structural levels.

PRAGMATIC SOLIDARITY AND BEYOND ON THE FARM

"Pragmatic solidarity" is the phrase used by the physician and anthropologist Paul Farmer to encourage his readers to join in practical ways with the struggles of oppressed people.[21] The academic project of denaturalizing social inequities must be accompanied by efforts at all levels of a micro to macro continuum. On the farm, pragmatic solidarity could mean such things as explicitly including pickers in English classes, improving pesticide safety education and decreasing pesticide usage, and developing fairer means of employee hiring and advancement. Over the past several years, the farm has begun transitioning several fields of blueberries to be certified organic. While this could hold great potential health benefit for blueberry pickers, the farm has been required by its organic label to change each of these fields, once certified as organic, to "machine pick." Caught in a harmful irony, my Triqui companions continue to pick in pesticide-covered fields while machines pick in those that are pesticide-free.

When farm executives and managers asked my advice on what should be done to improve the living and working conditions of the pickers, I offered to translate so they could ask farmworkers that question directly. One manager took me up on the offer. More often than anything else, my Triqui companions asked for gravel to be put in the roadways and English classes to be offered for the pickers. The gravel could keep the dirt from the roadways out of the shacks and food. Many pickers requested that English classes be offered on an evening after work, preferably located in one of the camps.

The farm managers responded to these requests by mowing the grass over the septic tank draining field, which they called "the soccer field." This was done despite the fact that the Oaxacan people on the farm wanted to play basketball regularly and did not show any interest in soccer. During my second summer on the farm, an ad hoc group of area residents collected a few hundred dollars for the graveling of the camp driveways and local college students offered to help put it in place. A group of Americorps volunteers offered to give free English as a Second Language classes in the camps once a week after the pickers returned from work. These classes were offered one summer and not repeated the following summer. These efforts toward pragmatic solidarity on the farm were helpful for farmworkers at the same time that they repeatedly pointed out the need for solidarity that moves beyond only the pragmatic, practical, or programmatic.

One of the residents who lived above the farm labor camp where I lived hosted my birthday the second summer of my fieldwork. She supported my inviting people from different parts of my life, including my mother from eastern Washington, my friends from local migrant and environmental advocacy organizations and PFLAG (Parents and Friends of Lesbians and Gays), my friend who kept daily vigil holding signs in front of the county courthouse (including my favorite, a handwritten "Don't Bomb Anyone" sign), and several of the Triqui families with whom I had become friends. During the birthday picnic of party snack platters made by my white friends mixed with homemade tacos made by my Triqui friends, people from different backgrounds played catch, petted bunnies on the porch of the house, and attempted to communicate with broken "Spanglish" and body language. During this afternoon, the hostess of the party began an intermittent ongoing friendship with three of the children in one of the Triqui families. They began spending afternoons together regularly in the labor camp or at her house with her bunnies, teaching each other English and Spanish.

As she got to know these children, this woman spearheaded an effort to stop the pollution of the stream running through the labor camp, in which the children often played on hot summer days. She became notorious enough among some of the ranchers that she received threats. In addition, she began writing articles in the local newspaper. Some of them were simply fun, human interest stories about gardening or local animals. However, she was fired shortly after her article challenging the use of the phrase "illegal alien" led to numerous complaints from other county residents. When I inquired with the editorial staff of the newspaper about her being fired after her well-written critique of the problematic phrase, I was told that letting her go had nothing to do with that article and the responses it triggered but rather that "we like to change up the column writers from time to time to be fair." This woman has since started her own blog, through which she attempts to uncover and confront questionable current affairs in the area. In these ways, human relationships and connections have led to local forms of solidarity that go beyond the pragmatic to challenge power structures and representations that are harmful to migrant farmworkers.

CRITICAL PUBLIC HEALTH AND LIBERATION MEDICINE

Chapter 4 explored the suffering of Triqui migrant laborers and the health disparities related to institutional racism and global economic inequalities. Chapter 5 discussed the medicalization of conjugated oppression, socially structured work injury, and political torture. By "medicalization," I mean to indicate the defining of an entity as primarily or solely medical while stripping it of its political, social, historical, and economic context.[22] By reducing suffering to its biomedical and behavioral components, health workers deny the forces that cause it and, therefore, lose the opportunity to confront it effectively. Due to the lenses through which health professionals have been trained to see their patients, they are unable to work alongside those who are suffering in order to prevent sickness through political, economic, and social change. These health professionals inadvertently use a narrow, reductionist definition of their own roles as health care providers. Scheper-Hughes writes, "Medicine is, among other things, a technical practice for 'rationalizing' human misery and for containing it to safe quarters, keeping it 'in its place,' and so cutting off its potential for generating an active critique."[23]

In another article, however, Scheper-Hughes discusses what she calls the "rebel body." She uses this term to point out the ways the body offers critiques of "social dis-ease" and, thereby, resists hierarchy when no other recourse is available.[24] More explicitly, she writes that illness "can contain the elements necessary for critique and liberation."[25] How might the practice of medicine change if clinicians paid attention to the social critiques presented by the suffering bodies in our offices? How do those of us in public health and medicine preclude the effective treatment and prevention of health problems by defining them out of context and treating them with mere Band-Aids, or worse? How would the role of health professionals be defined if we took seriously our call to relieve and prevent suffering while also remembering the structural forces fundamentally producing this suffering?

If health professionals responded to sickness by treating not only its current manifestations but also its social, economic, and political causes, we could create a realistically critical public health and a "liberation medicine."[26] This latter term alludes to liberation theology, in which a reflective engagement with those who are poor and suffering leads to new ways of thinking and practicing theology in order to achieve social justice. While there is genuine need for the skills of narrowly trained, competent biomedical physicians, I am convinced this is not enough.

As shown by the health care experiences of Abelino, Crescencio, and Bernardo, medical skills practiced without recognition of the social structures causing sickness are doomed to address only the downstream, biological and behavioral inputs into disease. This leads to ineffective health care at best and complicit, injurious health care at worst. Far from being unrealistic to encourage physicians to recognize and engage the causes of their patients' suffering, this commitment falls clearly within the model of biopsychosocial health purportedly subscribed to by health professional schools nationwide.

In the current version of this model in medical and public health education, the biological receives the bulk of attention, the psychological is reduced to behavioral risk factors and takes up a small minority of time, and the social is limited to the relational and mentioned in passing if at all. Adding social structural analysis to medical and public health education would move toward a more realistic and balanced version of the biopsychosocial model already explicitly claimed in contemporary health-professional training. More important, this would provide future physicians and public health professionals with the lenses to recognize the societal critiques available in sicknesses and their distributions. With such an awareness of the structurally violent social context of disease, health professionals could move effectively toward acknowledging, treating, and preventing suffering.

At the same time, the health care system in the United States is in dire need of economic restructuring. Currently, the wealthy who have no preexisting conditions can afford high-quality health care, while the poor and sick are relegated to hoping for and negotiating whatever health care safety net might exist in their area. The neoliberal form of capitalism structuring health care in the United States has led to those with the highest burden of sickness being simultaneously those with the least access to care. As many public health and medical social science scholars have shown, this system is not working. The United States spends more per capita on health care than any other postindustrial country, yet has the worst health outcomes. It is time we learned from our mistakes and worked toward a universal health care system based on equal access to high-quality patient care instead of corporate profit. A very promising health care structure for these goals is the single payer system, which has been modeled successfully in much of Europe. The Affordable Care Act so controversial during Barack Obama's first term as president is a promising, important step in the right direction, though it still leaves forms of inequality, including the exclusion of most immigrants and migrants.

Beyond treating individual patients more effectively, we can also begin to practice critical public health and liberation medicine by working alongside our patients for positive social change. Rudolf Virchow, a nineteenth-century German physician-pathologist, is considered the founder of the field of social medicine. He believed that the calling of health professionals to work with those who are suffering included seeking healthier forms of society. He wrote, "Politics is nothing more than medicine on a grand scale."[27] As a tool to bring such social analysis into clinical work, Quesada, Bourgois, and Hart have proposed a "structural vulnerability" scale to be used in the routine patient interview and hospital admission process, though it could easily be expanded for use in public health practice.[28] Acknowledging the social context of suffering, we can begin to envision solutions with those who are sick and move beyond a solely pragmatic version of solidarity to work toward positive, lasting democracy, equality, and health.

As discussed earlier, immigrant health research often holds strong assumptions of "acculturation" and "assimilation." Many scholars utilize these frameworks to develop statistical scales—based sometimes on as little as which language the individual speaks at home—and compare these scales with various health outcomes. Many authors blame poor health outcomes on a lack of acculturation or assimilation, utilizing poorly defined constructs such as "religiosity" or "machismo" as a proxy for culture. Others place the blame on too much acculturation or assimilation, evinced by such things as worsening diet. Regardless of the specifics of the research article, these frameworks include troubling assumptions of a unidirectional move from a "traditional" culture toward a culture of the assumed modern, unmarked white American middle class.[29] Health researchers must move beyond such antipolitical analyses of health as based only in individual or cultural behaviors and instead begin to recognize and point out the unequal social, economic, and political structures that produce poor health outcomes in the first place.

SOLIDARITY FROM SOCIETY TO GLOBE

In U.S. society at large, possibilities for solidarity include such things as promoting and buying the products of farms that treat workers fairly, lobbying the government to change immigration and border policies and practices, developing experiential education programs working against the exclusion of those considered different, and restructuring education and health care so that they are accessible for everyone. I hope that the field notes in chapter 1 expressed not only the mortal danger and fear inherent in the experience of crossing the border but also the incredibly dire circumstances making this trek necessary for many people. The ethnography shows that "closing the border" is unlikely to stop people from seeking a means for themselves and their families to survive. Instead, our focus should turn to the social and economic policies forcing groups of people to risk their lives in this way in the first place. The Domestic Fair Trade Working Group has attempted to launch a fair trade label in the United States, much like that available in Europe. The United Farm Workers and the Piñeros y Campesinos Unidos organize workers for better working conditions and treatment. Supporters of the Dream Act call for equal access to education for everyone in the United States, including immigrants. Supporters of education in California and other states demand the re-funding of public education from elementary school to university. Organizations like Physicians for a National Health Plan, the National Physicians Alliance, and others support universal health care for all. In Arizona, organizations like No More Deaths, the Samaritans, Healing Our Borders, Borderlinks, Border Action Network, and Humane

Borders seek to stop migrant death on the border by offering medical care to migrants in distress, placing water barrels in especially dangerous areas, and raising awareness through seminars on border issues. Other organizations, such as Community to Community and Skagitonians to Preserve Farmland, work to develop community conversations about and awareness of the importance of the future of agriculture in the United States. In the Skagit Valley, the People's Seminary and Tierra Nueva offer seminars in which area residents hear from farm owners, pickers, and Border Patrol agents in order to form more realistic perceptions of Mexican migration and farmwork.

American society gains much from migrant laborers and gives little back beyond criminalization, stress, and injury.[30] This dishonest relationship must change. As discussed briefly in chapter 6, the Triqui people I know told me repeatedly that being given legal temporary worker status would be their first hope. They have explained that they want to keep their homes in Oaxaca and work in the United States one season at a time. Ironically, the U.S. government's policies making it more risky and dangerous to cross the border since 9/11 mean that currently more migrant laborers stay in the United States for several years at a time before going home instead of remaining only during harvest seasons. My Triqui companions support a fair temporary worker system that does not increase the power differential between employers and employees, as any plan linking permission to be in the country to one specific work contract would likely do. Most of the Triqui people I know would prefer U.S. residency or temporary permission to work in the United States while keeping their Mexican citizenship in order to maintain their homes with their extended relatives in Oaxaca. At the same time, a path to citizenship, as included in Barack Obama's proposed immigration reform, is an important option for many immigrants. In addition, this seems only fair in the United States, a country in which all other immigrant groups through history (including European settlers and invaders and their progeny) have received this opportunity.

Globally, and perhaps most important, the formation of broad coalitions of people is necessary in order to envision and work for a more equitable international economy such that people would not be forced to leave their homes to migrate in the first place.[31] This includes, among other efforts, the campaigns of Global Exchange and other organizations to defeat the Central American Free Trade Agreement, activities of individuals and movements toward the dismantling and reformation of international economic institutions like the World Trade Organization and the International Monetary Fund, and myriad movements promoting local and independent producers instead of multinational corporations. Strong support of local (not to mention natural, organic, sustainable, non–genetically modified, fair wage, and non-exploitative) producers is especially important in the area of agriculture and the food we all eat. Moving toward increasing international equity requires that we uncover the hidden workings of hegemony such that the people and corporations in power cannot promote their own interests unequally. Broad coalitions of people must actively engage in the war of position via not only words and representations but also concrete legal, political, civil, and economic actions. All these means are necessary to ameliorate social suffering, confront its naturalization, and promote health, equality, and genuine democracy. With such a multifaceted approach, we can move toward a future in which our Triqui companions have access to humane and healthy living and working conditions and no longer have to migrate across a deadly border in order to provide us with fresh fruit in exchange for their broken bodies.

APPENDIX On Ethnographic Writing and Contextual Knowledge

(OR, WHY THIS BOOK HAS NO METHODS SECTION)

Occupying the worlds of anthropology and the health sciences simultaneously, I often find myself translating between two languages. I write in both languages, depending on which audience I address. Sometimes this translation leads to new insights and theories, sometimes to a loss of nuance or precision. Often, I am asked by public health and medical researchers some version of the following: How should we evaluate anthropology? How do we know if it is rigorous? How do we know if it is reliable, reproducible, valid? My answer is usually a variation of, "First read the ethnography, then think about whether the analysis makes sense or not." To an anthropologist, this seems straightforward. However, scholars in the health sciences are trained to consume academic work in a specific, prescribed form.

In the health sciences, we are trained to expect a background section on the importance of the research question; a methods section summarizing the ways in which the investigator accessed research subjects and collected and analyzed data; a results section in which the data and metrics of significance are presented; and a conclusion or discussion section in which the author interprets and theorizes the results. This standardization of structure offers certain benefits: speed of finding specific desired information; ease of comparison among different articles and authors; and the ability to synthesize the information efficiently when presented in the expected order. However, such standardization of the literature carries drawbacks as well, specifically, decreased flexibility of presentation style to match the topic and argument, decreased overall narrative flow to keep the interest of the reader, and, perhaps most important, the erasure of the subjectivity and positionality of the author in the presentation of the design and interpretation of the research. This last drawback carries with it the problematic implication that the findings and analysis are entirely acontextual and universal.

In cultural and medical anthropology in general, our writing is judged primarily on the strength of the theoretical analysis and the depth of the ethnography. Most anthropologists do not enumerate our methods in a separate section but rather write such that the circumstances through which we came to our observations make up part of the narrative. The long-term immersion of ethnographic fieldwork also helps to break down preconceived ideas and assumptions, opening new analytical and theoretical possibilities to the ethnographer and the reader. The simultaneous presentation of ethnographer and "Other" in the writing allows the reader to understand in clear language not only our methods but also our positionality. With a clear reflexive presentation of the social categories occupied by the anthropologist and how these may affect both our perceptions and the ways in which the other subjects of our ethnography respond to us and our questions, readers may make their own informed interpretations and analyses. Similar to the interwoven presentation of our methods, anthropological conclusions do not come packaged in sections separate from the ethnographic vignettes. Rather, the analyses and theorization are often woven throughout the ethnography in a manner that allows interpretation of ethnographic vignettes more directly and smoothly.

This interconnected manner of presenting ethnographic vignettes alongside both the circumstances under which those observations were made and the theoretical analyses of those vignettes not only allows for narrative flow but also invites readers to take stock actively and critically of the full context of the ethnography, its presentation and interpretation. This manner of writing is a reminder that the research was conducted by a particular human subject (or subjects) in particular social contexts. Thus this structure invites readers to be active participants in the interpretation not only of the ethnography but also of the author's interpretation itself. In these ways, readers are reminded (sometimes despite the author) that position, perspective, and context are always involved in the production of knowledge.

By design, this book has no methods section. (See Holmes 2006 for my attempt to translate anthropological methods for a health science audience.) Instead, my own positionality and the context and methods of my observations and analysis are presented interwoven in the ethnography. I hope this manner of ethnographic writing will invite the reader more fully and actively into the narrative as well as its analysis.

Notes

CHAPTER 1

1. The field notes (in italic in this chapter) have been edited to reduce redundancy and maximize flow while maintaining the authentic narrative as I typed and tape recorded during and immediately after the events.

2. The Triqui people are an indigenous Mexican group from the mountains of Oaxaca, Mexico, from the area commonly referred to as La Mixteca.

3. *Mestizos* (lit., "mixed") is used to refer to Mexicans of mixed indigenous and Spanish descent, often referred to simply as "regular Mexicans" or "Mexicans" in everyday language.

4. Marcus 1998.

5. The MULT (Movimiento de Unificación y Liberación Triqui) is a political movement of Triqui people in the state of Oaxaca.

6. Wolf 1957.

7. See Cornelius 2001, Green 2008, Massey et al., 2002 and *Migration News* 2003a for further discussions of border deaths.

8. One of the most powerful accounts is Ted Conover's *Coyote* (1987).

9. Burawoy 1976.

10. See Bandura 1997. See Massey et al. 2002, Portes and Bach 1985, and Wood 1982 for other critiques of the "push" and "pull" framework of migration.

11. Butler 2009. See also Chavez 2001, 2008; Grillo 1985; and Jain 2006 on the ways immigrants are framed.

12. See *Rural Migration News* 2003 and Stephen 2007 for further discussion of NAFTA and Oaxacan migration, as well as Edinger 1996 on migration from Oaxaca to the United States.

13. For a further description of the somatic, social, and historical categorization of bodies as racial, see Weismantel and Eisenman, 1988.

14. Althusser 1982.

15. Bourdieu and Wacquant 1992.

16. See Bourgois 1995: 11–18.

17. See Nader 1972.

18. Primo Levi writes in *The Drowned and the Saved* of the *mitmensch,* the with-man, the human being who is personalized enough to be conceived of as real and, therefore, is able to invoke compassion and solidarity.

CHAPTER 2

1. For "pragmatic solidarity," see Farmer 1999.

2. See Clifford Geertz, "Deep Hanging Out," *New York Review of Books,* October 22, 1998.

3. *Gabacho* is the word commonly used in parts of Mexico to denote white Americans, much like the word *gringo.*

4. Like the Triqui, the Mixtec people are an indigenous group from La Mixteca of Oaxaca, Mexico.

5. There are times and spaces in which my Triqui companions consider themselves to be defined as, above all, "the poor." Interestingly, in this phrase they identified themselves as belonging to a social class before a category of ethnicity (Triqui), nationality (Mexican), citizenship status (undocumented), or many other potential identifiers. As seen throughout this book, these categories are inextricably linked in the farm labor hierarchy and are differentially employed depending on who is doing the identifying and in what context.

6. Scheper-Hughes 1992: 23.

7. Stoller 1997: xv.

8. Wacquant 2005. See Estroff 1985 and Farquhar 2002 for other examples of embodied anthropology.

9. Scheper-Hughes and Lock 1987.

10. Merleau-Ponty 1996.

11. *Chakuh'* is my transliteration of the Triqui word for "Bald-head." Triqui people often refer to one another by nicknames loosely related to the appearance

of their head. As mentioned earlier, my informant, Samuel, was referred to as "Goat-head" because of his goatee. Samuel's brother, who also lived in the same slum apartment in California, was referred to as "Sheep-head" because his hair was often messy and looked like sheep's wool.

12. Bourdieu and Wacquant 1992.

13. See the concept of the anthropologist as clerk of the records in Scheper-Hughes 1992. See also Berger and Mohr 1967.

14. *Migration News* 2003b.

15. *Migration News* 2002.

16. Espenshade 1995.

17. Frank et al. 2004; Kandula, Kersey, and Lurie 2004.

18. *Migration News* 2003a.

19. Ibid.

20. Ibid.

21. *Rural Migration News* 2003.

22. Ibid.

23. Ibid.

24. See Bacon 2004, Simon 1997, and Stephen 2007.

25. *Rural Migration News* 2003.

26. Marcos 1995.

27. E.g., Marcos 1995; Ejército Popular Revolucionario 2002.

28. Amnesty International 1986; Franco 2002; INS 1998.

29. E.g., Sassen 1998: chap. 3; Grillo 1985; Bustamante 1983; Quesada 1999.

30. McGuire and Georges 2003. See also Fox and Rivera-Salgado 2004.

31. Rothenberg 1998.

32. Engels 1958.

33. See Bourgois 1988; Eber 1995; Farmer 1992, 1997, 1999; Kleinman and Kleinman 1994; Scheper-Hughes 1992, 2002, 2003; Singer and Baer 1995. Wacquant (2004) points out potential analytical pitfalls in the overly generalized, nonspecific use of the term "structural violence." In order to avoid conflating different forms of violence, I use the phrase narrowly, staying close to Johan Galtung's (1969) as well as Scheper-Hughes and Bourgois's (2003) focus on political economic domination. The effects of structural domination are thus analyzed separately from, among other phenomena, everyday physical violence, armed political violence, and symbolic violence enacted with the complicity of the dominated (see Bourgois 2001). The phrase is helpful in indicating that social structures can do "peacetime" violence that has the same effects as other forms of violence, though on a different time scale (Engels 1958). In addition, I illustrate ethnographically the ways in which structural violence is enacted on every level of the farm's social hierarchy, not solely on the poorest or most marginalized.

34. See Bourdieu 1997, 2001.

35. See Bourgois 1995, 2001; Scheper-Hughes and Bourgois 2003; Klinenberg 1999.

CHAPTER 3

Parts of this chapter were published in: Seth M. Holmes, "Parce qu'ils sont plus près du sol: L'invisibilisation de la souffrance sociale des cueilleurs de baies," *Actes de Recherche en Sciences Sociales* 165, no. 2 (2006): 28–51; Seth M. Holmes, "An Ethnographic Study of the Social Context of Migrant Health in the United States," *PLoS Medicine* 3, no. 10 (2006): e448; Seth M. Holmes, "Oaxacans Like to Work Bent Over: The Naturalization of Social Suffering among Berry Farm Workers," *International Migration* 45, no. 3 (2007): 39–68; Seth M. Holmes, "Structural Vulnerability and Hierarchies of Ethnicity and Citizenship on the Farm," *Medical Anthropology* 30, no. 4 (2011): 425–49.

1. See Besserer 2004, Hirsch 2003, Kearney 1998, and Rouse 2002 for discussions of transnationality.

2. In fact, one of the labor camps was mistaken for a collection of chicken coops by a housing developer who recently toured the valley.

3. Bourgois 1995; Holmes 2006a, 2006b.

4. Rothenberg's *With These Hands* (1988) is a notable exception, including a thick ethnographic description of growers as well as pickers.

5. See Bourgois 2001; Farmer 1992, 1997, 1999.

6. See Quesada, Hart, and Bourgois 2011.

7. Sakala 1987.

8. Cf. Orwell 1937. Other meanings of "dirt" are considered in chapter 6.

9. Ibid.

10. See chapter 6 for further discussion of the naturalization, normalization, and justification of social hierarchies on the farm.

11. See Bourgois 1995. See Stephen 2007 on the relationships between ethnic hierarchies in Mexico and the U.S.

12. See Bourdieu 1997.

13. Holmes 2006; Kandula, Kersey, and Lurie 2004; McGuire and Georges 2003; *Migration News* 2004; Mobed, Gold, and Schenker 1992; *Rural Migration News* 2005; Rust 1990; Sakala 1987; Slesinger 1992; Villarejo 2003.

14. See Wolfenstein 1955.

15. See Quesada, Hart, and Bourgois 2011.

16. As mentioned in chapter 1, I use ethnicity not as a genetic or biological given but as a biologized social phenomenon. I understand ethnicity to be akin to Althusser's (1982) use of the concept of interpellation, in which a human subject is

positioned by social and economic structures in a specific category or location within power hierarchies and simultaneously recognizes oneself and others to be a member of their specific categories. As will be considered further in chapter 6, I understand ethnicity and race, along with Weismantel and Eisenman (1998), to be simultaneously social and materializing. In this sense, the social position of a person (e.g., proximity to animals; access to dental care, showers, and soap) produces not only perceptions of that person as racialized in a certain way but also differential conditions under which her or his material body develops and changes over time.

17. Bourgois 1988. See Stephen's (2007) concept of "transborder lives," highlighting the ways indigenous Mexican migrants must cross multiple borders of class, race, nation state, etc.

18. The gendered nature of language not only affected the position of women and men in the farm hierarchy but also affected my ability to build rapport with them. While I learned many words and phrases in Triqui, I was unable to become fluent during my fieldwork, largely because the Triqui language has a difficult tonal nature and is not a written language. Unfortunately, my poor language skills in Triqui and the lack of fluency of some Triqui women in Spanish and English created a barrier to further direct interviews and conversations with them. Whenever possible, I attempt to counteract this difficulty with quotes from or observations related to both Triqui women and men.

19. Levi 1988.

20. Ibid., 40.

21. Scheper-Hughes and Bourgois 2003.

22. Sartre 1956.

23. Scheper-Hughes 1992.

24. These and other representations will be considered further in the conclusion.

CHAPTER 4

1. Scheper-Hughes and Bourgois 2004; Bourgois 2001.
2. Bourgois 2001: 8.
3. Galtung 1969; Farmer 1997.
4. Bourdieu 2001.
5. Scheper-Hughes 1992, 1997.
6. Bourgois 2001: 30.
7. See Quesada, Bourgois, and Hart 2011.
8. Kandula, Kersey, and Lurie 2004.
9. Villarejo 2003.
10. McGuire and Georges 2003.

11. Frank et al. 2004; Slesinger 1992.
12. Slesinger 1992.
13. Villarejo 2003.
14. Kandula, Kersey, and Lurie 2004.
15. Kauffold et al. 2004.
16. Bourdieu 1997.
17. Ibid.; Villarejo 2003.
18. Villarejo 2003.
19. McGuire and Georges 2003.
20. Ibid.
21. Frank et al. 2004.
22. Ibid.
23. Ibid.; Mobed, Gold, and Schenker 1992.
24. Frank et al. 2004.
25. Rust 1990; Slesinger 1992; Villarejo 2003.
26. Slesinger 1992; Mobed, Gold, and Schenker 1992.
27. Mobed, Gold, and Schenker 1992.
28. Ibid.; Sakala 1987.
29. Villarejo 2003.
30. *Rural Migration News* 2005.
31. Mobed, Gold, and Schenker 1992.
32. Sakala 1987.
33. Villarejo 2003.
34. Kauffold et al. 2004.
35. Health Outreach Partners 2010; Villarejo 2003; *Migration News* 2004.
36. Mines, Nichols and Runsten 2010. See also Bade 1999.
37. Slesinger 1992.
38. Kauffold et al. 2004.
39. Several elderly Triqui people in Oaxaca did not know their ages and often said "sixty or eighty," which seemed to mean simply, "I am considered old."
40. Taussig 1986.
41. Fanon 1963.
42. Scheper-Hughes 1992; Basaglia 1987.

CHAPTER 5

Parts of this chapter have been published in Seth M. Holmes, "The Clinical Gaze in the Practice of Migrant Health: Mexican Migrants in the United States," *Social Science & Medicine* 74, no. 6 (2012): 873–81.

1. See Kleinman 1988; and Farmer 1997, 1998.

2. More recently, other physician anthropologists—e.g., Cohen (2000), Fassin (2001, 2005), Hansen (2005), Holmes and Ponte (2011), Kalofonos (2010), Konner (1987), Metzl (2011), Nguyen (2010), Stoner et al. (2002), Stonington (2006), and Wendland (2010)—have expanded the focus to consider the economic and religious context of infectious diseases globally, the racialization of mental illness and addiction, the symbolic context of aging and death around the world, and the politics of inclusion and exclusion of immigrants, as well as the social and cultural processes by which medical professionals are produced.

3. Foucault 1994 [1963].

4. Ibid.: xviii.

5. This quote appears in various forms in different publications. For example, see Carrillo 1999.

6. Boyce 1994: 144–45; emphasis in original.

7. Hirschauer 1991.

8. Lella and Pawluch 1988.

9. Holmes and Ponte 2011. See Fox 1980 also on medical student uncertainty.

10. Konner 1987. See Holms, Jenks, and Stonington 2011 on the anthropology of contemporary clinical training.

11. Ibid.: 365.

12. Foucault 1990.

13. Davenport 2000.

14. Quesada 1999.

15. See Holmes and Ponte 2011 for further discussion of the "Subjective" and the "Objective" in the problem-based medical record.

16. www.migrantclinician.com.

17. See also Bade 2004.

18. Villarejo 2003; *Migration News* 2004.

19. Davis 2002.

20. Ibid.

21. Sachs 1991.

22. Martin 1992.

23. Orwell 1937.

24. Bourdieu 1997.

25. Brubaker and Cooper 2000. See also Pine 2008.

26. Rubel 1964; Rubel and Moore 2001.

27. See Holmes 2009.

28. Quinones 1998.

29. See Holmes 2009.

30. See Sesia 2001 and Stephen 2007 for background.

31. CONAMED n.d.

32. Grupo Autocolor de Oaxaca n.d.

33. See also Good 2001.
34. Ferguson 1990.
35. See Kleinman and Benson 2006.
36. Jenks 2011; Hester 2012; Willen et al. 2010.
37. Jenks 2011; Shaw and Armin 2011.
38. Metzl 2011.
39. See also Terrio 2004.

CHAPTER 6

1. See Besserer 2004, Hirsch 2003, Kearney 1998, Rouse 2002.
2. See Sangaramoorthy 2004; Chavez 1992.
3. Rothenberg 1998; Quesada 1999.
4. See also Wells 1996.
5. See Scheper-Hughes 1997.
6. Bourdieu 1997, 2001; Bourdieu and Wacquant 1992.
7. Bourdieu 2001: 37.
8. Bourdieu 1997: 166.
9. Bourdieu 2001: 35.
10. Bourdieu 1997, 2001; Bourdieu and Wacquant 1992.
11. Hunt et al. 2004.
12. Gutmann 1999.
13. See Gilroy 1989; Hall 1990.
14. Rouse 2002. See de Genova 2005 on transnational US-Mexican spaces. See Glick Schiller and Fouron 2001 on "long-distance nationalism."
15. See Fox 2005, 2006 on multilayered ethnicity and citizenship.
16. Douglas 1966: 2.
17. In Orwell 1937: 119.
18. Weismantel 2001: 34.
19. Weismantel and Eisenman 1998: 134.
20. Ibid.
21. Ibid.: 133.
22. Ibid.: 136.
23. See also MacLeod 1993.
24. Thompson 1999.
25. See Beck 2009 on the individualization of risk and responsibility.
26. Though helpful, Strauss's (1966) analysis is limited by its assumed universality. Scheper-Hughes (1992) and Brandes (1980) offer more contextual analyses of body position and imputed humanity.
27. Farmer 1992.

CHAPTER 7

1. Crapanzano 2008.
2. Miyazaki 2009.
3. Bourdieu 2003: 273.
4. Ibid.: 274.
5. Gramsci 1971.
6. Emmanuel Levinas, the French phenomenological philosopher, wrote specifically of suffering and its justification in "Entre Nous." He argued that our human responsibility is to understand the suffering of others as "useless" and "senseless" and to therefore work toward its amelioration. He called for "the end of theodicy," because he argued that placing a meaning on suffering ultimately justifies the production of that very suffering. The anthropologist Veena Das (1987) considers ethnographically the Bhopal disaster and massacres in India to make a related analytic move. She indicates that attempts to make meaning from suffering can function to validate patriarchal, unequal social structures while silencing the sufferer. Instead, she argues that suffering must be understood as illegitimate and chaotic in order to allow the continued existence of those who are suffering. Suffering must not be justified in order that sufferers might be comforted and also that further suffering might be prevented.
7. See Taussig 2012 on the multilayered nature of reality and Nader 1972 on the anthropological vertical slice.
8. I use *migrate, migrant,* and *migration* in this book because these are most commonly understood in this context. Yet I do not want to indicate an uncritical assent to the assumptions that are found behind these words.
9. See Besserer 2004, Kearney 1998, Rouse 2002. See Glick Schiller 2003 on "transnational social space."
10. See Gilroy 1989; Hall 1990.
11. Ong 1999.
12. At the same time, these words are used so commonly in society and in health research that it would be unwieldy to avoid them throughout this book. Thus, working against these drawbacks and prejudices in the terminology, I continue to use some of these words.
13. See Castañeda 2010, Stephen 2007, and Willen 2007 for further discussion of the experience of being considered "illegal."
14. See Morrissey 1986.
15. Gramsci 1971. See also Kissam and Jacobs 2004 for practical research suggestions related to Mexican indigenous communities.
16. See Hall 1986.
17. Gramsci 1971.
18. California's Proposition 187. Quoted in Quesada 1999.

19. Quesada 1999.
20. See Voss and Bloemread 2011.
21. Farmer 1992.
22. Illich 1976; Kaw 1993; Martin 1992; Scheper-Hughes 1990.
23. Scheper-Hughes 1994.
24. Scheper-Hughes 1990.
25. Scheper-Hughes 1992.
26. See Scheper-Hughes 1992; Smith and Hilsbos 1999.
27. Virchow 1985.
28. Quesada, Bourgois, and Hart 2011.
29. Hunt 2004; Gutmann 1999.
30. See Burawoy 1976; Rothenberg 1998; *Arizona Daily Star* 2005.
31. See Bacon 2013.

References

Althusser, Louis. 1982. *Montesquieu, Rousseau, Marx: Politics and History*. Trans. Ben Brewster. London: Verso.

Amnesty International. 1986. *Human Rights in Rural Areas: Exchange of Documents with the Mexican Government on Human Rights Violations in Oaxaca and Chiapas*. London: Amnesty International.

Arizona Daily Star. 2005. "3 Entrants' Bodies Found on Reservation; Toll at 178." July 20.

Bacon, David. 2004. "NAFTA's Legacy: Profits and Poverty." *San Francisco Chronicle*. January 14.

———. 2013. "Let's Stop Making Migration a Crime." *Truthout*. February 15. http://truth-out.org/opinion/item/14569-lets-stop-making-migration-a-crime

Bade, Bonnie. 1999. *"Is There a Doctor in the Field?" Underlying Conditions Affecting Access to Health Care for California Farmworkers and Their Families*. CPRC Report. [Berkeley]: California Policy Research Center, University of California.

———. 2004. "Alive and Well: Generating Alternatives to Biomedical Health Care by Mixtec Migrant Families in California." In *Indigenous Mexican*

Migrants in the United States, ed. Jonathan Fox and Gaspar Rivera-Salgado, 205–48. La Jolla: Center for U.S.-Mexican Studies / Center for Comparative Immigration Studies, University of California, San Diego.

Bandura, Albert. 1997. *Self-Efficacy: The Exercise of Control*. New York: W.H. Freeman.

Basaglia, Franco. 1987. *Psychiatry Inside Out: Selected Writings of Franco Basaglia*. Ed. Nancy Scheper-Hughes and Anne M. Lovell. New York: Columbia University Press.

Beck, Ulrich. 2009. *World at Risk*. Cambridge: Polity Press.

Berger, John, and Jean Mohr. 1997. *A Fortunate Man*. New York: Random House Vintage.

Besserer, José Federico. 2004. *Topografías transnacionales: Hacía una geografía de la vida transnacional*. Mexico City: Universidad Autónoma Metropolitana, Unidad Iztapalapa.

Bourdieu, Pierre. 2000 [1997]. *Pascalian Meditations*. Stanford, CA: Stanford University Press.

———. 2001. *Masculine Domination*. Stanford, CA: Stanford University Press.

———. 2003. "Gender and Symbolic Violence." In *Violence in War and Peace: An Anthology*. Malden, MA: Blackwell: 272–74.

Bourdieu, Pierre, and Loïc Wacquant. 1992. *An Invitation to Reflexive Sociology*. Chicago: University of Chicago Press.

Bourgois, Philippe. 1988. "Conjugated Oppression: Class and Ethnicity among Guaymi and Kuna Banana Plantation Workers." *American Ethnologist* 15 (2): 328–48.

———. 1995. *In Search of Respect: Selling Crack in El Barrio*. New York: Cambridge University Press.

———. 2001. "The Power of Violence in War and Peace: Post–Cold War Lessons from El Salvador." *Ethnography* 2 (1): 5–34.

———. 2005. "Missing the Holocaust: My Father's Account of Auschwitz from August 1943 to June 1944." Special Issue. *Bringing the Past into the Present: Family Narratives of Holocaust, Exile and Diaspora. Anthropological Quarterly* 78 (1): 89–123.

———. In prep. "Socially Structured Suffering among Aging Homeless Heroin Injectors." In *Festschrift for Arthur Kleinman*, ed. Veena Das and Paul Farmer.

Boyce, W. Thomas. 1994. "Beyond the Clinical Gaze." In *The Crisis of Care*, ed. S. Phillips and B. Benner, 144–48. Washington, DC: Georgetown University Press.

Brandes, Stanley. 1980. *Metaphors of Masculinity: Sex and Status in Andalusian Folklore*. Philadelphia: University of Pennsylvania Press.

Brubaker, Rogers, and Frederick Cooper. 2000. "Beyond 'Identity.'" *Theory and Society* 29: 1–47.

Burawoy, Michael. 1976. "The Functions and Reproduction of Migrant Labor: Comparative Material from Southern Africa and the United States." *American Journal of Sociology* 81: 1050–87.

Bustamante, Jorge A. 1983. "Mexican Migration: The Political Dynamics of Perceptions." In *U.S.-Mexican Relations: Economic and Social Aspects,* ed. C. Reynolds and C. Tello, 259–76. Stanford, CA: Stanford University Press.

Butler, Judith. 2009. *Frames of War: When Is Life Grievable?* London: Verso.

Carrillo, J. 1999. "Cross-Cultural Primary Care." *Annals of Internal Medicine* 130 (10): 829.

Castañeda, Heide. 2010. "Deportation Deferred: 'Illegality,' Visibility, and Recognition in Contemporary Germany." In *The Deportation Regime: Sovereignty, Space, and the Freedom of Movement,* ed. Nicholas De Genova and Nathalie Peutz, 245–61. Durham, NC: Duke University Press.

CBS News. 1960. "CBS Reports: Harvest of Shame with Edward R. Murrow." Nov. 26.

Chavez, Leo R. 1992. *Shadowed Lives: Undocumented Immigrants in American Society.* Fort Worth, TX: Harcourt Brace Jovanovich.

———. 2001. *Covering Immigration: Popular Images and the Politics of the Nation.* Berkeley: University of California Press.

———. 2008. *The Latino Threat: Constructing Immigrants, Citizens, and the Nation.* Stanford, CA: Stanford University Press.

Cohen, Jeffrey. 2001. "Transnational Migration in Rural Oaxaca, Mexico: Dependency, Development, and the Household." *American Anthropologist* 10 (4): 954–67.

Cohen, Lawrence. 2000. *No Aging in India: Alzheimer's, the Bad Family, and Other Modern Things.* Berkeley: University of California Press.

CONAMED (Comisión Nacional de Arbitraje Médico) and Cruzada Nacional por la Calidad Salud. "10 derechos del paciente." www.conamed.gob.mx.

Conover, Ted. 1987. *Coyotes: A Journey across Borders with America's Illegal Migrants.* New York: Vintage Books.

Cornelius, Wayne A. 2001. "Death at the Border: Efficacy and Unintended Consequences of U.S. Immigration Control Policy." *Population and Development Review* 27 (4): 661–85.

Crapanzano, Vincent. 2003. "Reflections on Hope as a Category of Social and Pscyhological Analysis." *Cultural Anthropology* 18 (1): 3–32. Doi: 10.1525/can.2003.18.1.3.

Csordas, Thomas, ed. 1994. *Embodiment and Experience: The Existential Ground of Culture and Self.* Cambridge: Cambridge University Press.

Das, Veena. 1987. "The Anthropology of Violence and the Speech of Victims." *Anthropology Today* 3 (4): 11–13.

Davenport, Beverly Ann. 2000. "Witnessing and the Medical Gaze: How Medical Students Learn to See at a Free Clinic for the Homeless." *Medical Anthropology Quarterly* 14 (3): 310–27.

Davis, Andrew. 2002. "Unusual Woodburn Office Helps Indigenous Mexicans." Associated Press Newswires.

De Genova, Nicholas. 2005. *Working the Boundaries: Race, Space, and "Illegality" in Mexican Chicago*. Durham, NC: Duke University Press.

Douglas, Mary. 1966. *Purity and Danger: An Analysis of Concepts of Pollution and Taboo*. London: Routledge and Kegan Paul.

Eber, Christine. 1995. *Women and Alcohol in a Highland Maya Town: Water of Hope, Water of Sorrow*. Austin: University of Texas Press.

Edinger, Steven T. 1996. *The Road from Mixtepec: A Southern Mexican Town and the United States Economy*. Fresno, CA: Asociación Cívica Benito Juárez.

Ejército Popular Revolucionario. 2002. "Sobre Chiapas y el magisterio." www.pengo.it/PDPR-EPR/comunicados/c_150502.htm.

Engel, George. 1977. "The Need for a New Medical Model." *Science* 196: 129–36.

Engels, Friedrich. 1958. *The Condition of the Working Class in England*. Trans. W.O. Henderson and W.H. Chaloner. Stanford, CA: Stanford University Press.

Espenshade, Thomas J. 1995. "Unauthorized Immigration to the United States." *Annual Review of Sociology* 21: 195–216.

Estroff, Sue E. 1985. *Making It Crazy: An Ethnography of Psychiatric Clients in an American Community*. Berkeley: University of California Press.

Fanon, Frantz. 1963. *The Wretched of the Earth*. New York: Grove Press.

Farmer, Paul. 1992. *AIDS and Accusation: Haiti and the Geography of Blame*. Berkeley: University of California Press.

———. 1997. "On Suffering and Structural Violence: A View from Below." In *Social Suffering*, ed. Arthur Kleinman, Veena Das, and Margaret Lock, 261–83. Berkeley: University of California Press.

———. 1999. *Infections and Inequalities: The Modern Plagues*. Berkeley: University of California Press.

Farquhar, Judith. 2002. *Appetites: Food and Sex in Postsocialist China*. Durham, NC: Duke University Press.

Fassin, Didier. 2001. "The Biopolitics of Otherness: Undocumented Immigrants and Racial Discrimination in the French Public Debate." *Anthropology Today* 17 (1): 1, 3–7.

———. 2005. "Compassion and Repression: The Moral Economy of Immigration Politics in France." *Cultural Anthropology* 20: 362–87.

Ferguson, James. 1990. *The Anti-Politics Machine: Development, Depoliticization, and Bureaucratic Power in Lesotho.* Minneapolis: University of Minnesota Press.

Foucault, Michel. 1990. *The History of Sexuality: An Introduction.* New York: Random House Vintage.

———. 1991. *Remarks on Marx: Conversations with Duccio Trombadori.* Trans. R. James Goldstein and James Cascaito. New York: Semiotext(e).

———. 1994 [1963]. *The Birth of the Clinic.* New York: Vintage Press.

Fox, Jonathan. 2005. "Unpacking Transnational Citizenship." *Annual Reviews in Political Science* 8: 171–201.

———. 2006. "Reframing Mexican Migration as a Multi-Ethnic Process." *Latino Studies* 4: 39–61.

Fox, Jonathan, and Gaspar Rivera-Salgado. 2004. *Indigenous Mexican Migrants in the United States.* La Jolla: Center for U.S.-Mexican Studies / Center for Comparative Immigration Studies, University of California, San Diego.

Fox, Renée. 1980. "The Evolution of Medical Uncertainty." *Milbank Memorial Fund Quarterly* 58 (1): 1–49.

Franco, Pilar. 2002. "Military Blamed for Murders of Two Indian Youths." Global Exchange. www.globalexchange.org / campaigns / mexico / news / 051699a.html.

Frank, Arthur, Robert McKnight, Steven Kirkhorn, and Paul Gunderson. 2004. "Issues of Agricultural Safety and Health." *Annual Review of Public Health* 25: 225–45.

Galtung, Johan. 1969. "Violence, Peace, and Peace Research." *Journal of Peace Research* 6: 167–91.

Geertz, Clifford. 1998. "Deep Hanging Out." *New York Review of Books.* October 22.

Gilroy, Paul. 1989. *"There Ain't No Black in the Union Jack": The Cultural Politics of Race and Nation.* Chicago: University of Chicago Press.

Glick Schiller, Nina. 2003. "The Centrality of Ethnography in the Study of Transnational Migration: Seeing the Wetland Instead of the Swamp." In *American Arrivals: Anthropology Engages the New Immigration,* ed. Nancy Foner, 99–128. Santa Fe, NM: School of American Research Press.

Glick Schiller, Nina, and Georges Eugene Fouron. 2001. *Georges Woke Up Laughing: Long-Distance Nationalism and the Search for Home.* Durham, NC: Duke University Press.

Good, Mary-Jo DelVecchio. 2001. "The Biotechnical Embrace." *Culture, Medicine, and Psychiatry* 25 (4): 395–410.

Gramsci, Antonio. 1971. *Selections from the Prison Notebooks.* New York: International Publishers.

Green, Linda. 2008. "A Wink and a Nod: Notes from the Arizona Borderlands." *Dialogical Anthropology* 32 (1–2):161–67.

Grillo, R. 1985. *Ideologies and Institutions in Urban France: The Representation of Immigrants.* Cambridge: Cambridge University Press.

Grupo Autocolor de Oaxaca. "Decalogo del buen paciente." Distributed by Comes Preocupados por la Salud de Oaxaca.

Gutmann, Mathew. 1999. "Ethnicity, Alcohol, and Acculturation." *Social Science & Medicine* 48 (2): 173–84.

Hall, Stuart. 1986. "Gramsci's Relevance for the Study of Race and Ethnicity." *Journal of Communication Inquiry* 10 (2): 5–27.

———. 1990. "Cultural Identity and Diaspora." In *Identity: Community, Culture, Difference,* ed. J. Rutherford, 222–37. London: Lawrence and Wishart.

Hansen, Helena. 2005. "Isla Evangelista—A Story of Church and State: Puerto Rico's Faith-Based Initiatives." *Culture, Medicine and Psychiatry* 29 (4): 433–56.

Health Outreach Partners. 2010. *Breaking Down the Barriers: A National Needs Assessment on Farmworker Health Outreach.* 4th ed. Oakland, CA: Health Outreach Partners.

Henderson, Gail, Nancy King, Ronald Strauss, Sue Estroff, and Larry Churchill, eds. 1997. *The Social Medicine Reader.* Durham, NC: Duke University Press.

Hester, Rebecca J. 2012. "The Promise and Paradox of Cultural Competence." *HEC Forum* 24 (4): 279–91.

Hirsch, Jennifer. 2003. *A Courtship before Marriage: Sexuality and Love in Mexican Transnational Families*. Berkeley: University of California Press.

Hirschauer, S. 1991. "The Manufacture of Bodies in Surgery." *Social Studies of Science* 21 (2): 279–319.

Holmes, Seth M. 2006a. "An Ethnographic Study of the Context of Migrant Health." *PLoS* 3 (10): e448; 1776–93. Doi: 10.1371/journal.pmed.0030448.

———. 2006b. "Parce qu'ils sont plus près du sol: L'invisibilisation de la souffrance sociale des cueilleurs de baies." *Actes de Recherche en Sciences Sociales* 165 (2): 28–51.

———. 2007. "'Oaxacans Like to Work Bent Over': The Naturalization of Social Suffering among Berry Farm Workers." *International Migration* 45 (3): 39–68.

———. 2009. "Don't Misrepresent the Triqui." *Monterey County Herald.* Jan. 29.

———. 2011. "Structural Vulnerability and Hierarchies of Ethnicity and Citizenship on the Farm." *Medical Anthropology* 30 (4): 425–49.

———. 2012. "The Clinical Gaze in the Practice of Migrant Health: Mexican Migrants in the United States." *Social Science & Medicine* 74 (6): 873–81.

Holmes, Seth M., Angela C. Jenks, and Scott Stonington. 2011. "Clinical Subjectivation: Anthropologies of Contemporary Biomedical Training." *Culture, Medicine, and Psychiatry* 35 (2): 105–12.

Holmes, Seth M., and Maya Ponte. 2011. "En-case-ing the Patient: Disciplining Uncertainty in Medical Student Patient Presentations." *Culture, Medicine, and Psychiatry* 35 (2): 163–82.

Holmes, Seth, and Scott Stonington, eds. 2006. "Theme Issue on the Relevance of the Social Sciences to Medicine." *PLoS Medicine* 3(10).

Hunt, Linda M., Suzanne Schneider, and Brendon Comer. 2004. "Should 'Acculturation' Be a Variable in Health Research? A Critical Review of Research on US Hispanics." *Social Science & Medicine* 59 (5): 973–86.

Illich, Ivan. 1976. *Medical Nemesis.* New York: Pantheon.

INS. 1998. "Violence against Indigenous Groups in Oaxaca." www.ins.usdoj.gov/textg/services/asylum/ric/documentation/Oaxaca.htm.

Jain, Sarah S. Lochlann. 2006. *Injury: The Politics of Product Design and Safety Law in the United States.* Princeton: Princeton University Press.

Jenks, Angela C. 2011. "From 'List of Traits' to 'Open-Mindedness': Emerging Issues in Cultural Competence Education." *Culture, Medicine and Psychiatry* 35 (2): 209–35.

Kalofonos, Ippolytos A. 2010. "'All I Eat Is ARVs': The Paradox of AIDS Treatment Interventions in Central Mozambique." *Medical Anthropology Quarterly* 24 (3): 363–80.

Kandula, Namratha, Margaret Kersey, and Nicole Lurie. 2004. "Assuring the Health of Immigrants: What the Leading Health Indicators Tell Us." *Annual Review of Public Health* 25: 357–76.

Kauffold, Andrea, Edward Zuroweste, Deliana Garcia, Carmel T. Drewes. 2004. *Breast, Cervical and Colon Cancer in Mobile Underserved Populations.* Migrant Clinicians Monograph Series. Austin, TX: Migrant Clinicians Network.

Kaw, Eugenia. 1993. "Medicalization of Racial Features: Asian American Women and Cosmetic Surgery." *Medical Anthropology Quarterly* 7 (1): 74–89.

Kearney, Michael. 1998. "Transnationalism in California and Mexico at the End of the Empire." In *Border Identities: Nation and State at International Frontiers,* ed. Thomas W. Wilson and Hastings Connan, 117–41. Cambridge: Cambridge University Press.

Kissam, Edward, and Ilene J. Jacobs. 2004. "Practical Research Strategies for Mexican Indigenous Communities in California Seeking to Assert Their Own Identity." In *Indigenous Mexican Migrants in the United States,* ed. Jonathan Fox and Gaspar Rivera-Salgado, 303–42. La Jolla: Center for U.S.-Mexican Studies/Center for Comparative Immigration Studies, University of California, San Diego.

Kleinman, Arthur. 1988. *The Illness Narratives: Suffering, Healing, and the Human Condition.* New York: Basic Books.

———. 1994. "Moral Orientations to Suffering: Legitimation, Power, and Healing." In *Health and Social Change in International Perspective,* ed. Lincoln

Chen, Arthur Kleinman, and Norma Ware, 139–67. Boston: Harvard School of Public Health. Distributed by Harvard University Press.

Kleinman, Arthur, and Peter Benson. 2006. "Anthropology in the Clinic: The Problem of Cultural Competency and How to Fix It." *PLoS Medicine* 3 (10): e294.

Kleinman, Arthur, Veena Das, and Margaret Lock. 1995. *Writing at the Margin: Discourse between Anthropology and Medicine.* Berkeley: University of California Press.

———, eds. 1997. *Social Suffering.* Berkeley: University of California Press.

Kleinman, Arthur, and Joan Kleinman. 1991. "Suffering and Its Professional Transformation: Towards an Ethnography of Interpersonal Experience." *Culture Medicine and Psychiatry* 15 (3): 275–301.

———. 1994. "How Bodies Remember: Social Memory and Bodily Experience of Criticism, Resistance, and Delegitimation Following China's Cultural Revolution." *New Literary History* 25: 707–23.

Klinenberg, Eric. 1999. "Denaturalizing Disaster: A Social Autopsy of the 1995 Chicago Heat Wave." *Theory and Society* 28: 239–95.

Konner, Melvin. 1987. *Becoming a Doctor: A Journey of Initiation in Medical School.* New York: Penguin Books.

Lella, Joseph W., and Dorothy Pawluch. 1988. "Medical Students and the Cadaver in Social and Cultural Context." In *Biomedicine Examined,* ed. M. Lock and D. R. Gordon, 125–53. Dordrecht, The Netherlands: Kluwer.

Levi, Primo. 1988. *The Drowned and the Saved.* New York: Simon and Schuster.

Levinas, Emmanuel. 1998. *On Thinking-of-the-Other: Entre Nous.* New York: Columbia University Press.

Lopez, Felipe, and David Runsten. 2004. "Mixtecs and Zapotecs Working in California: Rural and Urban Experiences." In *Indigenous Mexican Migrants in the United States,* ed. Jonathan Fox and Gaspar Rivera-Salgado, 249–78. La Jolla: Center for U.S.-Mexican Studies and Center for Comparative Immigration Studies, University of California, San Diego.

Macleod, Jay. 1995. *Ain't No Makin' It: Leveled Aspirations in a Low-Income Neighborhood.* Boulder, CO: Westview Press.

Malinowski, Bronislaw. 1922. *Argonauts of the Western Pacific: An Account of Native Enterprise and Adventure in the Archipelagoes of Melanesian New Guinea.* London: Routledge and Kegan Paul.

Marcos, Subcomandante. 1995. *Shadows of Tender Fury: The Letters and Communiques of Subcomandante Marcos and the Zapatista Army of National Liberation.* New York: Monthly Review.

Marcus, George. 1998. *Ethnography through Thick and Thin.* Princeton: Princeton University Press.

Martin, Emily. 1992. *The Woman in the Body: A Cultural Analysis of Reproduction.* Boston: Beacon Press.

Marx, Karl. 1972 [1867]. *Capital.* Translated by Samuel Moore and Edward Aveling. New York: International Publishers.

Massey, Douglas, Jorge Durand, and Nolan J. Malone. 2002. *Beyond Smoke and Mirrors: Mexican Immigration in an Era of Economic Integration.* New York: Russell Sage Foundation.

Mines, Richard, Sandra Nichols, and David Runsten. 2010. "California's Indigenous Farmworkers." www.indigenousfarmworkers.org.

McGuire, Sharon, Sr., and Jane Georges. 2003. "Undocumentedness and Liminality as Health Variables." *Advances in Nursing Science* 26 (3): 185–96.

Merleau-Ponty, Maurice. 1996. *Phenomenology of Perception.* New York: Routledge.

Metzl, Jonathan. 2011. *Protest Psychosis: How Schizophrenia Became a Black Disease.* Boston: Beacon Press.

Migrant Clinician Network. www.migrantclinician.com.

Migration News. 2002. "Census, INS: Data." *Migration News* 9: 4.

———. 2003a. "INS: Registration, Border, Polls." *Migration News* 10: 1.

———. 2003b. "Migration Trade and Development." *Migration News* 10:1.

———. 2004. "Labor, H-1B, Census, Health." *Migration News* 11: 4.

Miyazki, Hirokazu. 2009. *The Method of Hope: Anthropology, Philosophy, and Fijian Knowledge.* Stanford: Stanford University Press.

Mobed, Ketty, Ellen Gold, and Marc Schenker. 1992. "Occupational Health Problems among Migrant and Seasonal Farm Workers." *Western Journal of Medicine* 157 (3): 367–85.

Morrissey, James A. 1983. "Migration, Resettlement, and Refugeeism: Issues in Medical Anthropology." *Medical Anthropology Quarterly* 15 (1): 3, 11–14.

Morsy, Soheir. 1996. "Political Economy in Medical Anthropology." In *Medical Anthropology: Contemporary Theory and Method,* ed. Carolyn F. Sargent and Thomas M. Johnson, 21–40. New York: Praeger.

Moss, Michael. 2013. *Salt, Sugar, Fat: How the Food Giants Hooked Us.* New York: Random House.

Nader, Laura. 1972. "Up the Anthropologist: Perspectives from Studying Up." In *Reinventing Anthropology,* ed. Dell H. Hymes, 284–311. New York: Pantheon Books.

Nagengast, Carole, Rodolfo Stavenhagen, and Michael Kearney. 1992. *Human Rights and Indigenous Workers: The Mixtec in Mexico and the United States.* La Jolla: Center for U.S.-Mexican Studies, University of California, San Diego.

Nazario, Sonia, and Don Bartletti. 2002. "Enrique's Journey: Boy Left Behind." *Los Angeles Times.* Sept. 29.

Nguyen, Vinh-Kim. 2010. *The Republic of Therapy: Triage and Sovereignty in West Africa's Time of AIDS*. Durham, NC: Duke University Press.
Ong, Aihwa. 1999. *Flexible Citizenship: The Cultural Logics of Transnationality*. Durham, NC: Duke University Press.
Orwell, George. 1937. *The Road to Wigan Pier*. New York: Harcourt Brace Jovanovich.
Pine, Adrienne. 2008. *Working Hard, Drinking Hard: On Violence and Survival in Honduras*. Berkeley: University of California Press.
Portes, Alejandro, and Robert L. Bach. 1985. *Latin Journey: Cuban and Mexican Immigrants in the United States*. Berkeley: University of California Press.
Quesada, James. 1999. "From Central American Warriors to San Francsico Latino Day Laborers: Suffering and Exhaustion in a Transnational Context." *Transforming Anthropology* 8 (1–2): 162–85.
Quesada, James, Laurie K. Hart, and Philippe Bourgois. 2011. "Structural Vulnerability and Health: Latino Migrant Laborers in the United States." *Medical Anthropology* 30 (4): 339–62.
Quinones, Sam. 1998. "'Grapes of Wrath' South of the Border." San Samuel, CA: Special to the Examiner. *SF Gate*. Jan. 11.
Rothenberg, Daniel. 1998. *With These Hands: The Hidden World of Migrant Farmworkers Today*. Berkeley: University of California Press.
Rouse, Roger. 2002. "Mexican Migration and the Social Space of Postmodernism." In *The Anthropology of Globalization: A Reader*, ed. Jonathan Xavier Inda and Renato Rosaldo, 157–71. Oxford: Blackwell.
Rubel, Arthur J. 1964. "The Epidemiology of a Folk Illness: Susto in Hispanic America." *Ethnology* 3 (3): 268–83.
Rubel, Arthur J., and Carmella C. Moore. 2001. "The Contribution of Medical Anthropology to a Comparative Study of Culture: Susto and Tuberculosis." *Medical Anthropology Quarterly* 15 (4): 440–54.
Rural Migration News. 2003. "Mexico: Migrants, Nafta." 9 (1). www.migration.ucdavis.edu/rmn.
———. 2005. "Health and Insurance." 11 (1). www.migration.ucdavis.edu/rmn.
Rust, George. 1990. "Health Status of Migrant Farmworkers: A Literature Review and Commentary." *American Journal of Public Health* 80 (10): 1213–17.
Sachs, Wolfgang, ed. 1991. *The Development Dictionary*. London: Zed Books.
Sakala, Carol. 1987. "Migrant and Seasonal Farmworkers in the United States: A Review of Health Hazards, Status, and Policy." *International Migration Review* 21 (3): 659–87.
Sangaramoorthy, Thurka. 2004. "Invisible Americans: Migrants, Transnationalism, and the Politics of Place in HIV/AIDS Research." Unpublished MS.
Sartre, Jean-Paul. 1956. *Being and Nothingness*. London: Methuen.

Sassen, Saskia. 1998. *Globalization and Its Discontents.* New York: New Press.

Scheper-Hughes, Nancy. 1990. "Three Propositions for a Critically Applied Medical Anthropology." *Social Science & Medicine* 30 (2): 189–97.

———. 1992. *Death without Weeping: The Violence of Everyday Live in Brazil.* Berkeley: University of California Press.

———. 1994. "The Rebel Body: The Subversive Meanings of Illness." *Traditional Acupuncture Society Journal* 10: 3–10.

———. 1997. "People Who Get Rubbished." *New Internationalist,* no. 295: 20–22.

———. 2002. "Peace Time Crimes and the Violence of Everyday Life." *IDEAS: Journal of the National Humanities Center* 9 (1): 56–58.

———. 2003. "Why Violence: An Interdisciplinary Dialogue." Lecture, University of Massachusetts, Boston, Apr. 5.

Scheper-Hughes, Nancy, and Philippe Bourgois. 2003. "Making Sense of Violence." In *Violence in War and Peace: An Anthology,* ed. Nancy Scheper-Hughes and Philippe Bourgois, 1–31. Malden, MA: Blackwell.

———, eds. 2003. *Violence in War and Peace: An Anthology.* Malden, MA: Blackwell.

Scheper-Hughes, Nancy, and Margaret Lock. 1987. "The Mindful Body: A Prolegomenon to Future Work in Medical Anthropology." *Medical Anthropology Quarterly* 1 (1): 6–41.

Sesia, Paola. 2001. "'Aquí la progresa está muy dura': Estado, negociación e identidad entre familias indígenas rurales." *Desacatos,* no. 8: 109–28.

Shaw, Susan J., and Julie Armin. 2011. "The Ethical Self-Fashioning of Physicians and Health Care Systems in Culturally Appropriate Health Care." *Culture, Medicine and Psychiatry* 35 (2): 236–61.

Simon, Joel. 1997. *Endangered Mexico: An Environment on the Edge.* San Francisco: Sierra Club Books.

Singer, Merrill. 1998. *The Political Economy of AIDS.* Amityville, NY: Baywood Publishing.

Singer, Merrill, and Hans Baer. 1995. *Critical Medical Anthropology.* Amityville, NY: Baywood Publishing.

Slesinger, Doris. 1992. "Health Status and Needs of Migrant Farm Workers in the United States: A Literature Review." *Journal of Rural Health* 8 (3): 227–34.

Smith, Lanny, and Ken Hilsbos. 1999. "Liberation Medicine: Health & Justice." *Doctors for Global Health Reporter* 3 (1): 8–10.

Stephen, Lynn. 2007. Transborder Lives: *Indigenous Oaxacans in Mexico, California, and Oaxaca.* Durham, NC: Duke University Press.

Stoller, Paul. 1997. *Sensuous Scholarship.* Philadelphia: University of Pennsylvania Press.

Stoner, Bradley, J.D. Fortenberry, M. McFarlane, A. Bleakley, S. Bull, M. Fishbein, D.M. Grimley, and C.K. Malotte. 2002. "Relationships of Stigma and Shame to Gonorrhea and HIV Screening." *American Journal of Public Health* 92: 378–81.

Stonington, Scott. 2006. "Is There a Global Bioethics? End-of-Life in Thailand and the Case for Local Difference." *PLoS Medicine* 3 (10): e439.

Strauss, Anselm, and Juliet Corbin. 1990. *Basics of Qualitative Research: Grounded Theory Procedures and Techniques.* Newbury Park, CA: Sage.

Strauss, Erwin. 1966. "Upright Posture." In *Phenomenological Psychology: The Selected Papers of Erwin W. Strauss*, 137–65. New York: Basic Books.

Taussig, Michael. 1986. *Shamanism, Colonialism, and the Wild Man: A Study in Terror and Healing.* Chicago: University of Chicago Press.

———. 2012. *I Swear I Saw This: Drawings in Fieldwork Notebooks, Namely My Own.* Chicago: University of Chicago Press.

Terrio, Susan J. 2004. "Migration, Displacement, and Violence: Prosecuting Romanian Street Children at the Paris Palace of Justice." *International Migration* 42 (5): 5–33.

Thomas, Robert. 1985. *Citizenship, Gender, and Work: The Social Organization of Industrial Agriculture.* Berkeley: University of California Press.

Thompson, Hunter S. 1999. *Hell's Angels: A Strange and Terrible Saga.* New York: Modern Library.

Villarejo, Don. 2003. "The Health of U.S. Hired Farm Workers." *Annual Review of Public Health* 24: 175–93.

Virchow, Rudolf L. K., and L. J. Rather, eds. 1985. *Collected Essays on Public Health and Epidemiology.* Canton, MA: Science History Publications.

Voss, Kim, and Irene Bloemraad. 2011. *Rallying for Immigrant Rights: The Fight for Inclusion in the Twenty-First Century.* Berkeley: University of California Press.

Wacquant, Loïc. 2004. "On the Strategic Appeal and Analytic Perils of 'Structural Violence.'" *Current Anthropology* 45(3): 322–23.

———. 2005. "Carnal Connections: On Embodiment, Apprenticeship, and Membership." *Qualitative Sociology* 28 (4): 445–74.

Weismantel, Mary. 2001. *Cholas and Pishtacos: Stories of Race and Sex in the Andes.* Chicago: University of Chicago Press.

Weismantel, Mary, and Stephen Eisenman. 1998. "Race in the Andes: Global Movements and Popular Ontologies." *Bulletin of Latin American Research* 17 (2): 121–42.

Wells, Miriam. 1996. *Strawberry Fields: Politics, Class, and Work in California Agriculture.* Ithaca, NY: Cornell University Press.

Wendland, Claire L. 2010. *A Heart for the Work: Journeys through an African Medical School.* Chicago: University of Chicago Press.

Willen, Sarah S. 2007. "Toward a Critical Phenomenology of 'Illegality': State Power, Criminalization, and Abjectivity among Undocumented Workers in Tel Aviv, Israel." *International Migration* 45 (3): 8–38.

Willen, Sarah S., Antonio Bullon, Mary-Jo DelVecchio Good. 2010. "Opening up a Huge Can of Worms: Reflections on a 'Cultural Sensitivity' Course for Psychiatry Residents." *Harvard Review of Psychiatry* 18: 247–55.

Wolf, Eric. 1957. "Closed Corporate Peasant Communities in Mesoamerica and Central Java." *Southwestern Journal of Anthropology* 13: 1–15.

Wolfenstein, Martha. 1955. "French Parents Take Their Children to the Park." In *Childhood in Contemporary Cultures*, ed. M. Mead and M. Wolfenstein, 99–117. Chicago: University of Chicago Press.

Wood, Charles H. 1982. "Equilibrium and Historical-Structural Perspectives on Migration." *International Migration Review* 16 (2): 298–319.

Zabin, Carol, et al. 1993. *Mixtec Migrants in California Agriculture: A New Cycle of Poverty.* Davis: California Institute for Rural Studies.

Index

Italic page numbers indicate illustrations.

acculturation, 160, 186, 195
administrative assistants, *51*, 60–62, 83–84
Affordable Care Act, 195
Agricultural Labor Relations Act (1975), 102
agriculture, U.S., 31, 46, 86, 181; corporatization of, 52, 58; dependence on undocumented migrant workers, 65; ethnic-citizenship hierarchy in, 180, 182; fault lines of power in, 50; foreign competition and, 46, 55; future of, 197; hierarchy of suffering in, 95; overtime labor laws and, 62
Alaska, 103, 105, 110, 141–42
alcohol consumption, as self-medication, 98, *99*, 134
"alien smuggling," as legal offense, 22–23
allostatic load, 101
Althusser, Louis, 28, 206n16
anemia, 101, 102
Anglo-Americans, 49, 51–52, 84, *85*, 95. See also *gabachos*; whites
anthrax, 101
anthropology: anthropologist as record keeper, 39; embodied, 28, 33–40; participant observation, 3; physician anthopologists, 114, 116, 209n2; social theory terms and, 32. *See also* ethnography; fieldwork
anxiety, 101
apples, 58, 63, 73, 171
Arizona, 10, 13, 19, 31, 41
ascariasis, 101
assailants (*rateros*), as danger, 8, 11, 14, 16
assimilation, 186, 195
automobiles, 68–69, 77, 80–81, 104

back pain, 32, 34, 39, 88, 94; idiopathic, 74; migrants' accounts of, 75, 89, 93
bad faith, 86–87, 143, 157
Basaglia, Franco, 110

bathroom breaks, 62, 65, 73
Becoming a Doctor (Konner), 116
biomedicine, 135, 143–44, 152–53
biopower, 32
Birth of the Clinic, The (Foucault), 114–15
births, premature, 74
blacks, as migrant laborers, 126, 186
blisters, 20, 27
blood disorders, 101, 102
blueberries, 57, 66, 73, 84, 93, 191
Board of Immigration Appeals, 40
bodily differences, 138, 171, 173–74, 181
body position, in labor, 174–76, *175*
border, U.S.-Mexico: approach from Mexican border town, 13–17; crossing of, 18–21, *19*, *20*, 151; death of migrants in borderlands, 8, 26, 27; Mexican side of, 11–12; militarization of, 161, 185, 190; risks and suffering faced in crossing, 8–10, 196, 197; traveling to, 7–8
Border Action Network, 196
Borderlinks, 196
Border Patrol, U.S., 6, 8, 18, 75, 197; abuses committed by agents of, 9; checkpoints, 20; on contributions of undocumented workers to U.S. society, 187–88; Entry Without Inspection offense and, 22–23, 24; migrants apprehended by, 21–25, 92; suspicion of being spy for, 11; Washington State police and, 37
Bourdieu, Pierre, 31, 35, 44, 89, 185, 190; on being and perception, 135–36; on habitus, 35, 157, 183–84; on symbolic violence, 156–57, 183, 184
Bourgois, Philippe, 28, 195, 205n33; on "conjugated oppression," 50, 85; on violence continuum, 86, 89–90
Boyce, Tom, 115
Bracero Program, 103
Brandes, Stanley, 174
breast cancer, 96
Buber, Martin, 116
Burawoy, Michael, 12–13
Burger King, meals at, 36
Butler, Judith, 21

cabinas (cabins), 47–48, 99
cacti, as danger for border crossers, 8, 12, 18, 20, 92
cadavers, objectification of, 115–16
California, 3, 43, 80–83, 122; berry-growing regions, 10; Central Valley, 5, 82, 127, 129; clinics in, 36–37, 127, 139, 151; crops harvested in, 30; farm labor camps in, 163; labor relations legislation in, 102; migrants' relatives living in, 9; Proposition 187, 13, 40–41, 121, 190; white residents of Central California, 156, 158–60, 166, 169–70
capitalism, 107, 109, 194
carpal tunnel syndrome, 96
Catholicism, 150
Central America, migrants from, 9, 11, 81; Latino identity and, 100; migrant health and, 126, 127
Central America Free Trade Agreement (CAFTA), 26, 198
Charcot, Jean-Martin, 116
checkers, *51*, 68–71, *70*, 76, 79; body position in labor and, *175*; breaks taken by, 83; minimum-wage pay of, 83–84
children, 35, 81, 192; childcare for farmworkers, 82–83; childhood mortality, 146; citizen children of undocumented parents, 38, 39; education of, 91; health care and, 96; labor hierarchy recognized by, 80
Chile, agricultural competition from, 46, 55, 58, 59, 60
China, agricultural competition from, 46, 55, 58, 59–60
cholesterol levels, 101
citizenship, 13, 28, 32, 78, 158; acculturation and, 160; fault lines of power and, 50, 85; hierarchy of identification and, 204n5; Mexican, 197; racial profiling and, 37; right to vote and, 41; structural violence and, 43; violence continuum and, 95. *See also* ethnic-ctizenship hierarchy
civilization, hierarchy of, 84
class, social, 32, 43, 78; acculturation and, 160; communication problems and, 137; conjugated oppression and, 50; fault lines of power and, 50, 85; migration and, 187; structural violence and, 89; violence continuum and, 95
classism, 52, 147
Clifford, James, 32
clinical gaze, 114–17, 123, 124; acontextual medicine and, 152–53; apolitical cultural competency and, 153–54; of migrant health clinicians, 135–41; in San Miguel, Oaxaca, 144–51
"closed corporate communities," 5, 6
coccidioidomycosis (valley fever), 101, 129
collective bad faith, 87
Colorado, 13, 41
Community to Community, 197
conjugated oppression, 50, 85

coyotes (border-crossing guides), 1, 9, 11; author mistaken for, 2, 15; Border Patrol risk and, 18, 20–21; migrants' preparations for border crossing and, 14–16; payment of, 27, 42
Crapanzano, Vincent, 183, 184
crop managers, *51*, 53, 62–65, 79, 161, 180

Das, Veena, 211n6
Davenport, Beverly Ann, 116
"deep hanging out," 32
dehydration, 8, 12
dental problems, 101, 102, 138
deportation, 24, 27, 37, 40, 92, 101
depression, 138
dermatitis, 101
diabetes, 74, 101, 137, 138
diarrhea, 146
diaspora studies, 160, 186
difference, fear of, 159–60
dirt, 67, 68, 73, 174, 180, 191; living/working conditions of lower classes and, 164; as matter out of place, 163; pesticide residue thought of as, 172
doctor-patient relationship, 116
Domestic Fair Trade Working Group, 196
domestic violence, 133–34
domination, 43, 157, 184, 205n33
Douglas, Mary, 163
doxa (mental schemata), 157
Dream Act, 196
Driscoll (berry company), 49
"Driving While Brown," 37
Drug Enforcement Agency, U.S., 2, 107
drug smuggling, 2, 23
drug use, illicit, 101

Eisenman, Stephen, 165
encephalitis, 101
Engel, George, 153
Engels, Friedrich, 43
English language, 22, 27, 119; children of migrant laborers and, 56; English as a Second Language (ESL), 167, 191; gender difference among Triqui and, 86; labor hierarchy and, *85*; Mexican farmworkers blamed for not learning, 166–67; migrant health clinicians and, 130; pesticide danger sign in English only, 172, *173*; pickers excluded from English classes, 66, 167, 191; promotion in labor hierarchy and, 61, 66–67, 174
"Enrique's Journey" (*Los Angeles Times*, 2002), 9
ethnic-citizenship hierarchy, 56, 78, 95, 135, 153, 166; interrelation with labor and suffering hierarchies, 31; normalization of, 170; possibility of change and, 182; unfair promotion practices and, 178–79
ethnicity, 28, 32, 78, 187, 206n16; bodily differences, 138, 171, 173–74; changing perceptions of, 84; conjugated oppression and, 50; violence continuum and, 95
ethnocentrism, 139, 141, 151, 186
ethnography, 28, 37–38, 185, 196. *See also* anthropology; fieldwork
executives, farm, 51–60, *51*, 61, 84–85; breaks taken by, 83; hierarchy of suffering and, 95–96; racism unnoticed by, 180

Fair Labor Standards Act (1938), 102
Farmer, Paul, 114, 190
farm labor segregation hierarchy, 50–51, *51*, 78
fatigue, 101
Ferguson, James, 152
fieldwork, 8–9, 38, 182; embodied experiences of, 34; on the move, 3–7, 27; in San Miguel, 25; in Skagit Valley, 47. *See also* anthropology; ethnography
Foucault, Michel, 114–15, 116, 117, 124, 185

gabachos (white Americans), 6, 32, 38, 204n3 (ch. 2); perceived bodily differences and, 173; Triqui attitudes toward, 35, 36, 38, 79–80. *See also* Anglo-Americans; whites
Galtung, Johan, 205n33
gastritis, 74, 118, 143
gaze. *See* clinical gaze
Geertz, Clifford, 32
gender, 43, 85, 135; language and, 86, 207n18 (ch. 3); private/public spheres and, 86; structural violence and, 89
"Gender and Symbolic Violence" (Bourdieu), 184
Global Exchange, 198
globalization, 52
governmentality, 32
Gramsci, Antonio, 185
Grupo Beta (Mexican Army organization), 16, 23
Gutmann, Matthew, 160

Häagen-Dazs, 49, 59, 60
habitus (Bourdieuian concept), 35–36, 157, 160, 183–84
Hart, Laurie K., 195

"Harvest of Shame" (CBS news broadcast, 1960), 125–26
hate crimes, 156
headaches, 74, 90, 101, 110; migrant health care system and, 132–35; triggered by terms of abuse, 97–98, 132
Healing Our Borders, 196
health care, 13, 39; critical public health, 192–95; health disparities in context, 99–103; insurance, 103, 129, 130; liberation medicine, 195; in Mexico, 103, 111–13; migrant health field in social/cultural context, 125–28; Proposition 187 and, 40–41; reform in United States, 26, 194–96; structural competency and, 153, 154; structural factors and migrant health clinicians, 128–32; structure and gaze in, 117–25, 132–35, 141–44; Triqui traditional healers, 94, 114, 118–19, 128, 132–33; worker's compensation, 119, 123, 140
health fairs, in labor camps, 96–97
"healthy Latino paradox," 100
heart disease, 96
heat stroke (sunstroke), 8, 9, 12, 101
hegemony, 189, 190, 198
hermeneutic of generosity, 177
Hirschauer, Stefan, 115
"Hispanic," as category, 100, 142, 143, 161, 163
HIV (Human Immunodeficiency Virus), 97, 102
Holmes, Seth, 116
homelessness, 35, 92
homicide, 101
housing, 35, 95, 146, 169
Housing Act (1949), 102
Humane Borders, 196–97
Hunt, Linda, 160
hybridization, 160, 186
hypertension, 101

"illegal aliens," 187, 189, 192
indigenous Mexicans, 81, 95; "closed corporate communities" of, 5; excluded from "Mexican" category, 164–65; excluded from processing plant jobs, 78; health insurance and, 103; labor hierarchy and, 84, *85*; military repression in Mexico and, 25; number of, in United States, 42, 99; "regular Mexicans" distinguished from, 54, 61, 161–62, 164–65; suffering and illness among, 31; supervisors' attitudes toward, 67–68. *See also* Mixtec Oaxacans; Triqui Oaxacans
individualization, of risk and responsibility, 26
Institute of Medicine, 100
internalization, of symbolic violence, 172–74, 183
International Monetary Fund, 198
interpellation (Althusserian concept), 28, 206–7n16

Japanese Americans, 48, 84, *85*, 170
joint inflammation, 94

kidnappings, 8, 9
kidney function, abnormalities in, 101
Kleinman, Arthur, 114
knee pain, 39, 74, 93, 94, 117–25
Konner, Melvin, 116

labor hierarchy, 78–80, 83–87; administrative assistants, *51*, 60–62; body position in labor and, 174–76, *175*; in California, 81–82; checkers, *51*, 68–71, *70*; crop managers, *51*, 62–65; farm executives, 51–60, *51*, 61, 79, 95–96; field workers paid by weight (contract workers), *51*, 72–78; hourly field workers, *51*, 71; physical suffering and, 94; supervisors (crew bosses), *51*, 65–68
Latinos/Latinas, U.S., 63, 81; administrative assistants, 60; Border Patrol agents, 24; field workers paid by weight, 78; as "Hispanics," 161; hourly field workers, 71; labor hierarchy and, 84, *85*; "Latino" as metacategory, 100; Mexican migrant workers as seen by, 83, 164–65; as "Mexicans," 159–60; promoted over indigenous pickers, 178–79; supervisors (crew bosses), 65, 66, 161–62
lawyers, immigration, 9, 22, 23–25
Lella, Joseph, 115–16
leptospirosis, 101
Levi, Primo, 86, 204n18
Levinas, Emmanuel, 211n6 (ch. 7)
liberation medicine, 194
liver function, abnormalities in, 101
Lock, Margaret, 34
lunch breaks, 62, 93, 178–79

Malinowski, Bronislaw, 32
malnutrition, 101, 102, 146, 147
Marcus, George, 3
Masculine Domination (Bourdieu), 157
Medicaid, 103, 129
Medicare, 129

memory problems, 101
mental illness, 101, 209n2
Merleau-Ponty, Maurice, 34
mestizos ("regular Mexicans"), 1, 33, 43, 81, 203n3; attitudes toward Triqui people, 146–51, 167–68, 170–71; in California, 81; families left behind in Mexico, 68; field workers paid by weight, 73; health care clinics in Oaxaca and, 127–28; health insurance and, 103; health professionals and, 141; hourly field workers, 71; indigenous Mexicans distinguished from, 54, 61, 161–62, 164–65; labor hierarchy and, 84, *85*; pickers, 67; promoted over indigenous pickers, 178–79; in San Miguel, Oaxaca, 167; in Skagit Valley, 5; supervisors (crew bosses), 65, 67
Metzl, Jonathan, 153
Mexican Army, 2, 110; Grupo Beta, 16, 23; torture practiced by, 106–7, 142; Triqui people in, 173
"Mexican crews," 65, 72–78
Mexico, 42, 176; deportation back to, 24, 27, 40; health care in, 137; Institutional Revolutionary Party (PRI), 104; NAFTA and, 25, 41. *See also* Oaxaca (Mexican state); San Miguel, village of
Migrant Clinicians Network, 126
Migrant Health Act (1962), 126
Migrant Health Program, 102, 126
migrant laborers, 3, 29; age of, 100; checkers' attitudes toward, 68–71; crops harvested by, 30; field workers paid by weight (contract workers), *51*, 72–78; "Harvest of Shame" broadcast and, 126; health status of, 99–103; hiddenness of, 87, 155–56, 180; hourly field workers, *51*, 71; illness as manifestation of violence, 28; importance of, 40–43; labor hierarchy and, 84; migrant health clinicians and, 136–41; physical effects on body from picking, 74, 89–95; white residents' racialized views of, 158–66
migration: assimilation/acculturation and, 186; externalized costs of, 12–13; as forced movement, 186; individual motivations for migrating, 17–18; lower-class connotations carried by, 187; Skagit Valley nonprofit seminar on, 75; suffering involved in, 27
migration studies, 17–18, 132
Mills, C. Wright, 185
minimum wages, 55, 62, 70, 73, 102
Mixtec (Mixteco) language, 66, 67, 131, 132, 189
Mixtec Oaxacans, 5, 33, 42, 99, 142, 162, 168; excluded from "Mexican" category, 164; field workers paid by weight, 73; hourly field workers, 71; labor hierarchy and, 84, *85*; migrant health clinicians and, 131, 132; in Skagit Valley, 47; supervisor (crew boss) on Tanaka Farm, 65, 66–67, 171
Miyazaki, Hirokazu, 183, 184
MULT (Movimiento de Unificación y Liberación Triqui), 5, 104, 105, 106, 107, 203n5
Murphy, Sen. George, 171
musculoskeletal injuries, 96

Nader, Laura, 29
National Agricultural Worker Survey, 99
National Physicians Alliance, 196
naturalization, of inequality and racism, 29, 71, 176, 181, 182, 198
neoliberal policies, 25, 41, 125, 194
New York State, 43
No More Deaths, 196
nonsteroidal anti-inflammatory drugs (NSAIDs), 118, 121
normalization, 28, 110, 170, 176, 180, 182
North American Free Trade Agreement (NAFTA), 25, 26, 41, 92, 167
nurses, 28, 115, 127, 128, 136, 137, 146–50

Oaxaca (Mexican state), 1, 13, 30, 56, 203n2; bus ride to U.S. border from, 2; clinical gaze in, 144–51; extended Triqui families in, 30; health clinics in, 36–37, 127–28; housing in, 169; lack of jobs in, 76, 91; La Mixteca region, 42, 105; number of indigenous Oaxacans in United States, 99; Triqui Zone of, 38, 91, 104, 108. *See also* San Miguel, village of
Oaxacos (derogatory term for Oaxacans), 66, 164
Obama, Barack, 195
obesity, 101
Occupational Safety and Health act (1970), 102
Ong, Aihwa, 187
Operation Gatekeeper, 42
Oportunidades (formerly Progresa), 144
Oregon, 43, 131
organic crops, 57, 71, 191
Orwell, George, 164
Osler, Sir William, 115
overtime labor laws, 62, 102

Pawluch, Dorothy, 115–16
People's Seminary, 197

pesticides, 30, 71, 95, *173*; blame for exposure deflected from farm, 171–72; internalization of symbolic violence and, 172–74; machine picking and, 191; safety education and, 191; strawberry pickers poisoned by, 96
physicians, 28, 123, 125; biomedicine and, 152–53; clinical gaze and, 114–17; complaints about practices of Mexican patients, 137; language barrier and, 142; in Mexico, 137, 147; migrant health clinics and, 126, 128–32, 136, 138; physician anthropologists, 114, 116, 209n2; politics and, 195; rehabilitation medicine, 120–21, 123, 153; structural violence and, 125; worker's compensation claims and, 140–41
Physicians for a National Health Plan, 196
Piñeros y Campesinos Unidos, 196
Ponte, Maya, 116
poverty, 17, 146; culture of, 28; institutional racism and, 78; NAFTA and, 167; poverty line, 103; race and, 165; as spur to emigration from Mexico, 41
pragmatic solidarity, 190–92
prejudice, 28, 39, 56, 95; anti-immigrant, 52; hierarchy of labor and, 110; violence of, 43
Prison Notebooks, The (Gramsci), 189
profitability, 53, 54, 58, 95
Proposition 187, 13, 40–41, 121, 190
psychotherapy, 133
public health discourse, 25
"pull" factors, as migration motivations, 17
Purity and Danger (Douglas), 163
"push" factors, as migration motivations, 17

Quesada, James, 121, 190, 195

rabies, 101
race, 43, 165–66; fault lines of power and, 50, 85; racial profiling, 37; structural violence and, 89
racism, 17, 52, 151, 156; as grievance of striking workers, 178–79; growers' attitudes toward, 53; institutional, 78, 192; from Latino U.S. citizens, 83; medical, 147; of migrant health clinicians, 136; naturalization of, 181; stereotypes and, 98, 110; of supervisors (crew bosses), 65, 178
raspberries, 63, 71
rattlesnakes, 9, 12, 19, 27, 92; Border Patrol agent bitten by, 22; garlic on boots as precaution against, 18; slingshots for use against, 2
repetitive stress injuries, 96
reproduction, externalized costs of, 26
resistance, 28, 29, 90, 116, 177, 180
"ride-giver" (*raitero*), 82
Road to Wigan Pier, The (Orwell), 164
robbery, danger of, 9
Rothenberg, Daniel, 43, 206n4
Ruiz-Alvarez, Adolfo, 131

salmonellosis, 101
Salpêtrière Clinic, 116
Samaritans, the, 196
San Miguel, village of, 1, 3–5, 21, 73, 80, *112*; author's fieldwork in, 6, 25, 111–13; Centro de Salud (government clinic), 111–13, 127, 144–51, *145*; *mestizos* in, 167; money sent back to families in, 33; preparations for border crossing from, 10–11; risks of staying or leaving, 26; rumor about blood in corporate sodas, 177; seasonal return to, 42; transnational migration circuit and, 160; Triqui education levels in, 86, 131; Triqui extended community and, 160–61
Sartre, Jean-Paul, 87, 157
Scheper-Hughes, Nancy, 33–34, 174, 205n32; on "collective bad faith," 87; institutional violence studied by, 110; on the "rebel body," 193; on violence continuum, 86, 89–90
scorpions, danger from, 12
sexism, 52
sexuality, 43, 89
Skagitonians to Preserve Farmland, 197
Skagit Valley (Washington State), 5, 45–47, 80, 95, 197; farm labor camps in, 47–48, *48*, 49–50, 206n2; migrant health clinics in, 126–27, 128–29, 131, 136–37; as node in transnational circuit of labor migration, 155, 160; Tanaka Brothers Farm, 48–51; white residents of, 87, 156, 159, 161–63, 166, 169–70
sleep disturbances, 101
slipped vertebral disks, 74
smoking, 101
Social Security Act, 102
social theory, 32, 37
Spanish language, 2, 14, 33, 119; administrative assistants and, 61; Border Patrol agents' use of, 21; indigenous languages seen as "dialects" of, 189; indigenous Mexicans and, 76; labor hierarchy and, *85*; medical students at health fairs and,

97; migrant health clinicians and, 130, 131; mistranscription of names in, 130; racist treatment conducted in, 180; as second language for Triqui laborers, 104; spoken by Triqui men and women, 86; white checkers and, 68, 69
stereotypes, 43, 98, 110, 135, 184
sterility, 101
Stoller, Paul, 34
Strauss, Erwin, 174
strawberries, 10, 59; pay for pickers, 66, 73, 84; pesticides and, 172–74; physical effects on body from picking, 34, 73–74, 119–20; strike by pickers, 63, 177–80, *178*, *179*; on Tanaka Brothers Farm, 49, 50
stress, chronic, 101
strike, by pickers, 53, 63
structural violence, 8, 9, 43, 94, 205n33; market rule and, 52; of migrant farmwork, 43–44; naturalization of, 176; of neoliberal policies, 41; physicians and, 125; sickness as embodiment of, 28, 89; violence continuum, 86, 88–90, 95, 153; work-related physical pains and, 109. *See also* symbolic violence
structural vulnerability, 99
substance abuse, 138
suffering (*sufrimiento*), 8, 13, 37, 125, 182; amelioration of, 26, 31, 114, 185, 198, 211n6 (ch. 7); "contest of suffering," 121; depoliticization of, 154; embodied anthropology and, 35; ethnicity-citizenship hierarchy and, 31; ethnography of, 9; everyday life and, 8–9, 27; health care reform and, 193, 194; hierarchy of, 28, 85, 95–96, 180; meaning of, 211n6; medical professionals and, 136; narrative of ethnic succession and, 56; normalization and naturalization of, 169–70, 198; physical and mental/emotional, 89; social and symbolic context of, 29, 135, 143, 152; structural/symbolic violence and, 44, 86, 89, 110, 185; victims blamed and criminalized, 125, 153–54, 166–69, 181; violence continuum and, 88–90
suicide, 101
supervisors (crew bosses), 36, *51*, 65–68, 94; checkers and, 68, 70; degrading treatment from, 77, 95
susto (culture-bound syndrome), 137
symbolic violence: defined, 44, 156–57; internalization of, 172–74, 183; as naturalization of inequality, 71; political violence (war) and, 86; possibility of change and, 184; of stereotypes and prejudice, 43. *See also* structural violence

Tanaka, John, 53–56, 168, 169, 170, 179
Tanaka, Rob, 56–58, 67, 180
Tanaka Brothers Farm, 48–51, 81, 83, 88, 103, 151; bank used to pay pickers, 176; English classes hosted on, 66, 167; ethnicity-citizenship hierarchy on, 48–51, *51*, 166; executives, 51–60, 161; health care and, 118–23; indigenous languages seen as "dialects," 189; Latino crew bosses, 65, 66, 161–62, 165; strike by strawberry pickers, 177–80, *178*, *179*
tendonitis, 94
tetanus, 101
Tierra Nueva, 197
torture, by Mexican military, 106–7, 142, 143–44, 152
Triqui language, 4, 14, 21, 67, 128, 149; difficulty of learning, 207n18 (ch. 3); nicknames in, 33, 204–5n10 (ch. 2); referred to as "dialect," 189
Triqui Oaxacans, 3, 33, 99, 111–13, *149*, 203n2; border crossing by, 9–10; in California, 83; children of, 56; doctors as seen by, 112–13, 124; excluded from "Mexican" category, 164; extended families in San Miguel, 160–61; family life in camps, 67, 79; field workers paid by weight, 73, 74–78, *74*; habitus of, 36; health care in San Miguel, 144–51; health status of, 100–101; hierarchy of suffering and, 96; hunting in mountains of Oaxaca, 19; identification as "poor," 30, 204n5; internalization of symbolic violence, 173–74, 176; labor hierarchy and, 84, *85*; Latino identity and, 100; legal temporary worker status and, 197; as majority of farm labor in U.S. regions, 42–43; marriage practices, 138–39, 186; migrant health clinicians and, 131; migrants' return to hometowns, 13; migration as recent phenomenon, 42; origin story of Triqui people, 107–8; in Skagit Valley, 47, 90, 93; strike by pickers, 177–80, *178*, *179*; suffering of, 44, 90–95, 150–51; on Tanaka Brothers Farm, 53; in town apartment outside of labor camp, 103–4; trust of, 38; violence and, 108–9, 168. *See also* migrant laborers
tuberculosis, 101–2

unemployment compensation, 102
United Farm Workers (UFW), 102, 173, 196

United States: application for residency in, 150; fair trade label in, 196; family farming in, 46–47; farm subsidies raised by, 41; health care system in, 194–95; immigrant population of, 40; migrant laborer population in, 100; migration routes from/to Oaxaca, 4; NAFTA and, 167; number of indigenous Mexicans in, 42, 99; taxes paid by undocumented workers, 188; undocumented immigration into, 2
urinary tract infections, 101
U.S.-Mexico Border Counties Coalition, 40

Ventura Morales, Santiago, 132
"vertical slice," of social hierarchies, 29, 185
vigilantes, armed, 8, 9, 92
violence. *See* structural violence; symbolic violence
Virchow, Rudolf, 195
vision problems, 102

Wacquant, Loïc, 34, 205n33
Wagner Act (1935), 102
war of position (Gramscian concept), 189–90, 198
Washington State, 3, 6, 122; berry farm labor camp in, 32; clinics in, 36–37, 151; crops harvested in, 30; Department of Labor and Industries (LNI), 117–25; migrant health clinics in, 139; minimum wage, 55, 73, 176; police in, 37
weather, 57, 62; exposure to, 30, 94, 95; work schedule and, 54
Weismantel, Mary, 28, 165
welfare, 140, 159, 168
whiteness, 165–66
whites, 79, 84, 127; administrative assistants, 60–61; Central California residents, 156, 158–60, 163–64, 166, 169–70; checkers, 68–71, *70*, 170; crop managers, 63–65; farm executives, 58–60; migrant farmworkers, 126, 158, 186; Skagit Valley residents, 87, 156, 159, 161–63, 166, 169–70; supervisors (crew bosses), 65, 67–68; teenage field pickers, 72, 187. *See also* Anglo-Americans; *gabachos*
With These Hands (Rothenberg), 206n4
Wolf, Eric, 5
women, clinical objectification of, 116
World Trade Organization, 198

Zapotec Oaxacans, 100

CALIFORNIA SERIES IN PUBLIC ANTHROPOLOGY

The California Series in Public Anthropology emphasizes the anthropologist's role as an engaged intellectual. It continues anthropology's commitment to being an ethnographic witness, to describing, in human terms, how life is lived beyond the borders of many readers' experiences. But it also adds a commitment, through ethnography, to reframing the terms of public debate—transforming received, accepted understandings of social issues with new insights, new framings.

Series Editor: Robert Borofsky (Hawaii Pacific University)

Contributing Editors: Philippe Bourgois (University of Pennsylvania), Paul Farmer (Partners in Health), Alex Hinton (Rutgers University), Carolyn Nordstrom (University of Notre Dame), and Nancy Scheper-Hughes (UC Berkeley)

University of California Press Editor: Naomi Schneider

1. *Twice Dead: Organ Transplants and the Reinvention of Death,* by Margaret Lock
2. *Birthing the Nation: Strategies of Palestinian Women in Israel,* by Rhoda Ann Kanaaneh (with a foreword by Hanan Aashrawi)
3. *Annihilating Difference: The Anthropology of Genocide,* edited by Alexander Laban Hinton (with a foreword by Kenneth Roth)
4. *Pathologies of Power: Health, Human Rights, and the New War on the Poor,* by Paul Farmer (with a foreword by Amartya Sen)
5. *Buddha Is Hiding: Refugees, Citizenship, the New America,* by Aihwa Ong
6. *Chechnya: Life in a War-Torn Society,* by Valery Tishkov (with a foreword by Mikhail S. Gorbachev)
7. *Total Confinement: Madness and Reason in the Maximum Security Prison,* by Lorna A. Rhodes
8. *Paradise in Ashes: A Guatemalan Journey of Courage, Terror, and Hope,* by Beatriz Manz (with a foreword by Aryeh Neier)
9. *Laughter Out of Place: Race, Class, Violence, and Sexuality in a Rio Shantytown,* by Donna M. Goldstein
10. *Shadows of War: Violence, Power, and International Profiteering in the Twenty-First Century,* by Carolyn Nordstrom

11. *Why Did They Kill? Cambodia in the Shadow of Genocide,* by Alexander Laban Hinton (with a foreword by Robert Jay Lifton)
12. *Yanomami: The Fierce Controversy and What We Can Learn from It,* by Robert Borofsky
13. *Why America's Top Pundits Are Wrong: Anthropologists Talk Back,* edited by Catherine Besteman and Hugh Gusterson
14. *Prisoners of Freedom: Human Rights and the African Poor,* by Harri Englund
15. *When Bodies Remember: Experiences and Politics of AIDS in South Africa,* by Didier Fassin
16. *Global Outlaws: Crime, Money, and Power in the Contemporary World,* by Carolyn Nordstrom
17. *Archaeology as Political Action,* by Randall H. McGuire
18. *Counting the Dead: The Culture and Politics of Human Rights Activism in Colombia,* by Winifred Tate
19. *Transforming Cape Town,* by Catherine Besteman
20. *Unimagined Community: Sex, Networks, and AIDS in Uganda and South Africa,* by Robert J. Thornton
21. *Righteous Dopefiend,* by Philippe Bourgois and Jeff Schonberg
22. *Democratic Insecurities: Violence, Trauma, and Intervention in Haiti,* by Erica Caple James
23. *Partner to the Poor: A Paul Farmer Reader,* by Paul Farmer, edited by Haun Saussy (with a foreword by Tracy Kidder)
24. *I Did It to Save My Life: Love and Survival in Sierra Leone,* by Catherine E. Bolten
25. *My Name Is Jody Williams: A Vermont Girl's Winding Path to the Nobel Peace Prize,* by Jody Williams
26. *Re-Imagining Global Health: An Introduction,* edited by Paul Farmer, Arthur Kleinman, Jim Kim, and Matthew Basilico
27. *Fresh Fruit, Broken Bodies: Migrant Farmworkers in the United States,* by Seth M. Holmes, PhD, MD